C'est ma vie

my life

Muriel Kiefe Bessinger

MAKB Publishers
New York, New York

C'est Ma Vie — My Life by Muriel Kiefe Bessinger

ISBN: 978-1-66784-401-5

First Edition: April 2022

Cover and book design by Stephen Bodkin

Cover photography by Gerald Bessinger

MAKB PUBLISHERS
New York, NY
United States

Email: makbpublishers@gmail.com

Printed in the United States of America

Table of Contents

Dedication

This book is dedicated to the memory of my husband, Jerry, who lovingly encouraged me to write my life story. His warm support is felt in these notes, written to me more than thirty years ago:

writing is _never_ a waste of time —
if in _your_ words and represent _your_
thoughts and feelings.
these remain as a perpetual reminder
of who you are, who you were, to
those who love you, care for you —
and those who wish they knew
and knew you...
One of those who loves you — always.
4-10-92   Your Husband!

Jerry, your love still inspires me.

CHAPTER 1

Lestelle

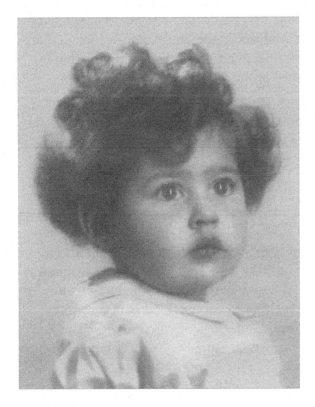

I was only a little girl when the Second World War reached France. At the time, my parents, Andre and Sybil and I were taking a family vacation on the Cote d'Argent, in a charming and ideal summer place called Bidart.

My grandmother had built a villa there, perched on a steep hill, overlooking the Atlantic Ocean. Bidart was and still is a fine beach resort close to Biarritz, first made fashionable and popular by Empress Eugenie.

Discerning that the political atmosphere was worsening for Jews, my father Andre hastened back to Paris, where he headed with his uncle and cousin, a well-known business firm founded by his grandfather. But, under the circumstances, he could not stay in Paris. He assembled some cash and stocks and prepared his departure from the capital, as rapidly as possible, to return to his little family in the southwest of France.

The war was so drastically changing the world, and France was no exception. The Germans had invaded the country and the surrender of 1940 had created two zones. Northern France was under German military control, while the so-called "Free Zone" had a semblance of independence under the leadership of Marshal Petain, with Vichy as its capital.

Andre met a Belgian refugee, Catinette, through relatives. She was struggling to pass from the Occupied Zone to the Unoccupied Zone. Andre offered to help her. But as they both approached the line of demarcation, a sharp and loud voice stopped them. Andre and Catinette had been caught by the Nazis and were incarcerated in the prison of St. Palais.

These were bad times, growing dangerous. Jews were being deported to camps. Andre had been rushed into a cell and might never see daylight again. Even more shattering was the overwhelming possibility that he might never see his wife Sybil and his two-year-old daughter Muriel again.

Sybil was, at that time, expecting their second child. Andre was in prison, doubtful and frightened about the future.

Days went by. Deprived of his liberty, Andre's dreams of freedom were distorted by the nightmares of reality. But, Andre spoke German and was brought before the officers as a translator. His fluency in the German language turned out to be his salvation. Two weeks after his incarceration, Andre was able to humor the interrogator with his witticisms and talk himself out of prison. Meanwhile, Catinette had apparently left the premises and was able to make it to the Unoccupied Zone.

Several weeks later, when Andre and Sybil returned to the villa with their groceries, they found Emilia the maid, crying.

"Mon-mon-sieur, Ma-ma-dame," she tried to articulate in half-broken syllables.

"What is it, Emilia? You are trembling. Stop crying. Tell us!" Sybil implored.

"I can't — I don't know," Emilia whispered with a dazed look on her face.

"We don't understand! Please tell us what is going on," Sybil begged with persistence.

Emilia wiped off her tears and took a deep breath. "The Germans, the Germans — they are here! They have moved in with us," she said, pointing to the stairs.

Was this possible? Andre and Sybil's questions were soon answered: a commanding officer and his orderly had actually moved in and had taken the nicest rooms!

I was far too young to understand or to remember the puzzling situation. But certainly, it could not have been easy for Andre and Sybil to live side by side for several months with the enemy.

It was during this period of great upheaval that Sybil gave birth in Biarritz to Ghislaine, a fair-haired little pink-skinned baby. "It was far from being a favorable time," Sybil recounted so often. "The doctor no longer had his car and could not make it on time, so Ghislaine was born without his help, but Andre was there to assist the nurse in the delivery of the baby," Sybil would impart in reverie. I thought that my father playing the role of a midwife was very funny.

The war was so drastically changing everything. Andre and Sybil could no longer ignore the situation, but they could not leave yet. Ghislaine was a newborn and Sybil was recovering from a long bout of phlebitis.

Monsieur Malric, an elderly Catholic acquaintance of the family, offered to take me to Pau, in the Unoccupied Zone, by train. The tumultuous atmosphere gave Andre and Sybil, no choice.

I was two years old. I was way too young to remember anything about that specific time. When my parents would later recall that episode to me, I would feel a chill in my spine. It certainly could not have been easy to part with one's little girl. Apparently, my mother had made me wear all her jewelry; every piece was sown in the lining of my coat. She wanted to make sure that I would have something, should she be unable to join me or ever see me again.

On our arrival in Pau, Monsieur Malric entrusted me to my Aunt Huguette, Andre's sister, who had managed to reach the Unoccupied Zone sooner, with Francois and Nicole, her children. For the next few hours after my arrival, I was a real problem for my aunt. With a very firm hold, I hugged my teddy bear and clutched my small handbag. I would not let go and I would not take my coat off. I was going to wait for my mother. My aunt tried and tried in vain. She did not want to traumatize me more. Poor Aunt Huguette just went on trying to convince me to take off my coat, but I just hugged my teddy bear and begged for my mother. In desperation, Huguette had to call upon a friend to help out in the matter. Seemingly hours later, my grip lessened and exhausted, I fell asleep.

I was in Pau for several weeks, far too young to remember my sojourn there and far too young to appreciate the beautiful city overlooking the Gave.

Meanwhile, the war was growing in intensity. Andre and Sybil were more convinced than ever that they could no longer postpone their departure from Bidart.

For days they discussed ways to escape and save some of their assets. Andre had an idea. Determined to safeguard his cash, stocks and bonds, he carefully dismantled the lining of my magnificent baby carriage and padded the whole perambulator with the securities. Then, with care, he accurately stitched back the interior covering. No one but Sybil knew of his shrewdness. Emilia would send the carriage with a few other important personal belongings by railway to a forwarding address.

Andre and Sybil had to wait for the propitious moment to leave the villa and best elude the commanding officer and his orderly, who had lived with them, under the same roof, for over seven months.

A couple of days later, Andre, serious and worried, whispered to Sybil, "Last night I thought about it — we must no longer delay our departure, I think right now is a good time." Hypnotized for a moment by his words, Sybil stared at him, as he took a big puff on a cigarette. Tears were pouring down her face, but there was nothing else to do. They had to go.

There was no question of carrying luggage. They had to wear what they were taking. Wrapped in several layers, they prepared to leave with baby Ghislaine in their arms. Coming to the doorway, they looked back with a strange feeling in their hearts. However, the idea of a possible reunion with their little girl in Pau gave them the fortitude to face their uncertain future.

The courage and bravery of my parents, which were demonstrated in the early stages of the war, were only the preamble of what was yet to come.

First, they traveled by train, but when the risk increased and the situation became extremely dangerous, they walked by night, crossing fields, rivers and creeks. On occasion, they waded in water up to their waistlines. All this was complicated by the fear of being caught at any moment. They had to be careful in order to assure themselves that no enemy forces could see them or hear them. Not only was it necessary to watch each step with great care, but it was mandatory for Ghislaine to remain totally quiet during the escape. Holding Ghislaine, who was all wrapped up in blankets, Andre led the way quietly and cautiously for Sybil. Andre and

Sybil were certainly nervous and frightened — so much could go wrong — but they knew that they had to remain strong and help each other's self-assurance and level of optimism. They sought to give an appearance of courage, in the belief that they could make it and that Andre's experience of being caught at the line of demarcation with Catinette would not repeat itself.

Their precarious journey along the border to the Unoccupied Zone was a steady but slow advance.

After hours and hours of walking, they finally reached Pau.

Andre and Sybil did not want to stay in Pau. They were anxious to get out of troubled France and reach Spain. They picked me up and together we left the picturesque town with its remarkable medieval chateau of King Henri IV and headed for the Pyrenees Mountains, with their snow-capped peaks, which stood out so amazingly clear against the sky.

This was the early spring of 1941. It was still quite frigid. The trees, bare of leaves and distorted by the winds, had not yet blossomed. But where southwestern France and Spain merge lies a very attractive part of France. We headed for the scenic mountain areas hiding old villages. We came upon Lestelle, a quaint village with a small group of dwellings in a magnificent setting surrounded by the Pyrenees. Situated close to Lourdes, Lestelle was, in contrast, totally unknown.

My father intended to spend one night there before resuming our journey. However, Pension Arricaud, located next door to the church on the main square, ended up being our abode for the next four years.

There, we lived in an almost claustrophobic bedroom on the second floor. The room was dismal and completely devoid of charm. The walls, covered with worn-out yellowish paper, were bare of pictures. The only ornamentation was a large crucifix over my parent's bed.

Catholicism, in France and particularly in that region, was predominant, and adorning each room with a cross was customary.

The room had exactly what it required to make it livable. My parents shared a full-size bed, and Ghislaine and I had small cots. A large wooden armoire held our clothing and the few belongings we had with us. In a corner next to the window, there was a small wash basin under which my mother kept a few laundering products, hidden by a short curtain. To the right of the window, there was a plain wooden table with two rickety wooden chairs with rattan seats. The table was covered with spots and marks, but we could depend on its solidity.

On the table, Andre kept an old-fashioned radio that did not work well, but its hissing and crackling noises did not prevent our parents from listening to the daily newscasts.

The reports were of extreme importance because all contingencies had to be taken into consideration for any emergency.

I will never forget the heating stove in the middle of the room. My parents took turns in feeding the archaic furnace, which was supposed to keep us warm during the severe winters of the Pyrenees. Unfortunately, the wood was often damp and the oppressive odor caused by the fumes was so bad that we had no choice but to open the windows. We were lucky when my father could get the wood we needed.

On the creaking floor, the old grey carpet brought very little warmth to the room. It had barely any color left in it and was worn out.

There was a feeling of tenebrous dimness to the room. The ceiling light flickered frequently and lacked luminosity. During the early morning, the sunshine came across the room, but it soon disappeared!

Facing north, the windows opened on the courtyard, which was spacious but almost entirely barren except for an isolated fig tree adjacent to a square shed where the garden implements were stored. I remember climbing often to the top of the shed with my friends and sitting with our feet dangling off the side, eating sweet figs with much delight. We talked and laughed together, while the sun caressed and warmed our skin. Wisterias flourished along the sidewalls that separated the yard from the little road going down to the river. Their scent was subtle and pleasant, their delicate and lustrous mauve color brightening the courtyard.

At the end of the courtyard, a mini-gate made way to another area with a pigpen lodging three pigs; across from it chickens and rabbits lived in their crowded coops. The dirt in the muddy and wretched pigsty was shocking, but the farm animals amused all the children in the little pension.

Another small gate led to a vegetable garden, where Monsieur and Madame Arricaud, the pension owners, planted among other things, potatoes, turnips, and Jerusalem artichokes.

The vegetable garden marked the end of the property.

On the other side of the wall, a narrow meadow, bordering the river, was often the site of an encampment of gypsies. They were very different from the villagers and spoke their own language, which had no similarity to French, nor to the patois used by the rustic local folks. Their clothes were colorful but torn and dirty. Their badly cut, heavy masses of thick hair and their belligerent gaze gave them a rather alarming appearance. Furthermore, numerous terrifying accounts were told about them. They were often regarded as thieves, stealing food and valuables from the villagers. But the most frightening of all was the legend about their kidnapping children and selling them to the troubadours, minstrels and other street entertainers. I do not know how factual these tales were, but we were rebuked severely by the villagers if we were seen near the gypsies' wooden caravans.

The view from our window might have been considered rather peaceful. But this semblance of tranquility could not possibly wipe out the stress and anxiety caused by Hitler's appalling measures against the Jews and the haunting anti-Semitism in Europe.

Andre had finally abandoned his plan to leave France and decided to settle down, at least for a while, in Lestelle. Consequently, the baby carriage and the suitcases were forwarded to us by railway, as Andre had arranged with Emilia.

My father had accomplished an absolute "coup de maître." He had out-smarted the pro-Nazi French and Germans. Surreptitiously, he had been able to pass his assets from the Occupied Zone to the Unoccupied Zone. I can only admire my father's brilliant stratagem and dexterity with which he was able to contrive his clever scheme.

Everything was paradoxical during the Occupation. Our parents told us to be honest, while dishonesty and ruses were frequently needed to survive.

Our new life in the hamlet was far from the lifestyle to which my parents were accustomed.

Sybil had a comfortable but strict childhood in her native England. She was raised in London by her father David, whom she worshipped, and by Elizabeth, a rather austere Protestant stepmother, who converted to Judaism.

"Why did they ever send me, me a Jewish girl, to La Sagesse?" Sybil would wonder, as she related her stories to me. "My parents believed that I would receive a top education there, but life in the convent was wretched. We slept in unheated white-washed dorms where we had to dress and undress in our own curtained cubicle, under our nightgowns of course! For looking at ourselves would have been improper and a definite no-no."

"Really!" I interjected, with surprise.

"Yes my darling, I assure you." The rules were established and we were supposed to abide by them. Many girls submitted to the nuns' authority, but I had strong impulses to do things my way and that got me into trouble! I was often punished for what I realized later were just normal childish pranks. I must have been about seven years old when I was taken to the Reverend Mother for talking in my dorm after the lights had been put out!

"My poor child, God only knows what you will become!" the Reverend Mother cried out. "I felt damned for life," said Sybil.

I was horrified to hear my mother's story. How could a Reverend Mother utter such words to a little girl?

However, notwithstanding the rigorous upbringing of her stepmother and the rigid Catholic boarding school she attended for about two years, Sybil grew to be a lady of the greatest charm and sensitivity. She radiated warmth and was in every way a beautiful person. It was not surprising why my father fell in love with her when she was only seventeen. He was at the time nineteen years old. They were both so young, but they already knew that they wanted to share the rest of their lives.

Sybil married Andre seven years later, despite the exasperation and difficulties engendered by their respective families, who were not in favor of a Franco-British alliance.

My father was reared in a completely different setting from my mother's milieu. He was born into an extremely affluent Franco-Jewish family. Therese, his mother, was brought up in extravagant and opulent surroundings, but she married into a more traditional family. Unfortunately, Victor, his father, was killed during the First World War, leaving her at the age of 27 alone with her two offspring. Andre was only five years old and his sister Huguette was barely three when their papa died.

Andre's governess was more like a sergeant when it came to his education. Nevertheless, he was doted upon and served diligently by his mother, his grandmother, and his sister, since he was the only male in the household. Yet the luxury of gracious living did not prevent him from becoming a remarkably industrious and diligent man. His fortitude was exceptional, particularly through the traumatic circumstances of this period.

Our new abode was terribly unsophisticated. But we were cozily together and nothing mattered more.

Monsieur and Madame Arricaud had two children: Francoise, a rather haughty girl a few years older than I, and Jean Claude, our playmate, who was exactly of Ghislaine's age. In addition, there were two noticeably old-fashioned, white-haired little ladies who gave the appearance of being meek and submissive, but who in reality were matriarchs. They dominated their nephew, Monsieur Arricaud, who had a rough countenance, but who was indeed a warm-hearted individual, trying to keep his place going under the prevailing troublesome years of war.

Madame Arricaud was a simple and kind woman who was, for the most part, helpful.

Since the bathrooms were never heated, she invited Sybil down to the main kitchen, to bathe her two little girls in a portable metal tub placed next to the old-fashioned black stove. I am not sure whether this was due to water shortage or to the cost of heating water, but the same water was used for Jean Claude, Ghislaine and myself. In any case, we had to be thankful for the few luxuries we had, however modest!

Our meals at the pension were meager. The undersized portions of potatoes, turnips, salsify, Jerusalem artichokes and airmail-thin slices of cheese were by no means enough to satisfy any appetite.

Basic requirements were extremely hard to obtain. Bread, meat, fish, eggs, vegetables, fruits, butter and soap were just about nonexistent.

My father who had never soiled his hands, decided to go and work on a farm to supplement the nourishment of his two little girls. His toil in the fields was far from the glamour he had experienced. His hours were long and tedious. He shared the labor with the peasants and soon discovered their strenuous rural way of life. With punctuality, Andre would reach the farm before sunrise. He would drink a hot bowl of milk and share some dark bread with the farmers. Once he had recognized the earthy roughness of these men, he discovered their humanity. They had sympathy and understanding for my father's secret. They knew he was Jewish, and that it was important to keep it among themselves. They grasped the problem of his predicament and they wanted him to know that they were there for him. In exchange, he was only too happy to give his best and worked the fields with tremendous zeal.

After a while, Andre and Sybil knew everyone in the village. They encountered many admirable people who graciously opened their homes to them and shared with them the uncertainty and bewilderment caused by the hostilities of the war. The accumulation of adversities brought out the best in everyone. Families, relatives, members of the community went all out to help each other.

Lestelle was never a battleground. Yet it had not been completely spared by the German heel. Occasionally our family had to seek refuge with some courageous Catholic friends, who took it upon themselves to hide us in their vast estate on the outskirts of our village.

Notwithstanding the dangers in protecting a Jewish family, Monsieur and Madame de Richecourt concealed our whereabouts and went all out to endow us, vulnerable refugees, with their kindheartedness. Andre and Sybil were touched by their friendship and retained a fondness for the family de Richecourt, long after the war ended.

The family de Richecourt was not quite ordinary. The world was madness, but Monsieur and Madame de Richecourt and their twelve children succeeded, in simplicity, in keeping their noble demeanor and projecting an image of distinction and refinement at all times.

We were often invited to their impressive mansion for an afternoon. The gatherings were organized about the adults, who enjoyed a peaceful tea time while the older siblings kept their younger brothers and sisters and their friends occupied and out of the way. The de Richecourts' affection and devotion during this remarkably troublesome period were heartwarming. Anytime, day or night, we could knock at their door and they were ready to help us.

My mother, with her heart of gold, played her part by giving a helping hand to the Pochard family. Impoverished indigents, they lived in a small shack located in one of the back streets of Lestelle. The shanty was dilapidated and the filth was unbelievable. Monsieur Pochard appeared emaciated and haggard. His favorite pastime was the bottle. He was rarely sober and did very little for his family. Madame Pochard looked worn out and exhausted. The brutality of her terrible existence, with all the suffering and deprivation, left her sullen and melancholic. The ravages from her numerous childbearing years had left their mark. Whenever Sybil could, she would bring them food and the clothing Ghislaine and I had outgrown. Sometimes we accompanied her, but Ghislaine and I were somewhat terrified by the Pochard clan. Their neglected appearance and the frightening atmosphere brought out in us a feeling of alarm and apprehension.

Like any ordinary hamlet, Lestelle had a mixed community. There were not only the wealthy and the poor, but the priest, the pension owners, the farmers, the store-keepers, the postmaster, the teacher, the dressmaker, the blacksmith, the cobbler — and then, there was Dr. Naudet.

Dr. Naudet lived with his wife and their two daughters in an old-fashioned house directly across from our pension on the same square. As I visualize Dr. Naudet, walking with his determined gait, I remember the man with his prematurely white hair and his excessively red face. Just like everyone else, Dr. Naudet had no car. Gasoline supplies had long run out; not even a physician could obtain a drop of the precious fuel. Yet Dr. Naudet would be seen, in all seasons, pedaling his bicycle from one side of the village to the other, and throughout the sparsely settled agricultural country surrounding Lestelle, to heal the sick. He was truly a remarkable man. Absolutely dedicated to his vocation, he could be reached day or night. No hour was unacceptable for Dr. Naudet; he would always go to the bedside of his patients.

As a matter of fact, I owe my life to Dr. Naudet. I must have been approximately five or six years old when I was taken to Pau by my parents for a tonsillectomy. The whole episode was like a nightmare. The doctor in Pau who performed the surgery was more like a butcher than a surgeon. He operated on me with no anesthetic and without even taking my temperature or checking my throat! I prefer to leave out the gory details, but to this day, I am still terrified to open my mouth in a dentist's chair!

After the operation, Andre and Sybil brought me back to Lestelle. By the time I was set down to rest in bed and recuperate from my horrifying operation, I was running an exceptionally high fever. My mother assumed that it was simply due to the tonsillectomy. Little did she know! It so happened that Ghislaine had an acute temperature, as well. Immediately, Sybil sent for Dr. Naudet. With his usual promptness, the good doctor came to see us. Both Ghislaine and I were critically ill. We had contracted diphtheria.

There was an epidemic spreading rapidly in the village. Men, women and children were dying every day as a result of the contagious disease.

Andre and Sybil were quite naturally disheartened by the dumbfounding news, especially when Dr. Naudet added, in an abrupt and frank manner: "I will do everything in my power to cure Ghislaine, but I may not be able to save Muriel!" Andre and Sybil were left wandering about the room in a daze.

Day after day, Dr. Naudet came back and forth to inject our stomachs with a quart of serum. The injections were extremely painful, but Dr. Naudet had little choice.

Ghislaine was slowly recovering, and she was up on her feet long before I could sit up. My case was far more serious and had surely been aggravated by my tonsillectomy.

One day when I was lying in bed, far too sick to be moved, my parents had to leave me for a few hours in the care of Madame Arricaud. That afternoon, some German authorities came to the pension to carry out an investigation. I can still hear the echo of the strong German accent in the room where I was bedridden. Madame Arricaud was questioned about my health. Distressed, she disclosed the gravity of my malady. The officer pulled my blankets off and uttered: "Why bother! She is dying anyway!"

As sick as I was, I didn't want to remain uncovered in the presence of a stranger, but I lay there, unable to show my anger. Shocked by his insensitivity, Madame Arricaud sat for a moment unable to move. Then she got up from her chair and whispered, as she picked up the blankets to tuck me in, "Don't worry little girl, I'll take care of you."

After a few moments of consideration, the officer left the room followed by Madame Arricaud, and I continued my silent fight for life!

It took me weeks to recover completely from diphtheria, but without my parents' love and the magnitude of Dr. Naudet's complete devotion, I would not be here to tell my story.

I have many recollections about those days in Lestelle; some are clear and some are half-remembered. One scene, however, is very clear in my mind.

It took place at the pension when I was about five years old. My mother had to go on an errand and there was no question of leaving Ghislaine behind. Devilish as quicksilver, my little sister would get herself into some unbelievable predicaments. Once, she maneuvered her head between two parallel bars of a wooden chair while my mother was trying to feed her! Ultimately, a bar had to be sawed off to free her! Then, there was also the crisis when Ghislaine managed to inhale a pearl high into her nose! It took the ingenuity of several persons to make her sneeze and blow the bead out. Ghislaine's mischievousness always got her into trouble. Contrary to my dear sister, I rarely got into trouble. So my mother had no qualms about leaving me behind.

For a moment that afternoon, Sybil looked at me as though she was going to take me with her. But then she saw that I was happily playing in the courtyard with Jean Claude. "Be a good girl," she said, as she gave me an affectionate hug before she went out with Ghislaine.

However, when Sybil and my sister returned to the pension the whole place was in turmoil. What could have happened to cause such a commotion and aroused such terror?

Had the Nazis reached Lestelle?

A mass of people congregated around her and affronted her with insults and abuse.

"This is outrageous!" Monsieur Arricaud yelled out as he thumped the table.

"You'll have to pay for this!" Marguerite, one of the old aunts, shouted out.

"Yes, it is an outrage. You must pay!" Isidorine, the other old aunt, growled.

"Do you realize what your wicked child did to mine?" Madame Arricaud screamed over her shoulder, as she was trying to calm down Jean Claude.

Almost speechless, Sybil stood there, realizing that something very serious had occurred during her brief absence. She had a puzzled expression in her warm and grayish-blue eyes.

I ran into her arms and cried.

"What on earth are they trying to say?" She asked me excitedly as she picked me up and plopped me onto the table in the main kitchen. I could not explain, but I was the culprit.

Jean Claude was thirsty, so I invited him up to my room. I knew that my mother kept bottles under our sink behind the short curtain. But I did not realize that, in my kindness, I had offered my playmate Javelle water, a strong bleaching agent that I mistook for lemonade. Fortunately, Jean

Claude spat out the few drops he had in his mouth, but his shrieks were so piercing that his mother thought that he had swallowed some. She alerted her whole family and everyone at the pension. Soon, half of the villagers were there as well. The emotional outburst was spreading.

Suddenly, a stillness replaced the hullabaloo and Jean Claude pushed his way towards me and said, "Come on Muriel, let's play." The crowd stood about, watching the reconciliation.

Sybil frowned at me slightly. "Go ahead!" She finally said."Go and play!"

Jean Claude and I were soon prancing in the yard. The outrage was soon forgotten and the incident was only remembered as an innocent gesture of a young child.

Jean Claude was a great playmate. However, Ghislaine and I had many friends in the hamlet. We played all sorts of games, indoor games and outdoor games. But our favorite hideout was the church. The church doors were never locked, but we crept through the doors hurriedly, in order not to be seen. Its inspiring sense of mystery and wonder was the perfect place for our little gang to play hide and seek. In the shadows of dim lights, a few treasures for the consecration to the eucharist shone on the altar. Behind the altar, the large cross of Jesus Christ evoked a certain fear in us, but these apprehensions soon transferred themselves into a great thrill, as we hid and looked for each other.

The sound of our echoed steps banished the silence. The creaking floor, which led to the elevated lectern, was a dead give-away, but we loved to get up there and look down at the luminosity of the burning candles.

Catching a glimpse of our good friend Nadette in her concealment behind the holy-water stand, I flew down to surprise her. "It's not fair, you saw me from the top!" she groaned. I had already discovered our comrade Jacques in a confessional booth.

There were three confessional booths. We often sat in the enclosed wooden compartments and confessed to all sorts of make-believe wickedness, to a make-believe clergyman who listened on the other side of a dense brown curtain. Oh, how we wished that the confessional booths could talk and tell us all about the real intimate secrets disclosed by the devout every week!

Just like anywhere else, Lestelle had its share of tainted characters: one was unfaithful, one was dishonest, another was foul-mouthed. Whatever the infamy, the sinner confessed to the priest and repented in the hope of being given absolution for his or her wrongdoings. But, so frequently, the penitent asked for forgiveness only to persist in his or her disruptive behavior.

I often pondered the irony of such incongruity. How could one violate the law, then return to the priest to implore for pardon, only to turn around and commit more evil? I came to the conclusion that a truly religious person is not necessarily the individual who adheres to a monastic order, but rather the person whom each day leads a life of moral rectitude, kindness and tolerance for others.

My friends in the hamlet were all Catholics. We didn't, of course, ever discuss religion. But with the extermination of the Jews all over Europe at the hands of the Nazis, my parents decided to have Ghislaine and me baptized. As the war reached its climax, I can well understand Andre and Sybil's intense despair. If a baptismal certificate could in any way save their little girls from the persecutions, the compromising of their principles prevailed. I do not remember the Christian sacrament that occurred on that day in 1941. But I do have the certificate proving that it did happen!

The war was going on, but people were still getting married, having babies, and were still observing the holidays. My curiosity was roused when a baptism, a communion or a wedding took place in the little church next door. Of course, weddings were my favorite. The ritual of a marriage ceremony emanated an aura of nobility and a sensation of romanticism in which I delighted.

However, the gloomy mood of a funeral procession, with all the despairing mourners dressed in black, gave me feelings of jittery uneasiness. As a little girl, I could never walk in front of the house of a deceased. Just the sight of the front door, framed with a thick black cloth crowned by a huge, clipped-on, embroidered white initial of the deceased person, terrified me. I knew that it was the custom to keep the body in the house several days before the burial. A death in the village was inclined to affect the small community. Most villagers were at great pains to make a visit to the bereaved family. As they arrived in front of the door, they would stand for a moment, sighing and weeping. Then, nervously fixing their appearance, they would enter the house.

"Maybe you'd better run along girls," Sybil would implore as she increased her step. It was almost a relief to be forced away from these distressing sights.

Despite the preoccupations the villagers had with the war, the Catholic holidays were fully observed in the hamlet. I was, of course, far too young to attend any midnight mass, but I do remember vividly, the Easter parades commemorating the resurrection of Christ. I wormed my way through the crowd to see it all. I gazed at the pageantry, in awe. The processions were headed by a young boy carrying a golden cross, followed by the priests wearing a long black cassock with a short, white, loose-fitting gown with full-flowing sleeves, and by others from the clergy, in white or red cassocks. The various members of the church, dressed in their best clothes for the holiday, walked behind them. The sound of the church bells echoing all the way back from Rome, as tradition had it, had an unforgettable tone and were uncommonly splendid.

The luncheon we ate at the pension on Easter Sunday was definitely superior to our everyday meals. We never had enough to eat, but somehow for the occasion, Madame Arricaud managed to make it somewhat festive.

The slightest necessity was a difficult proposition during these war years. Lestelle had two small general stores, Mattock and Magros. Their unusual assemblage of disparate supplies and miscellaneous articles was similar to a bazaar, where foods, notions, housewares, clothing and shoes were mingled in disorder and confusion. The stock was lacking and the choice was notably inadequate.

The rationing and the restrictions were so acute that many resorted to buying their goods on the black market. If people did not have the money or simply did not want to pay the outrageous prices, they merely had to do without the articles. Bartering was also popular among the villagers. I remember my mother exchanging a few cakes of Savon de Marseille, a yellow household soap, for a few yards of fabric to clothe her little girls. The lines outside the stores were always very long; everyone was so desperately trying to get the indispensable. There were, of course, the few undisciplined characters who tried to move ahead by infiltrating themselves in the middle of the crowd. That, obviously, caused an outburst of melodramatic arguments. People were frustrated, but somehow the pulse of continuous life managed to recharge their weariness.

As arduous as it seemed, in the midst of these troublesome years, Lestelle was still, with its lovely countryside, a kind haven for our family. The peaceful scenery surrounding our hamlet, with its large fields and widely dispersed old farms on one side and with Betharram, a place of pilgrimage, on the other side, still remains so vivid in my mind.

Not as famous as Lourdes, Betharram is noteworthy for its cathedral, a beautiful 17th-century sanctuary with bas-reliefs depicting the Stations of the Cross. There were grottoes nearby. I only remember visiting them once. Beneath the arch of mud the light was poor, but as we filed down the steep path of the corridors, one by one, the galaxy of stalactites and stalagmites riveted my whole attention. In the feeble rays, their strange forms conveyed all kinds of mysterious spectral sculptures. I admired them with a certain trepidation. In the damp atmosphere, an occasional drip of water plopped against the rock and broke the silence. Of course, roaming around the grottoes was kind of adventurous. But I must admit that I was glad to step out of the dark and see the blue sky!

At no great distance, the continuous rhythmic flowing of the Gave de Pau could be heard. Almost all day, along the embankment of the river, in the shadow of the trees, the fishermen would sit still for endless hours in the hope of a big catch. From a little bridge above, where we often stopped, we would watch them at a distance. They lacked refinement with their grimy appearance and their high rubber boots. But their harmonious and poetic relationship with the environment was formidable. Nothing else mattered; patiently waiting for a jolting of the rod, they hoped for a good-sized trout!

Whenever they could, Andre and Sybil rode their bicycles to the neighboring villages. Ghislaine was seated behind Maman on her bike and I would sit behind Papa on his bike. The beauty of the landscape along the tree-lined roads was peaceful. The red poppies and the blue cornflowers contrasted so delicately with the yellow corn. The countryside was magnificent. If only the anguish of the distressing period could have been alleviated, our stay in the Pyrenees would have been most rewarding.

Unfortunately, the war was still going on and was spreading. My parents had little contact with their relatives. My mother was totally alienated from her family in England. My father's relatives were scattered in various directions. His sister and brother-in-law were trying to escape with their children to Spain. They stopped over in Lestelle and left shortly after. Andre's mother and grandmother also came to Lestelle. They settled down for a while. However, when the situation worsened, they admitted that they wanted to go into hiding. So, my father decided to have a family conference. But it was not easy; both Grand-mere and Meme (we referred to our Great-grandmother and our Grandmother in these terms) were hard of hearing. Grand-mere was completely deaf. She had at the time a remarkably odd apparatus, something like an ear-trumpet, which amplified the sound. With this device, she could lend an ear and pick up the essence of the conversation when a person spoke clearly and loudly into acoustic.

During that troubled time, it was definitely not advisable for anyone to exchange loud discussions concerning future plans and finances. To apprise Grand-mere of the precarious situation and to analyze the measures that had to be ascertained, it was vital to find a place where my parents, my grandmother and my Aunt Huguette could talk without the chance of being overheard. The fear of denunciation was always there. Andre decided that the most opportune spot would be in the middle of a vast field.

The decision was made, but how to get Grand-mere into the open expanse of land was another question. She was about 85 and was far too elderly to ride a bike, especially since she had broken her hip. I wonder if Grand-mere had ever cycled in her life. Her method of conveyance had been a horse and carriage until the automobile and chauffeur had replaced them.

It took the ingenuity of my father to realize such a brilliant contraption. He attached, with extreme care, a sort of two-wheeled wagon to his bicycle. On this wagon's small platform he placed an armchair, which he roped with great meticulousness so that he could take his grand-mother out of the village and into the heart of the countryside.

Grand-mere stepped onto her improvised carriage with her usual grace and charm. She ascended and seated herself with such harmonious simplicity that one could have been oblivious to the reality of the situation. My father replaced the horses and the wagon superseded the carriage. Grand-mere's fashion sense was always refined and renowned for its class and elegance. Her garb on that particular day could have been worn to a garden party among her circle of wealthy Parisian friends. She was sophisticated and the pressure of the war and inconveniences were not going to put an end to her distinguished mode of existence. Her beautiful black and white outfit complemented her style. Nothing was missing; her smart wide-brimmed black hat, lavishly embellished by a well-proportioned black velvet bow, contrasted well with her white hair. Her black kid gloves and her black high-heeled shoes splendidly rounded out her already exquisite outfit.

I wonder if Grand-mere fully understood the effort undertaken by her favorite grandson. In order to conquer the hilly road of the rural region, he had to pedal with such vigor and vitality. Despite Grand-mere's slight stature, the load my father had to pull was, nevertheless, weighty.

After some thoughtful and lengthy consideration, it was decided that both Grand-mere and Meme would leave Lestelle for a convent, a short distance away from Lourdes, under the protection of a Mother Superior and a group of nuns.

I was sorry that they had to leave. I cherished both of them, but I was especially close to Meme. Her joviality was unbelievable. Meme's beautiful big brown eyes glowed with "la joie de vivre." She always had the knack of overcoming any intricate or complicated situation with high spirits. She loved life and was not going to concede and withdraw because matters were not going her way. She was a fighter. Her early widowhood (she was 29 years old when Victor, her husband, was killed in the First World War) and her complete responsibility in the upbringing of her children as a single parent did not overburden her. At all times, she overcame the crisis and secured her wholehearted devotion to them.

Both Grand-mere and Meme were wonderful human beings, but it was quite extraordinary to imagine that they were related. No mother and daughter could have been more dissimilar. Grand-mere was tall and slender, while Meme was on the short side with a definite excess of weight. Grand-mere was elegant and extremely precise, while Meme was, far from being as fastidious as her mother, more relaxed in manner. She dressed in a more casual way. Grand-mere valued etiquette and decorum, while Meme hated conventionalities and preferred spontaneity. Both maintained a high standard of living, but Grand-mere was more parsimonious than her daughter, who was a born giver.

After a few weeks with us, Grand-mere and Meme moved on to the convent, where they subsisted up to the end of the war. I am not sure why they were kept apart; after all, they were in the same convent. Regardless of what happened to separate them, they withdrew from the world to live in a very austere environment. The entire furnishings in their small, unheated, whitewashed cubicles consisted of an iron bed, one chair and a sort of rod to hang their clothes.

I can very well imagine with what ominous horror they remained confined to their dreary abode. Their loneliness must have been really unbearable and the drastic severity of it all must have been surpassingly stressful on both Grand-mere and Meme, who had been fortunate enough to know and appreciate a sumptuous and graceful existence. But the agitating time gave them no alternatives. The crucial question was to seize, no matter what, the opportunity that could possibly reduce their exposure to risk and peril.

The supercharged atmosphere was rapidly growing in intensity. The Germans were advancing and their military operations had escalated. In 1942, when the line of demarcation between the two Zones collapsed, Andre became a member of the French Resistance. Opposed to the Nazi occupation and the pro-Nazi elements in the Vichy government, he joined the Maquis in Tarbes, in a small town, near Lestelle. I can still picture papa in his heavy military khaki outfit, with a happy smile as he sank down in a chair and held his two little girls on his lap. He always wanted to know about us, what we were up to, but he never talked about the war or his activities in the Maquis de Tarbes. Meanwhile, Sybil rejected despair with a formidable stamina. She shielded Ghislaine and me from her anxieties. We were obviously too young to understand the danger and the horror of it all.

For the next few months, our life as refugees in Lestelle, continued with its economic restrictions and uneasiness. Yet, with all the deprivations and problems my family had to deal with, they were still more fortunate than most Jews in France. The Gestapo had ordered Jews in much of France to wear a yellow star, to identify them. Fortunately, the Jewish badge decree was never wholly enforced in the Unoccupied Zone and we were able to avoid wearing the star. However, the atmosphere of the crisis was intensifying and the danger of deportation hovered over the Jews every day. My family was haunted by the horrible revelation that Hitler had begun the mass extermination of the Jews. Shocked and stricken, Andre and Sybil received the harrowing news that several cousins had been deported from Paris. It just seemed like no one listened or cared; the Nazis just advanced further and further.

At first, the Americans were against becoming directly involved in the war. However, in 1944, General Dwight Eisenhower of the United States, commander of the Allied Forces in Western Europe, and thousands of

American and British troops, were preparing to enter France, massively and forcefully, from England.

On June 6th, 1944, the Allies landed in Normandy. Before long, the Allied troops were moving expeditiously from the Northern coast across France. American and British planes controlled the skies and bombers made raids against innumerable enemy-held cities. One last major counter-offensive by the Germans was instigated and failed in December 1944.

Soon, throughout France, Jews and non-Jews combined their efforts to work with the Americans to put an end to the Holocaust.

At the end of 1944, my father left Lestelle to fight alongside the Americans. Sybil had long accepted the situation as an unavoidable inconvenience and was able to keep her emotions to herself. That was until papa came back, on leave.

Sybil's devotion and adoration showed as she ran to meet him. She looked at him with her warm blue eyes, their extraordinary love for each other bursting out with such radiance that for a moment they were alone, forgetting everything and everyone around.

I remember so well my father and his American comrades. These young men were in France to liberate the country and free its people from German oppression and persecution. But now and then they would take a little time from their tremendous task and bring brief moments of joy to the refugees. Ghislaine and I had an abundance of fun with them. Not only did they entertain us with their merrymaking and joking, but they frequently indulged us with a variety of tasty treats. The assortment of American chocolate bars delighted us and surprised us too. We had never devoured anything with such pleasure. The diversity was heavenly. Ghislaine and I discovered for the first time the taste of coconut, caramel and nuts. It was all so good. But I must admit that, above all, we were fascinated by the chewing gum — it really tickled our fancy. Undeniably, the Americans possessed distinctive qualities that had unaccountable effects on us. We were also charmed by their generosity and their brotherly warm-heartedness. Language was not a problem; they had a way to gesture their friendship. Their spontaneity was real and their impulse toward laughter was wonderful.

Seemingly I was too young to realize everything that had happened in my country throughout these four years in Lestelle. But I will certainly never forget that day in April 1945, when Adolf Hitler killed himself in his bunker.

The emotional elan in Lestelle was profound, ardent and heartfelt. The villagers' uncontrollable vehemence and the intensity of their repugnance for Hitler exploded with a colossal and huge manifestation of their feelings. A vulgar and crude dummy, fashioned in the likeness of Hitler, was carried all over the village. Then, as the crowd clustered around the main square, this symbol of the Third Reich was hung and burned.

I will always remember the exceptional and extraordinary condemnation demonstrated by the villagers as they watch Hitler's crude effigy being destroyed with fire.

"Murderer!" they shouted.

"Oppressor! You have made people suffer for years! We want our revenge," they yelled out, as they watched, with pitiless hatred, the flames and the smoke progressing and moving toward the sky.

Before long, the villagers were holding each other's hands and were dancing around the blaze, with vitality and dynamism. Soon, they also began to chant the "Marseillaise" and many other ballads and melodies.

How could I ever fail to recollect this momentous and incredible event? It was, to say the least, extraordinary and phenomenal.

****

The end of the war was close by. People were breathing more easily as they perceived a ray of hope after the long years of struggle and fear. It was time for my father to return to Paris, and carry on his collaboration with the American troops.

My mother recognized that it was still too early for her and her two little girls to make the move back to the capital with papa. It seemed only natural to her that she should stay in Lestelle, to maintain a sort of routine for Ghislaine and me.

By then, I was going to school, but no ordinary school. Two sisters, known as "Les demoiselles Perey Saint-Pierre," controlled the unique classroom in the village. It was open to all primary school children, no matter their age. The high school students had to leave the village and travel to Betharram.

The demoiselles Perey Saint-Pierre's capability to give lessons was remarkable and outstanding. They never failed to encourage us. Whenever we had the right answer they would reward us with a "hostie," a communion wafer, that they would get from the priest. They certainly knew how to inspire their young students to handwrite in cursive script. I still have an example of my achievement, a letter I wrote to papa when he left Lestelle to join the American troops to liberate France.

The demoiselles Perey Saint-Pierre look like were like characters from one of Dickens' novels. They were both massive old women in heavy black dresses, wrapped tightly in large black shawls. Their unfortunate image became seemingly aggravated by their grand stature, their lack of make-up, and by their severe straight and short haircuts. However, as they rose their eyes every morning to where we sat with a warm smile upon their lips, they began their day with a cordial "Bonjour les enfants," which we echoed with a "Bonjour." "They just do not look the way they sound," I thought.

The demoiselles Perey Saint-Pierre were kind ladies, who went about their daily pursuits in a quiet manner. They were devoted to education. For many long years, they taught the basics of simple arithmetic, reading and writing to their young students. The demoiselles Perey Saint-Pierre's classes seem so, so far away and somewhat blurred, but as I reflect upon my first days of school, I could never forget my very first teachers.

When the German leaders signed the Allied surrender terms on May 7, 1945, the war in Europe was over. It was a time to rejoice over the victory. The despair and terror evaporated and suddenly gave way to a sensation of relief and merriment. The blue, white and red French flags were flown high all over the country. Elated crowds met in the streets. Everyone, young and old, sang and danced together. There was such joy everywhere. Bonfires, fanfares, illuminations and fireworks cheered the entire nation.

Lestelle was no exception; the emotion was so great. It was not jubilation alone, but it seemed to me that everyone mingled to kiss, to cry, to laugh, to exhibit all kinds of feelings. They had survived the war and now they were desperate to get on with their lives.

As I entered the pension that afternoon, there was a serenity in Sybil's appearance. Her radiant countenance was wonderful.

"Come, darling, come," she called out to me, holding out her arms.

I sat on her lap and she kissed me. I held her tight with my arms around her neck. I had the feeling that she had something important to say. I knew how much she felt the void left by Andre's absence. "I am so glad to see the war end," she said smiling. She kissed me again and turned her beautiful blue eyes on me. "Now, Mumu," she said, "the time has come for us to return to Paris and meet up with your father."

I had forgotten that the end of the war would absolutely ensure our return to the capital. My mind wandered. I guess that I was puzzled and disturbed at the idea of leaving the village and my friends.

The moment had arrived for us to say goodbye. It was an emotional and poignant "au revoir." We were departing from the hamlet that had been a safe haven for our family for the last four years. Madame Arricaud was so much affected by our departure that she kissed us quickly and murmured, "My dear family from Paris is leaving." Overwhelmed with tears in her eyes, she retired.

Before boarding the bus, Sybil, Ghislaine and I stood there, for some time, trying to articulate and vocalize our last goodbyes. "Adieux" was never easy.

"We will miss you too," cried Monsieur Arricaud. "We will miss you all."

"We will miss you too," replied Sybil, "but we will come back and visit, I promise."

And with these good words, we boarded the bus for Tarbes. There we could catch the night train straight to Paris. After a considerable delay, the coal-powered locomotive approached the station slowly and halted with its long string of passenger and freight cars. How could one locomotive pull so many cars? I wondered.

There was tremendous confusion when the train stopped. So many people wanted to get on the train to Paris. Fortunately, we had our reserved seats.

"What a muddle!" Sybil said, shaking her head.

Holding onto her dress, Ghislaine and I followed her as she zigzagged her way through the crowd to get to our carriage. As soon as we ascended the steps into our compartment, the ticket inspector came and quickly converted our seats to two triple-deckers. The carriage was full, but I have no recollection as to who was sharing it with us.

"Well my darlings, we are on our way to Paris," Maman exclaimed as the train started to move slowly down the track.

Since it was already nighttime and far too dark to turn our eyes on the passing scenery, we placed ourselves on our sleepers. But not for long. The train was now moving at an amazing speed; the shaking and the rocking were unbelievable. Convulsed with laughter, Ghislaine and I fell on the floor several times. "You might as well be on the floor." Sybil uttered as she arranged a makeshift bed for us.

Probably the most miserable discomfort we suffered during our voyage was the lack of ventilation in the carriage. The only alternative was to open the window, after which the compartment was right away filled with smoke and soot, particularly when we passed through a long tunnel.

In the early morning, the train arrived at the spacious Gare d'Austerlitz. We had reached our destination. We were somewhat tired and extremely dirty from the smoke and soot. However, we were very happy to be reunited with Papa and we were so glad that the return voyage was over with our safe return to Paris.

CHAPTER 2

21 Rue de la Faisanderie

Paris weathered the German occupation and emerged with an undaunted spirit.

The Parisians who had fled the capital due to their prodigious fear of deportation were slowly returning to the city.

My parents' house in the suburbs was no longer available. Their home had been completely emptied by the Germans. Their furniture and their personal belongings had all been taken in a surreptitious way by the Nazis. However, both Andre and Sybil showed courage and determination.

We were alive and well and that was of sole importance to them. Too many members of our family and friends had been touched by suffering and bereavement. Things could always be replaced!

Fortunately, Grand-mere's mansion, a beautiful estate situated on the west side of the city close to the Bois de Boulogne and the Avenue Foch, had been protected by Madame Durel, my father's governess.

"We have arrived," Andre announced, as we approached 21 of the Rue de la Faisanderie.

Sybil's eyes brightened up and she began to smile.

We entered the sturdy wrought iron gates.

Andre opened the front door. On the left side, an elegant flight of steps led the way into the magnificent townhouse. Sybil went in, followed by Ghislaine and me.

Everything about the vestibule contributed to a sense of mystery that aroused my imagination. Poorly lit and shadowy, the hallway had a rather somber aspect. The heavy tapestries on the walls with their pictorial designs in subdued beiges, blues and greens reminded me somewhat of spectral beings! The massive brown wooden chest and the four large tapestry chairs under the wall hangings did little to liven up the crimson Persian rug. For sure, the soft darkness and the quiescent atmosphere were far from ordinary. With a curious inward stillness, I looked around.

"Come on Ghislaine, come on, don't you want to see the house?" I called out.

I opened the first double doors on the right side of the hallway. We walked into a beautiful petit salon. The sitting room was, according to Meme, used by Grand-mere to entertain her close friends.

From the petit salon, we pressed onward and proceeded through double doors, to sally forth into the grand salon. I was startled and amazed to look at such a grandiose and flamboyant room. "A prince and a princess could have lived there!" I thought.

The two reception rooms were unbelievably astonishing with their compelling resplendence and magnificence.

After the simplicity I had known in the Pension Arricaud, I gazed with enchantment and fascination at the beauty of it all. The high ceilings, with their richly patterned golden designs around the edge, the golden frames around the doors, the high and magnificent marble mantel pieces, the lovely rugs scattered on the fine parquetry and the rich satin curtains framing the tall French windows all complemented the glorious rooms with a definite refinement.

The furniture, however, was scarce and insufficient to fill the large rooms. Madame Durel, my father's governess, had propitiously removed several pieces of furniture and a major part of Grand-mere's sterling silver collection. Skillful and proficient, she was able to move Grand-mere's valuable possessions to a storage place before the Nazis availed themselves of Grand-mere's mansion as one of their headquarters.

Across from the reception rooms we entered into an enormous dining room directly connected with the pantry and the servants' hall. The pantry was later remodeled into a kitchen and the vast kitchen in the basement was no longer utilized.

For a moment I stood still. I tried to imagine the way of life that Grand-mere and her family were fortunate to have had and thrived in. Looking at these rooms with the sun and shadow flickering through them, my eyes turned toward the tall windows. I stepped on the small balcony and watched the passersby with excitement. I just loved the idea of being in a big city.

Feeling very happy, I hurried back into the vestibule to see more.

Straight across from the main entrance door, at the bottom of the staircase, an imposing and majestic white marble statue of a woman in a draped toga stood erect.

"Oh my, she is gigantic!" I uttered, staring at her with surprise. Ghislaine and I glanced at each other and burst out laughing.

"Come on, silly girls, let's go upstairs," Sybil suggested.

Both Ghislaine and I complied with the desire to go on and see more.

Discovering Grand-mere's house was indeed a joy for us. The wide staircase with its gold-leaf handrail led the way to two additional floors, where an impressive number of bedrooms, playrooms, antechambers and bathrooms were to be found. Ghislaine and I had great fun running from room to room.

"Open the windows! There is a musty odor about the house!" Sybil called out, as she reached the top floor.

"Yes, you are right! We really need to ventilate the rooms with a breeze of fresh air," echoed Andre. He looked at Ghislaine and me, grinned, and added: "Don't just stand there — you heard your mother."

We gave a helping hand to Papa and Maman to open all of the windows.

With a mix of impassioned and earnest emotions, I wanted to discover the rest of the property.

"Ghislaine, let's go to the garden," I called out with enthusiasm.

"It's still early, go ahead," Sybil responded calmly.

The attractive mansion, made out of natural ashlar stones, stood on spacious grounds.

From the entrance gates, a long gravel path led the way, through a vast garden, to a sizable courtyard, where a simple red brick house marked the end of the estate. The building consisted of two large stables which had been converted into garages after the introduction of the automobile. The servants' quarters were above the garages.

Ghislaine and I ventured around. It was pretty dark. We could almost see our footprints on the dusty floors of the hallway, which led to the many small rooms.

"They are certainly different from the chambers of the mansion!" I said with a swift glance at the space and the scope of the cubicles.

"Let's get out of here and see the garden," Ghislaine finally insisted.

When we came downstairs, we hurried about the grounds. The courtyard was separated by a short stone wall on one side and by a dense growth of shrubs on the other side. We had to return to the gravel path to go into the garden.

The garden had a neglected appearance and showed the ravages of the war. The grass was long and full of weeds; many plants and flowers had not survived the lack of care. Yet the lilac trees, which I particularly favored with their rich clusters of purple flowers and their wonderful fragrance, were still blooming. In fact, whenever I come across a lilac tree with its unique and distinctive scent, my thoughts go back to Grand-mere's garden, Rue de la Faisanderie.

Centered in the middle of the lawn was a beautiful grey stone statue of a woman on a high pedestal. I preferred her graceful naked form and refined traits to those of the massive lady standing at the foot of the staircase in the entrance hallway.

Ghislaine and I stopped for a pause on one of the green wooden benches along the alley. No words were exchanged. Exhilarated and filled with high spirits, so much went through my mind.

I was so excited and inspired by the discovery of my great grandmother's domain.

I was in awe and amazed by her grand residence.

Unfortunately, the graceful townhouse would never see again the splendor, the dazzle nor the ostentatious lifestyle it had known before the war with my great grandfather, my great grandmother and their three children. They had, from what I was told, at their service cooks, butlers, chambermaids, valets, laundresses, baby-nurses, chauffeurs and gardeners.

Now, Grand-mere's dazzling existence had ceased. World War II had taken care of that.

We had to be thankful that the townhouse had endured adversity and was providing a haven for most of our family. Like ourselves, they had been dispossessed of their property.

Before long, our mother called for us. Ghislaine and I left the garden and hurried back into the vestibule, anxious to get familiar with our new surroundings.

We were the first ones to reach Paris, but very soon afterward, the other family members followed.

I am not sure of how these arrangements came about, but I guess that compliance and yielding were, under the circumstances, the only reasonable things to do. The mansion was promptly divided into separate apartments and suites of rooms. Aunt Huguette, Uncle Roger and their two children, Francois and Nicole, occupied the main floor. Yvonne (Andre's cousin) arrived alone with her three children; her husband having been deported. They lived in Grand-mere's magnificent suite on the first floor until they could return to their lovely flat. Grand-mere and Meme occupied two bedrooms on the same floor. And the entire top floor was allocated to us.

There were no beds. For the first few nights, we had to sleep on mattresses laid down on the floor. The magnificent bathrooms were fully equipped and remarkably spare. Naturally, there was no kitchen on that floor, so one of the rooms had to be promptly remodeled and refurbished into a kitchen.

The moment had arrived to adjust and reconcile with the Parisian way of life. Shortages and scarcity in food and everything else faced millions of people in a war-torn Europe. Everyone was touched to some degree; so many industries had been destroyed.

We were very fortunate to have some wonderful American friends. Sympathetic to our circumstances and to our lack of basic essentials, they mailed packages of corned beef, Spam and other canned products to us. Clothing was also sent, as well.

Oh, how I remember the pretty dresses I inherited from the daughter of Andre's American friends! They were so colorful and so different from the average post-war French dresses. When I tried them on and looked at myself in a mirror, I felt a sudden quiver of emotion. At the age of seven,

I had already acquired the characteristics of femininity and was definitely style-conscious! My American clothes enchanted me to no end.

For Ghislaine and me, living in Grand-mere's stately residence was most definitely a new and exciting episode in our lives.

Of course, we did not have the responsibilities and problems our parents had to face. Andre and Sybil had to start from scratch and had to gradually round up the indispensable to make our home a home. For a while, we used the garden table and chairs as our dining room furniture. It did not matter; we were together and that was of sole importance. In retrospect, I cherish and value the memories of my childhood in Grand-mere's mansion.

The next seven years of my life were spent there, in an environment of close family relationships. They most certainly embraced the complexities of interwoven feelings of felicity and disenchantment, but nevertheless, these years were special and unforgettable.

The summer months were soon over. The schools opened their doors in early October. Too young to go to the Lycee, Ghislaine and I were enrolled in a neighborhood public school, a simple unassuming building standing on a fairly large playground. I have few recollections concerning these early school days.

But I will never forget the eighteenth of December 1945. Sybil was in labor, in the room next door to mine. I wanted to see my mother. The nurse stopped me from going into the room and insisted that I get ready to leave for school. I did not want to go to school that morning. I could not understand the inflexible standards and the lack of sensitivity of the nurse. I was almost hysterical. I cringed at the idea of having to yield to her authority. But lashing into a fury would not change the woman's mind. She was not young and she was not accustomed to resistance and defiance. She expected docility from me and insisted, with firmness, that I obey.

Finally, she had achieved her goal. I attended classes that morning. The morning progressed at a snail's pace. The monotonous voice of the teacher irritated me a great deal. I was tired of the dullness and tediousness of the lessons. I was there in school, sullenly aloof and withdrawn. I wanted to be home.

At long last the bell rang. I was elated. A sudden outpouring of emotions overwhelmed me as I scrambled to gather up my books. Rushing impetuously, I dashed down to the playground. Ghislaine and our maid were waiting for me.

"You have a baby brother," the lady bellowed.

I hardly could contain my jubilation. Eager to get back, I quickened my step. I left Ghislaine and our maid behind and I ran down the Rue de Longchamps, all the way home. I did not feel the cold of the winter. Cheerful and carefree, I swiftly ran up the two flights of stairs. I was ecstatic and tickled pink at the idea of having a baby brother.

I raced to the cradle and gazed at him with amazement. I felt a sudden intense emotion passing through my entire body. He was such a darling baby with his defined features, his light blond hair and his wonderfully soft and fair skin. He was precious, he really was.

"How could such a perfect and complete little being come out of my mother's womb?" I wondered.

Dazed and speechless for a moment, I was trying to absorb it all.

Then, carried away by a sudden impulse, I threw myself into mother's arms and hugged her tightly.

"May I take Christian out of his cradle?" I implored with boundless enthusiasm.

"Yes Mumu, you may hold him, but you must be very careful and very gentle."

Although this was my very first experience with a newborn, I was not scared. I was fascinated and totally enthralled to have him in my arms. The size of his hands and feet were so deliciously small and cute. I really was impressed and excited by the perplexity of life in this tiny human being.

Before long, Christian was sitting up and walking. I enjoyed him immensely. So often, I got down on the floor and played with him with his cars and trucks. I spent most of my pocket money on my little brother. I just loved to watch his eyes gleam every time I gave him a new toy.

Sybil claimed that it was just about impossible to raise Christian. Whenever he would get into trouble, I would cry and Ghislaine would scream!

Meanwhile, Aunt Huguette had also given birth to a boy. Daniel was born three months after Christian.

Notwithstanding the fact that Daniel was a pretty wild little boy, contrary to Christian, who was more calm and reserved, the cousins became very close playmates. They spent hours and hours together, sharing a great deal of naughtiness.

They were not the only ones! Daniel's older siblings, Francois and Nicole and aunt Yvonne's children, Michel, Liliane and Bernard — not forgetting Ghislaine and "petit moi"— were buddies, often mischievous, playfully annoying and prankish!

We all possessed a vivid imagination, and Grand-mere's spacious grounds provided us with incredible potential for the ingenious creativity of our games and schemes.

Francois, who was five years older than me, participated rarely in our play. However, when he did get involved, we were in for a thrill. He was audacious, fearless and incredibly daring. I will never forget our adventure with him through the sewer. Little did we know what was waiting for us!

It was an unparalleled experience.

Our clique had agreed to meet after lunch in the large kitchen down in the basement, where Francois had discovered a secret trap door. Ghislaine and I were able to leave our room unobtrusively and creep quietly downstairs. Fully equipped with flashlights, ropes and whistles, we were ready to start our mysterious adventure.

Past the trap door, a short flight of stone steps led the way down to a dingy pitch-black passage on which numerous corridors converged. One behind the other, holding onto our rope, we trampled about. The darkness was dreadful. The humidity and the chilliness of the premises overpowered us. An unsettling and bewildering feeling possessed everyone.

Yet, as horrified and frightened as we were, we did not voice our dismay right away!

The situation became even more terrifying when Francois started to intone alarming and exaggerated tales of ghosts. Furthermore, using his flashlight, he brandished images of ghostlike shadows on the walls. He insisted that the place was full of spirits and spooky specters. With his practical jokes about phantoms and supernatural beings, Francois attained a rush of excitement at our expense!

Our curiosity had surely been gratified to excess. We had had enough; we wanted to go home and leave this frightful and repulsive environment, but Francois ignored us and continued his tour.

"Walk with prudence," he yelled out with coolness. "The place is infested with rats."

Hearing his remarks chilled my blood. I barely could breathe.

And as if this was not enough to scare us out of our wits, in high pitched shrieks, Francois howled: "I see them! I hear them!"

Scared out of our wits, we cried out in a common accord: "We want to go back! We want to go back!"

"I hope that I can find the way," Francois retorted, as he stopped suddenly, and he added with sarcasm: "You know, this is like an 'oubliette' — a sort of dungeon with a trap door, where people were thrown down and forgotten forever!"

By tears or voice, we expressed our resentment and our dislike for it all. "You villain! You scoundrel! Get us out of here," we insisted with passion and fervent vehemence.

Our cruel fate condemned us to remain in that dreadful place until our leader, Francois, had found his way back to the trap door.

When we finally emerged from the dark, we stood there for a moment, taking a deep breath of relief. We were all gasping for air.

"Will you be able to get back all right?" Francois inquired in a bubbling voice.

"Of course!" we answered spontaneously, as we started to run upstairs.

"Where were you girls?" Sybil interrogated us with a worried look on her face. "I called you several times and you did not answer."

I do not recall whether we were reprimanded or not for our escape, but I do remember that being home felt so good.

Francois was basically a lovable boy, but an incorrigible tease! Without a doubt, his most obnoxious and sadistic trick was the dead chicken's head he placed in my bed!

I realize now that I was indeed my cousin's favorite target because I simply broke down into hysterics, and there was nothing more amusing to my dear cousin than my clamorous hullabaloo for his lousy jokes.

However, it was with Francois' sister Nicole that Ghislaine and I shared an abundance of fun. Blessed with an amazing imagination, Nicole improvised all sorts of games for us. At times though, our dear cousin was so intense in her world of make-believe that she was almost oblivious of the risk liable to have been incurred had we followed her command.

I will never forget the time when Ghislaine and I refused to plunge head-first into the courtyard from the stone wall separating the patio from the garden. Nicole was playing the role of a gym teacher. She was using the courtyard as our imaginary swimming pool, and she wanted us to jump head-first into the so-called pool!

She gave the impression of being a slight and delicate little girl with her hazel eyes and curly brown hair. But she had a distinctive desire to take advantage of her seniority over us to boss us around. Should we not comply with her wish, she would frown upon our insubordination and say: "The game is over! I am going to my room to read a book!" We did not like that at all. We were her fans and wanted to have fun without risking our lives!

Nicole's imagination and inventiveness could not to be believed.

I will never forget the day when Nicole, with her creative use of resources, substituted an old and huge black trunk for an imaginary vessel. We conjured up the vision that we were all in the midst of a hurricane on the high seas and that the strong winds were forcefully blowing against our ship. Our fantasy became a true nightmare. "Watch! We are hitting a large rock. It's a violent collision; we may lose our people," Nicole called out at the top of her voice.

The terror expressed in her loud scream horrified us. Soon the whole situation led to a terrific pandemonium! We were all playing our parts intensely!

Full of energy and enthusiasm, our gang could never stop inventing and creating all kinds of eccentric and weird situations together.

How could I ever forget the day when we decided to stage and produce an emotional and melodramatic performance of a funeral. The 'mise-en-scène' was strange and somewhat uncomfortable, but nothing suppressed our determination to get on and contrive our scheme. Our cousin Bernard, a fragile, pale-faced small boy, was elected to play the role of a cadaver. The entire sacrament was purely made up of our imagination; none of us had ever witnessed a burial.

All dressed in black, we formed a funeral procession and walked to a remote corner of the garden where we had shoveled enough soil to make a large hole in which we placed poor Bernard!

I still wonder what impulse motivated our morbid inkling! It was obvious that our world of make-believe really expounded on all sorts of ideas, conceptions and interpretations.

Conjuring up evocations of my childhood memories, my thoughts turn back to the many enchanting hours our clique spent together, producing and enacting all sorts of plays and performances. On one particular afternoon, I was the scenario-writer. I was reading aloud my farcical skit to my family, friends and babysitters. That was until I started mimicking cheerfully Mademoiselle Osgan, our babysitter. She was sitting there, quietly, among my attentive audience.

Mademoiselle Osgan seemed ancient to Ghislaine and me. Petite and slight, with her tightly twisted grey chignon pinned at the top of her dark-complexioned face, she put forth a rather austere aspect. Yet she was, in reality, a sweet elderly single lady whose job was certainly far from easy! Full of mischief, Ghislaine and I loved to tease her and witness her outbursts of rage; they amused us to no end. And the more excited and agitated she got with our pranks, the more amused we were! Despite our buffoonery, we were fond of her and loved her vivacious personality and her strong Turkish accent.

Well, as I started to mimic Mademoiselle Osgan, my mother got up hastily and simply seized the manuscript out of my hands. I was perplexed and disconcerted. All kinds of emotions stirred within me. A strange sense of helplessness fell upon me. Mortified by Sybil's action, I hurriedly left the room.

My mother did not realize at the time that to spare Mademoiselle Osgan, she had hurt my feelings. The impact of her gesture was formidable. I was a typical ten-year-old, exuberant and expansive. My overflowing high spirits led me to assume that everyone perceived things the way I did! Now, all of a sudden, I was thrashed with opposite winds. The burst of energy and enthusiasm with which I had earlier performed was followed by frustrations and tears. My acting days were over!

That day I realized that I was not free from social expectations and I became worried about expressing my feelings and how I would appear to the external world.

Lying on my bed, shattered and infuriated, I sighed myself into a good cry.

Shortly afterward, my mother was there, standing at the door. Her lips were moving, but I did not hear a word. I wasn't at all happy to see her there. My mind was still flaming with wrath. I thought she might still be angry, but that was not the case; she was staring at me, calmly. Distinguished in her appearance and demeanor, she looked lovely, small, slender and trim, with her fair skin that contrasted so exquisitely well with her soft brown hair and her deep blue eyes which reflected so much her keen intelligence and sensitivity.

I sat up on my bed and watched her as she moved closer. I felt so hurt; I did not think that I could ever forgive my mother. But her warmth emitted such a radiant glow, that I knew, deep down in my heart, that she was only trying to display the compassion and kindness she harbored for others. It was therefore impossible for me to hold a grudge towards her. And without a word, we embraced each other tenderly.

It would be unrealistic to say that our seven years in Grand-mere's mansion were free of worries and concerns for anyone. After all, elbowing and jostling, each and every day, with extended family members of all ages, temperaments and sensibilities could not have been easy! It must have been a true challenge for all. But our feelings were surpassed by our strong bond, mutual loyalties and affection for each other. I was always conscious of the strong family ties we had.

The mixture of strong emotions, of joy, tears, laughter, sorrow, good humor, teasing and conflicts, indeed, generated and produced for me many unforgettable moments.

I particularly cherished the uniqueness of our gatherings in Grand-mere's vast bedroom. Due to her advanced age and a broken hip, Grand-mere was, for the most part, bedridden.

Furnished with sumptuous black and gold Napoleon III furniture, her bedroom reflected opulence in its luxury and style. After lunch, whenever possible, the family, young and old, would cluster around her bed.

The adults were served black coffee in translucent porcelain demitasses, and Anisette liqueur in tiny delicate crystal glasses. The children were allowed to dip one sugar cube into their parents' Anisette. What a treat it was! We felt so important just being there.

Frequently, the animated and spirited discussions and exchanges during our great family gatherings resulted in a somewhat confused babble of loud voices. But the commotion and the euphoria did not disturb Grand-mere, who was very deaf. Despite her impediment, she was by no means left out. We all took turns communicating with her by speaking loudly and distinctly into her acoustic.

As we honored Grand-mere, the togetherness and intimacy of our close family was mutually rewarding.

I remember distinctly spending hours alone with Grand-mere, completely fascinated by her wisdom and experience. I listened attentively to her extraordinary stories. She had lived through three wars. Her past was so rich in memory. Unquestionably, she had the benefit of experiencing so many different occurrences, from the beginning to the end, in her full and great existence.

Attentive and mindful to each and every detail of her appearance and her magnificent bedroom, she had a significant quantity of astounding night-gowns for daytime and another batch for nighttime. Just as she changed her vesture daily, she adorned her bedroom every morning by embellishing the furniture with refined small lace doilies; every evening she would remove them and store them away in a box, until the next day.

It might have seemed perfectly ridiculous to some, excessively boring to others. But with her high sense of organization, Grand-mere believed in a strict routine for herself. The presence of Juliette, her maid, did not prevent her from tending to little things. Each and every day she would check her daily menus with her. Then, she would write in a precise penmanship, item by item, a list of the soiled clothes and linens she was giving her to be laundered. And once her laundry was returned to her, she checked her list in the same fastidious manner to make sure that nothing was missing.

Every Sunday she expected her great grandchildren to line up and collect their weekly pocket money of five 'sous' from her. Of course, Francois tried several times to cheat, by placing himself repeatedly in line. But invariably, Grand-mere's efficiency outsmarted my cousin's cunning dexterity. She was not going to be usurped by her oldest great-grandson! She had her ledger and could verify if he had had his share. And when it came to candy distribution, we were rationed to one a day and no more! I will always remember Grand-mere's contempt for Francois' greediness when she discovered him gorging on sweets!

When I look back to the wonderful holidays during my childhood, Christmas was one of the most amazing events of merry-making in our home. Jews in France, unless they were Orthodox, would partake in the Christmas festivities.

The choice of the tree was very important. Ghislaine and I would go with Papa to select the perfect one. With care, we inspected all the spruces until we found the right one. We needed a tall, deep green tree, bearing a thick growth of evenly divided branches.

The jollity of the atmosphere surrounding us was considerable. But the frosty temperatures were terrible. I felt sorry for the old man who was there, for hours and hours, selling the trees on the street corner. Slowly he would pace up and down the corridor between the lines of adjacent pines and yell at the top of his lungs: "Christmas trees! Christmas trees!"

"We shall take that one," Papa finally mumbled, as he pointed to a large pine tree.

Bringing it home was always hard to manage. But the enjoyment we would derive from it against the burden of the load determined the worth of our efforts.

There was a certain 'joie de vivre' walking down the streets on Christmas Eve. The sidewalks were bustling with activity. Notwithstanding the cold weather people, young and old, were running to complete their holiday shopping.

"Come on, come on, I'll show you the displays in the store windows," Andre uttered, with a big smile on his face.

Of course, Ghislaine and I loved looking at the enchanting Christmas displays. We did not mind waiting on the long lines until it was our turn to admire the superb tableaux, and marvel with curiosity at the magnificent spectacles of animated dolls and stuffed animals.

Beaming with excitement, we watched them in their fantasy world, as they moved in a lifelike manner.

I really enjoyed the remarkable and outstanding window scenes, but 'Pere Noel' (Santa Claus) had in my childhood an even greater appeal.

My very first visit to the Galeries Lafayette, after the war, was a revelation. I had never seen such a wide variety of merchandise in my life. Lestelle's two small general stores had absolutely nothing in common with this wonderful department store.

Although it was far from easy to get through the crowds, discovering the toy department was absolutely heavenly for me. There was so much to look at. The dolls and the playhouses interested me the most. But I also enjoyed watching the miniature trains as they followed their winding route, before their disappearance into a tunnel and their stop at a little station.

As I was glancing at a small mechanical bear tapping his fingers on the sides of the drum as he danced around and around, I heard Papa calling out, in a loud voice: "Muriel, Ghislaine, follow me! I want you to meet Pere Noel."

We approached the gigantic arm chair where Pere Noel was sitting in his red suit. I just stood there, startled and surprised, admiring his long white beard.

"Come, come," the jolly overweight man insisted. "Sit on my lap and tell me what you want for Christmas."

I whispered and mumbled a few words.

"What did you say?" he asked gently.

"Dolls, rollerskates and games," I repeated nervously.

He assured me that he would not forget me.

But Ghislaine and I were not about to take any chances. We made sure to post our long letters filled with wonderful ideas in the vast mailbox placed in the center of the store.

The outdoor scene on Christmas Eve was certainly thrilling as well. However, for me, the enchantment of the holiday was even greater within our home. With her British background, Sybil was able to combine the warm tradition of an English Christmas with the traditional French Noel. The blending of the two traditions resulted in enchanting, astonishing and delightful festivities.

As soon as we were old enough, we took part in the decorating of the tree. While we were actively adorning and embellishing the tree with all kinds of trimmings and ornaments, Sybil would put on the radio for us to listen to the joyous Christmas carols on the BBC.

There was always something very special about that evening. Looking back on it as I write about it, I believe that it was not only the magic of Christmas which delighted me so much, but the warm intimacy of our family gathering, superseded by the glowing effect produced by my mother's tender and caring radiance.

"Isn't the tree marvelous?" Sybil finally said, as she attached the last star. The tree was indeed lovely; in fact, the whole room looked like a picture. The scattered holly with its bright red berries and glossy evergreen leaves added color and brilliance to the already attractive room.

"It's time to attach the mistletoe sprig to our chandelier," Sybil declared.

Ghislaine and I looked at each other and laughed. The mistletoe, with its tradition, would always occasion giggles on our part. We thought it was very funny to see people kiss and naturally we wanted to cash in on more laughter by luring men and women underneath it as often as possible.

Before our going to bed on Christmas Eve, Ghislaine, Christian and I would each place an empty pillowcase and a pair of shoes by the fireplace. The shoes had to be polished. Sybil assured us that Pere Noel would not go near dirty shoes! We believed her and we were not going to take a chance!

Even long after we stopped believing in Pere Noel, we continued to lay down our shoes and pillowcases on the floor.

The excitement and agitation of our eager anticipation made falling asleep on Christmas Eve invariably difficult. The night would last forever! Ghislaine and I were growing impatient for dawn. Our inability to endure the wait was measured by our restlessness; incapable of sleeping, we were looking forward to the moment when we could dash out of bed and hastily thrust ourselves into the family room. But we knew that we could not wake up our parents or touch anything until seven in the morning.

At seven o'clock sharp, I went up to Ghislaine and whispered, "Let's go." Her smile stretched across her face.

We entered the room and discovered our pillowcases overflowing with gifts and our shoes totally stuffed with favors. We were momentarily overwhelmed and speechless. The amplitude and largesse exceeded our dreams and expectations. We were never more radiant. The jubilation was enormous. Ghislaine, Christian and I were dazed. We marveled at the fact that many of our wishes had been fulfilled.

The gaiety brought about by the unwrapping of the presents was beyond words. Each time we plunged our hands into the pile to take a package, we were filled with curiosity. Would it be a dream come true, such as the doll or the game we yearned for, or would it be a joke? Sybil had a sharp sense of humor and a marvelous imagination. She knew how to obtain chuckles. She would include a few ridiculous items among the things haphazardly gathered in the pile. I will never forget the bursts of laughter exhibited by all of us after I had opened a beautifully wrapped box in which I found a potato!

When we had finished opening our presents, the room was a panorama of widespread disorder. The chaos was phenomenal and unforgettable! Papers, strings, ribbons, boxes, presents, pillowcases and shoes were widely dispersed and mingled all over the floor in total confusion.

As we gathered around the table to have our breakfast, the disorder and chaos did not fluster us. Our predominant mood was characterized by good humor and animation.

After our temporary pause for breakfast, we would sort out our newly acquired treasures from the jumble and clean up the room with energy. We were eager to try on our new clothes and play with our new games. Later our father would take us to the Avenue de Bois, the avenue that extends from the Arc de Triomphe to the Bois de Boulogne. Wearing our best dresses and coats, Ghislaine and I at first would be inclined to be somewhat supercilious with our new skates or our new bicycle. But our clumsy performance and visible lack of grace would remind us that we should forget our haughtiness and learn how to skate and ride a bike!

"Be careful!" Papa would cry out.

But it would be too late. I would lose my balance and fall. Laughing out loud, Ghislaine would not be able to contain herself.

"I am so sorry, but your shaky style is really funny!" she would say with a gleam in her eyes.

I would be so embarrassed, I would want to cry for a moment, but her laughter was always catching. Then I would joyfully whisper, "It's your turn to do something funny."

Andre grinned as he watched us. "All right girls, it's time to go home," he would say as he rose from his bench.

By the time we reached the house, the entire extended family would be there, sitting together around the table for the traditional Christmas lunch. Sybil's jovial mood seemed to fill the whole room and impart graciousness. She would delight in preparing an attractive and beautiful table for the occasion. She would take pleasure in adding all kinds of tasteful little touches to the enchanting setting.

Crackers, with their decorative paper wrappings and favors, did not only enhance the festive layout, but they played a hilarious role in striking more laughter and joy when the time came to snap and crack them.

It was a typical Christmas luncheon. A roast turkey with all its flavorful trimmings and a most succulent chestnut puree was soon served, followed by a string of wonderful delicacies, such as the exquisitely rich and creamy French traditional Buche de Noel and the tasty English plum pudding filled with currants, raisins and spices. I was so fond of these parties with their cheerful equilibrium of shared warmth and joy. They were so precious and so sweet.

New Year's Day was also a rather special and out-of-the-ordinary day for us. At around nine o'clock in the morning, Ghislaine and I would leave our home with Papa to convey our good wishes for the new year to all the elderly members of the family — grandparents, uncles and aunts, cousins and distant relatives. With the exception of the leisurely and great family luncheon at Aunt Huguette's and Uncle Roger's home, we would be on the road all day until late in the evening.

Andre was a man of habits and was definitely inclined to follow the social conventions and gallantry of his generation. Courteously attentive, with his chivalrous and polite greetings, he would bring the same present to each. He would have a different theme every year. One of his well-chosen items could have been a box of elegant stationary, a pleasant eau de toilette, an exotic assortment of fruits confits, some succulent marrons glaces or a box of exquisite Swiss chocolates. He would simply select one suitable item for everyone and multiply his pick by the number needed for the circumstance.

At these customary stop-overs, Ghislaine and I would sit exactly where we were told to do so. The homes we visited were, for the most part, elegant and refined. The conversation exchanged between the adults was courteous and cultivated. The topic often alluded to the ancestry or the brilliance of a noteworthy young descendent.

At times, though, the words between the adults would fade into a murmur. "What could their whispers and innuendoes be about?" I would wonder. This was the plight of being a child: the adult world had little secrets, which they often tried to conceal from juvenile ears.

Inquisitive I was. But I would say nothing. Looking into the other direction, I would perk my ears, here and there, to catch a few broken syllables. After all, there was always a wicked one who would feverishly thrust allegations upon some relatives' endearment, deploring the marriage of a certain one or pointing out the sentimental indiscretions of another married one. This of course added a flutter of excitement to the conversation.

"Really! You don't say!" Andre would murmur in profound disbelief. Then he would rapidly try to change the subject, with tact. Andre did not really care for rumors. Unconcerned and indifferent, he loathed the folly of gossip and intrigue.

However, there are always exceptions…

On the impulse of the moment, as Papa was driving Ghislaine and me to our next place of a visit, he once decided to divulge the story of our great uncle's passions. Felix, a well-to-do, confirmed ladies' man, had apparently candidly admitted that there were two women who had really counted in his life. "They were both rather special to Uncle Felix. He loved them both dearly and could not give up one for the other," Andre sighed, as he turned his head slowly to glance at us and watch our reaction for a moment.

Ghislaine and I were surprised. We never expected that Papa would disclose the fact that our great uncle Felix adored two women and that one of his passions was none other than Madame K., the lady we were going to visit.

Ghislaine and I did not utter a word at first, then we looked at each other and giggled.

"Why do we visit Madame K. every year?" I finally cried out.

"She is a good friend of the family," Papa answered, looking somewhat embarrassed.

"I don't understand; she hasn't got anything to do with us," I blurted out, excitedly.

Papa smiled, shook his head and turned to Ghislaine and me. "She inherited all of Uncle Felix's shares in the family business. So, in a way, we are all still connected," he said as we listened carefully. But then I looked at my father and asked about the other lady in Uncle Felix's life.

"Madame H. lives in Switzerland," Andre retorted without hesitation. Ghislaine and I stared at our father, speechless. We never spoke again about our great uncle's immorality and his flamboyant love for two women.

New Year's Day, with its usual conviviality, diffused a certain feeling of profound awe and respect, enhanced by Andre's gentlemanly behavior. I regarded these polite visits with much reverence. I was glad that I was able to taste a little grace and style of the older generation.

When I reflect and conjure up visions of Christmas Day and New Year's Day during my childhood, I remember them so well. I could never forget them. Oh yes, how sweet they were! The warm memories will always exist in my heart and in my soul.

****

It was within a year after our arrival in Paris that Sybil suggested that I join the British Girl Guides.

"I promise, you will not regret it. You will learn English and take part in numerous social activities outside of your home and your school," Sybil said in a soft but convincing voice.

I was a shy little girl, but nevertheless, I thrived on new experiences and decided to become a member.

Miss A., the scout leader, greeted me warmly at the door. "Come in! I want you to meet the other girls," she said as she took me by the hand. It was obvious that it would not take me long to get acquainted and enjoy the weekly meetings.

Among the group, there was Lilian who had the same Franco-British background as I did. From the very beginning, we both shared a rather special friendship. Lilian was an only child and was somewhat the "poor little rich girl" who craved the warm and affectionate atmosphere she detected in my family home. She was particularly receptive to our hearty and lively ambiance. All in all, she was grateful that we shared so many happy hours together, and to this day she remains my faithful friend.

I could never forget, though, that our long friendship was born in the lap of the Girl Guides.

Life was never dull there; our activities expanded rapidly, in many directions. Displaying energy and vitality, our leader responded to our group's enthusiasm by planning picnics, campfires and hikes. Avid for adventure, camping in the wilderness for a couple of weeks at a time, was for me, without a doubt, the most exciting of all.

Packs upon our backs, we sang as we walked along the trail until we reached the area where we were supposed to pitch our tents and fasten the canvas to ground pegs. That was the hard work, but we did not mind. Our craving for an unusual experience was prodigious.

Our needs were modest. Yet the urgency was there.

To cook, we had to build a fire. At times, we had to go cross-country for a least a mile to find the necessary wood. We needed to collect sticks for kindling and logs to keep the fire going. What a relief it was when we could return with a batch of dry wood!

When it came to the water, we had to journey several times a day to the nearest pump or fountain to fill up the jugs with fresh water. The containers were heavy. Carrying them back to our camping site without splashing or scattering the water about was an art!

The jobs were divided up. Fire-makers, cooks and wood collectors would take turns and alternate. Cleaning up was always the worst job of all. Greasy pots and pans were, to say the least, a real nightmare!

On a more creative side, we built tripods to hold our washbowls, and racks to keep our towels and clothing off the ground. The makeshift rustic furniture was in perfect harmony with the woodland surroundings.

There was nothing I enjoyed more than sitting around a glowing campfire in the dark and singing songs or telling stories. The fire gave the warmth, but the friendships and togetherness radiated, for me, far more fervent emotions.

The yellow and red blaze of the flames would emphasize the darkness of the evening, but the soft clarity from the fire illuminated the bright and beaming faces of our inspiring unit.

I lived the life of a camper intensely. It encompassed fabulous moments of laughter and jauntiness with occasional annoyances and irritations!

I shall never forget our secret midnight feasts. We were certainly not supposed to have them. Just trying to get out of our tents in the middle of the night without being noticed by our leader was no easy operation.

Afraid to speak and afraid to hear our own breath, we braved the silence of the night to find the ideal spot for our nocturnal get-togethers.

Triumphant, we walked in our pajamas, flashlights in our hands, across the prairie. The green carpet under our feet was filled with crawling grasshoppers but they did not bother us. But on one occasion, as we were walking down a little path heading to another fenced field, I stopped and howled "Aie! Aie!" Tears were trickling down my face. To my horror, I discovered that I had just stepped on a small hedgehog! The pain was real and the shock was terrible, but the incident did not deter me from having more midnight feasts with my dear friends. I just remembered to wear shoes the next time!

Camping was not only an adventure, but it enabled us to discover several magnificent areas of France, England and Denmark.

Infinitely varied, the scenic beauty of Normandy and Brittany with their delightful and quaint little villages offered us the unique charm of the French countryside. I was especially impressed by our visit to Mont St. Michel, a medieval town built on a steep rock topped by a formidable abbey. Surrounded by the high tide, it was quite extraordinary to realize that, for centuries, the small walled city had resisted the ravages of seawater and damp weather. Climbing up the old narrow cobblestone streets and wandering around the scenic restored monastery with its beautiful view of the English Channel was, for me, a remarkable sight and an unforgettable experience.

Camping in Great Britain was fascinating as well.

I was seduced by England's pretty countryside. The fields and the flowers, the woodlands and the orchards were sensational. The charming old villages with their thatched houses contrasted well with the coastal scenery.

As our boat approached the rugged cliffs on the western end of the Isle of Wight, we were surprised to see, standing in the water, three huge chalk rocks known as the Needles. It was a most incredible sight.

The island was exquisite with its lush vegetation and old forests. The woodland was just ideal for riding its famous shaggy ponies.

With the exception of our first night there, our camping vacation in the Isle of White was delightful.

Soon after our arrival, we pitched our tents and managed to eat a little something before retiring in our tents for the night.

Two or three hours later, a huge thunderstorm with lightning and abundant rain came down from the heavens with such force that everyone woke up. We got on our feet, frightened, speechless for a while. Only our leader's strong voice brought us back to our senses.

"You must take your tent down immediately and move away from the tree!" she cried out anxiously as she lifted the canvas flap of our tent.

So, under a black sky inflamed by the flashes of lightning and the heavy rains, we hastened to dismantle our tent and move it to a safe spot. What a terrifying experience it was! We were drenched through and through. Needless to say, after that night we had learned our lesson: not to ever pitch a tent under a tree!

My camping vacation in Cornwall was also most rewarding. I will always treasure in memory the unequaled beauty of the Celtic land with its old fishing villages and wild seascape overlooking the fine golden stretch of sandy beaches with their multicolored shells. The subtropical climate and vegetation added atmosphere and warmth to the already enchanting region.

Camping in France and in England was always lovely and fun-filled for me. But the most striking trip of all with the Girl Guides was my journey to Scandinavia. Our group was invited to join an international camp in Denmark. The exuberance and high spirits of our joyous international gathering was marvelously invigorating.

Our sojourn in the Nordic nation was divided into two parts. Our first two weeks were spent camping in the scenically beautiful Jutland. I will never forget the warm and friendly welcome bestowed on us by the Danish Girl Guides. They did all the cooking, the cleaning, and last but not least, they entertained us. We were all treated like stars! What a fabulous camping experience it was. I loved it. Our hosts were determined to give us a great and unforgettable time in their beautiful country.

I remember our journey to the delightful old city of Odense, on the island of Fyn, where we visited Hans Christian Andersen's famous little dwelling. I fell in love with the children's storyteller's house, which had been converted into an attractive museum comprising a fine collection of his precious pictures and mementos.

When our camping stay was over, we headed for the charming city of Copenhagen. The boat ride was enchanting, the sea was not rough, and the seagulls with their grey and white plumage were flapping their long wings as they followed the ferry to the Danish capital.

The following ten days were spent in the charming city of Copenhagen. There we were all separated and invited to stay in one of the Danish Girl Guides' homes.

Ingrid's family lived in a somewhat modest home. Not given to exuberant manifestations of their feelings, her parents were nevertheless affable and gracious. They only spoke Danish. The inconvenience of not speaking the same language was actually not of great importance for me. When there is a need, there is a way! Smiling and making gestures were very useful, especially when I was hungry!

It seemed peculiar to me, coming from France, that dinner would be served at five o'clock in the afternoon! And then, to add to my surprise, we started our dinner with a sweet appetizer, which was followed by a very salty fish! At first, I was amazed to discover that countries would have so many different customs and ways of life. But it certainly did not stop me from eating the repast with gusto!

When it was time to go to bed, I was astonished to discover that my bed had no top sheet and no blanket! The bed just had a huge eiderdown on it! How could it be possible? I would not be able to tuck in the heavy comforter to secure myself cozily for a good night's sleep, as I was accustomed to. Little did I know that today it is the trend in many homes around the world to forget sheets and blankets and just use comforters! "Oh, it is just one more unusual custom to get used to!" I reflected as I closed my eyes.

Of course, by the morning hours, I was ready to start a new day with Ingrid. I do not recall much about her looks at all, but I was amazed to discover that her closest school friend was indeed one of Denmark's princesses. I never imagined that a member of the royal family would ever intermingle with a commoner. I really liked the idea of democratic social equality.

The whole next ten days were spent in Copenhagen, visiting the sights. I loved the beautiful capital of Denmark with its old houses, museums, palaces and canals. And then there was the enchanting promenade along the sound, with the warm wind gently caressing my skin. As I walked, I stared at the famous Little Mermaid statue, inspired by Hans Christian Andersen's fairy tale. She appeared so dainty and well-defined.

As I reflect upon my sojourn in Copenhagen, two very exciting occasions come to mind. For one, my whole group of Girl Guides was invited to the British Embassy for a 'smorrebrod.' I had never seen such a choice of open sandwiches, appetizers and delicious pastries. The Nordic specialties were attractively prepared. The ambiance, too, was festive. In the happy mood of good-hearted camaraderie, we felt important and proud to be there, in such lavish decor, as the ambassador's guests.

But the greatest thrill of all was the spectacular and unforgettable evening with the girls at the world-famous Tivoli Amusement Park. This place really held magic. The magnificent illuminated garden, with its rides, concerts, fireworks, restaurants and cafes, was an open-air paradise.

My trip to Denmark with the Girl Guides was not only an extraordinary experience, but the grand finale of my camping days.

****

Our beginnings after the war were humble. Indeed, they were. And I don't exactly remember how long it took Andre to beat the early deprivations and buy something special for himself. But I will never forget that afternoon when he entered the living room, grinning.

"Come, come, I have a great surprise for you," he said, as he pointed to the door. We followed him. And to our greatest astonishment, a huge black motorcycle was parked in front of the house.

"Look at my new toy," Andre exclaimed with excitement. One would have thought that it was the greatest moment of his life. Too startled to say anything, Sybil stared at the gigantic two-wheeler for a while and then burst into uncontrollable laughter.

Ghislaine and I were amused by it all. But when my father drove off with me, through the Bois de Boulogne, I was terrified to say the least.

"Please stop, Papa, don't go so fast," I begged. But Andre did not hear me as he raced on. My screaming could not muffle the echoing and reverberating sounds of his machine.

Andre seemed to genuinely enjoy his experience. The next day though, the black motorcycle had disappeared as quickly as it had appeared in our lives! "Heaven knows why I bought this. It was, in fact, a very bad choice," Andre admitted.

"There's no point in having a motorcycle for two when one has a family," he added with a smile.

Everyone was surprised but relieved to hear that Andre had decided to give up his motorcycle.

A few weeks later, Andre came home with a new little car. It was a Renault 4CV, a 4-door supermini automobile. Squeezed together in the small compact vehicle, Andre, Sybil, Ghislaine, Christian, Nicole and I traveled together to innumerable countries. Our luggage had to be reduced to the smallest common denominator. Sybil's expertise in knowing how to pack for six people, and making sure to have exactly what we would need for any given circumstance or for any weather change during a two weeks' vacation, was really admirable.

Traveling through France and abroad with Papa was unforgettable. He could actually stay behind the wheel for hours and hours, without too much effort. Much to my mother's distress, he would increase his speed as if he were pushed by an impelling force, so much so that the milestones indicating the distances on the tree-lined roads would pass out of sight with rapidity.

Governed by whims, Papa refused to make reservations for hotels in advance. So haphazardly, we stumbled upon all kinds of different accommodations. We never knew in advance where we would spend the next night. One night we would stay in an upscale, sophisticated and luxurious hotel, while the next night we would find ourselves in the countryside in a small inn.

Oh, how well I remember one terrible night! All the hotels and inns were fully booked, and our only recourse was to stay overnight as paying guests in a private home. We ended up in an eerie, stale, old-fashioned French residence belonging to an elderly doctor. Everything about that house induced a sensation of fear in Ghislaine and me. We shared a bed in a vast and poorly lit room on the second floor. The creaky floor and the dark, dilapidated furniture all contributed to the dreadful and dismal atmosphere of the room. The abode reminded us of a haunted house with the wind shrieking through the fissures of the cracked shutters. Footsteps could also be heard on the staircase. Immobilized with disbelief, the realm of our vivid imaginations conjured up such weird images that

Ghislaine and I were too petrified and too hopelessly paralyzed with terror to join our parents one flight down. I do not believe that either of us slept a wink that night. But as soon as daylight first appeared, the two of us bolted for our parents' room.

Papa wanted us to have all kinds of experiences. He yearned for us to appreciate the value of comfort and leisure. But he wanted us to understand that unanticipated situations could present themselves and that we would have to face the predicament and cope with the circumstances the best we could.

His earnest attempts to educate us never ceased either. In the car, he would repeatedly test our knowledge of history and geography. He would want an immediate response. "I press on a button and I need to have your answer." He would vociferate in a loud voice. Whenever my answer to the question was wrong, he would put me down with intolerable affronts. I felt so intimidated by him.

On our way, we would stop in every historic town to visit every medieval and gothic church and every museum in sight. Each town had its own unique atmosphere, exotic or romantic, intriguingly unusual or beautiful. Andre wanted to communicate to us his enthusiasm for their inherent mysteries and history.

My wildest aspirations toward traveling were definitely inspired by the marvelous diversity of the multifaceted countries I visited with my family. Whether we vacationed in France's popular resorts or toured along Switzerland's magnificent lakes and Alpine passes or enjoyed Italy's irresistible charm or discovered exotic Spain or visited beautiful Portugal, in my zest and exhilaration, I loved it all.

At times, Andre would bring the family together to look at a list of different countries and places where we could possibly go on our next trip. We read the choices carefully and quietly contemplated the potential towns, villages and coastlines of these diverse suggestions on Papa's list.

"It's time to vote! Choose one destination," Andre would clamor as he handed out a slip of paper to each family member. We promptly scribbled the name of the country we wished to visit and explore. "Fold your piece of paper once and then fold it again," he said as he glanced at all of us, sitting around the table.

"When you are ready, toss your ballot into the hat!" Andre insisted.

"All right, I will now mix the ballots." The shuffling of the little notes was the only audible sound in the room. Andre would then turn his eyes away from the hat and, looking in the opposite direction, grab one of these folded-up little notes. Then, overcharged with energy and cheerfulness, he would announce our lucky destination.

I will never forget the day when my father pulled my little ballot out of the hat! "Good! We are off to Spain," he announced happily. "We should travel to Portugal as well and stop in Lestelle on our way back," Papa proposed with a smile on his face.

At first, we all gazed at him in astonishment. And then, instantaneously, the room seemed to palpitate with high spirits. Throbbing with the pulse of excitement and exhilarated by the results of the vote, I was jumping up and down, totally ecstatic.

The most enchanting trip of all was about to begin. I was twelve or thirteen years old. Fascinated by the different customs of each country, I was captivated by their striking dissimilarities.

So close to France and yet so different, Spain was my favorite of all. With its contrast and its own characteristics, the Iberian Peninsula really enchanted me. People there never seemed to be in a rush. It was easy for them to say, "Mañana, por la mañana" — tomorrow, tomorrow, it can be done tomorrow!

There was no point in trying to get lunch before two or three o'clock in the afternoon or dinner before ten o'clock at night. The food, too, was very different. Each dish smelled with a strong olive oil flavor, but most pleasing to the palate was, at least for me, the famous and succulent paella.

Beautiful Andalusia was certainly for me the highlight of our trip through Spain. Granada, once the heart of Moorish Spain, with its fabulous castle of the Alhambra and its breathtaking view of the Generalife's superb terraced gardens, captivated me. But above all, I loved Andalusia's flamenco with its forceful rhythms of guitars and castanets. Watching the Gypsies dance was a pure joy for me. Guided by masterful and strong men, the women dressed in their flamboyant and colorful dresses, with a flower or two attached to their coiled-up chignon, danced with seductive charm and passion.

As I reminisce and reflect about the Gypsies, I will never forget the day we were heading for the Sacromonte Hills, where Gypsies were living in caves. Suddenly, a swarm of squealing, dirty and impoverished children literally prevented our vehicle from moving. They climbed all over the car, gripping their arms and their legs tightly. They would not let go. Their helpless condition clutched my heart. I had not seen such poverty since my exposure to the Pochard family in Lestelle during the war years. Andre gave them some money and decided to forget our plan to watch the cave-dwellers dance the flamenco.

Somewhat disappointed, we turned around. But, on our way down, we came upon a most touching scene. A group of young children was depicting the Passion of Christ by staging a delightful procession. Their realistic pictorial presentation was extremely moving and thrilling to witness. After all, it was Holy Week.

Strongly impressed by Granada's splendor, I was equally marked by Sevilla's charm as we walked through innumerable picturesque winding streets in the old quarter and visited the captivating ocher-colored Giralda and the Alcazar fortress.

Early Easter Sunday morning, Nicole slipped out of the room. She had heard something going on in the street. "Get up, get up, you must see what is going on in the street down there," she said resolutely, as she pushed the door wide open.

Ghislaine and I growled; we wanted to sleep. But a few moments later, Andre, Sybil and Christian entered our room. "Lazy girls, get up; let's get on with our day!" Andre uttered loudly.

Instantly, we got ready and made it to the Gran Via. Hundreds of people were looking at the spectacular religious procession of hooded penitents. It was a poignant scene. It really turned out to be something very special. Guided by sentiment and emotion, I could feel their strong conviction.

Then, strolling through Sevilla's most exotic park, filled with gorgeous flowers and elegant fountains, we discovered the graceful deer and the blue and green peacocks roaming around at liberty under the shade of the palm trees, the lemon trees and the orange trees. As we walked around, we caught sight of a little pond where children of all ages came to feed the multicolored ducks. We watched the feathered beauties as they struggled for supremacy. There was always one greedy little duck!

As I stood there, Andre grabbed me by the arm and said: "There is a magnificent mini-golf over there. I suppose you might want to play with us."

"Yes Papa, I most certainly would," I answered without any hesitation. Shortly thereafter, we began our game. When one of us would miss the hole, wanting to be playful and humorous, we laughed and applauded!

"Ah-hah! I am going to show you how to play," Andre blurted out with a smile on his face. He made a good speech and showed us how to hold the club. But when he propelled his club in the wrong direction, poor Christian was hit by the hard ball and was left with a black eye.

I felt sorry for my little brother, but I refused to let this incident cloud with gloom my spectacular stay under the sunny skies of my revered Andalusia.

The road from Sevilla to the border and throughout the Portuguese sun-scorched hills and villages was a feast for the eyes. Despite its geographic closeness, Portugal seemed surprisingly different from Spain. In Spain, I had the feeling that I was transported into a completely different world, whereas I found Portugal much more like France.

During our stay in Lisbon, we took side trips. We spent wonderful hours in L'Estoril, a true paradise where the elegant beaches and coast reminded me somewhat of the reputed Cote d'Azur. And rolling on, we stopped in Sintra, a resort town in the foothills of Portugal's mountains. Sintra is a delightful place where an abundance of luxuriant and green vegetation flourish and add splendor to the hilltop where we visited a noble Arab fortress and a Capuchin monastery.

In Porto, our main objective was to meet up with some far-distant relatives who had settled in Portugal during the war. The father had been killed by the Nazis and the mother had fled Germany with their son and daughter. For almost two days we were together and we realized that the mother had never quite reconciled herself to the tragedy of losing the love of her life.

Leaving Portugal behind, our return trip through northern Spain was great — that is, until we reached the Cantabrian Mountain range.

Andre was driving down a treacherous, steep hill when suddenly and unexpectedly he developed a terrible feeling of dizziness. To add to his dismay, rain was coming down heavily and the road was extremely slippery. The car was swaying from side to side. Andre tried to pull the hand brake to slow down. That, too, was in vain, and the car continued to zigzag from one sharp turn to another! Papa was pale. The perspiration was rolling down his face; he had lost his usual self-assurance. The car skidded atrociously. I thought that an accident was inevitable. When he drove close to the edge of an extremely steep precipice, we all turned ashen white with fright. Fortunately, we all remained very quiet. The slightest shriek could have provoked a catastrophe. Despite the overwhelming odds against him, papa was able to conquer his emotional anguish and skillfully control his car down the tortuous and abrupt mountain roads to our safe arrival in San Sebastian.

We smiled with great relief at the sight of the vast white sandy beaches of the Bay of Biscayne. In spite of the inclement weather, we went swimming. But I am not about to forget the incident with the policeman standing on the boardwalk in his khaki uniform, whistling and whistling until he got Nicole's attention. Then, shouting and gesticulating, he made her come out of the water. Looking at her with a stern expression, he told her that she was indecently dressed and that it was offensive and immodest to show so much of herself! "A bikini is strictly prohibited on our beaches," he said, as he opened his book to give her a fine.

Nicole was stunned and somewhat confused. She was worried that she had made a pitiful spectacle of herself. But her Uncle Andre intervened, and in a broken Spanish, he begged the officer for forgiveness. "She is a child; she is fifteen years old," he uttered with excuses.

The policeman shrugged his shoulders and ordered Nicole to cover herself, immediately. Then, cutting off any further discussion, he walked away.

As I recall this little episode, I realize how different things were in the early fifties, especially in Spain.

Back in the car, we burst into uncontrollable giggles over the Spaniard's criticism. But as we approached the border, and were about to leave Spain, I felt a pinch in my heart. I had found such great excitement in our fascinating grand tour of the Iberian Peninsula.

Andre drove on. The French roads were definitely in a far better condition than the dusty ones we had left behind. We were on our way to Lestelle, and spent the night there.

Sporadically and faithfully, we would return to the little village in the Pyrenees that nested us during the war years. Like ourselves, several people had left Lestelle. Some villagers had died. But the Arricaud family was always there in their little pension to give us a warm welcome. We would hug each other, laugh together, and with a certain nostalgia, Andre and Sybil would reminisce about the past with them.

I remember our visit to a farm the next morning. The sunshine came across the fields as we were bouncing around, lighthearted and happy. Then, as we were ready to leave, something unpredictable happened. A medium-sized black dog emerged. He had a beautiful face, with very expressive eyes. Taking the mutt in his arms, the farmer urged us to stroke him.

"Do you want him? He's a strong healthy dog," he said loudly.

Andre and Sybil understood right away, looking at Ghislaine, Christian and me, that we would indeed love to have a dog. And that's how we ended up with Wonk, a most undomesticated and notoriously amusing one-year-old farm dog.

We took an immediate liking to our new playmate. But quickly we grasped the fact that our task was not going to be easy. As soon as we opened the car door on Lestelle's main square, Wonk escaped and the chase began. Sybil's face was a picture of bewilderment, but Andre gave directions to Nicole, Ghislaine, Christian and me to encircle the escapee and, with the help of several villagers, we were able to catch our pup.

Traveling back to Paris in the small, already crowded Renault with our mischievous Wonk was by no means easy. We took turns holding him, but our pup was used to his liberty in the fields and hated the confinement of the car. His enormous strength, together with his incredible vitality, exhausted us. Much to his contentment, we stopped regularly to give our Wonk a chance to bounce around. But he was not accustomed to wearing a collar, nor to being kept on a leash. He hated the restrictions on his independence.

"Good heavens! What on earth did we do to ourselves?" Sybil exclaimed with a pang of bitterness as she watched our unruly mutt in the rear of the car.

"I am amazed and somewhat stupefied that we consented willingly. But everything happened so fast!!" Andre retorted.

Sybil sighed. "Will he ever be able to adapt himself to Grand-mere's mansion?" she questioned as we were reaching the French capital.

"Oh! He is fantastic," I blurted out. My heart started pounding like crazy. I was worried that Andre and Sybil might have a change of heart.

"Muriel, we're not going to change our minds. Wonk is coming home with us," Sybil said gently.

As soon as we crossed the threshold, we met Aunt Huguette. Her look said it all. She stood by the door of her bedroom, looking at Wonk with such a cold stare of disdain. I knew that from the very first moment she laid her eyes on him that she hated him. Wonk seemed to decide that the best way to pay her back was to defecate every morning in front of her door! No matter how early Andre took him out, he would wait to return to the house and make his "business" in front of Aunt Huguette's door! What on earth could Andre do? This, of course, created plenty of altercations between Andre and his sister.

Then there were the times when Andre and Sybil gave our farm dog his bath. Wet and full of soap, he would escape and run all over the mansion, splashing everyone and everything in sight.

"He escaped!" Sybil would cry out.

"What do you mean, he escaped? Can't you get rid of him?" Aunt Huguette would say virulently.

But as turbulent and naughty as Wonk was, he was demonically funny and we loved him.

****

It was May 1, 1952 — Labor Day in France. We all congregated after lunch around Grand-mere's bed for our usual family gathering. Her room was filled with lilies of the valley, for it was, and still is the custom in France, to give family and friends a small bouquet of the fragrant flowers to bring the person good luck and happiness.

The gleaming sun bathed Grand-mere's room and added warmth to the already affectionate ambiance. I never saw Grand-mere so radiant and happy. Soon after the coffee hour, Grand-mere expressed her desire that she needed to take a nap.

My mother explained that Grand-mere had gone into a deep sleep and that she was now in another world. I could not believe that I would never see Grand-mere again.

I did not attend the funeral, for Sybil felt very strongly that children whose parents were alive should not attend a burial.

Many years later, I was told the amazing story that Grand-mere had converted to Catholicism during the Dreyfus Affair and that nobody, including her husband, knew that she had changed her religion.

With Grand-mere's death, another episode of my childhood was ending. Her estate had to be divided and her mansion had to be sold. We all had to go our separate ways.

Meme moved to a hotel near the Champs Elysees, where she could have a staff of servants at hand. Uncle Roger, Aunt Huguette and their children relocated to an apartment in Auteuil. Meanwhile, Aunt Huguette had given birth to Jean-Pierre, her fourth child.

My parents decided to live on the Left Bank. They bought a beautiful apartment in walking distance of the Luxembourg Gardens, my favorite park in Paris.

Disheartened, we had to give our Wonk away. But we knew that, in all fairness to him, he was definitely not a dog for an apartment and that he would be much happier back in the fields and meadows where he really belonged.

Spending the last days in the mansion was a mixed bag of emotions. On one hand, my heart was beating with excitement at the idea of a new beginning. And then, on the other hand, there were the moments of sadness and reflections.

As though it was a dream, a series of images and emotions passed in reverie through my mind, as I went from room to room. When I reached the top of the elegant staircase, I could still see Nicole, Ghislaine and I staring at Francois' parties. Considered to be far too young to be invited, we followed the jollity from our observation post. Our eyes saw more than we expected. In their full skirts, the young girls and their partners were dancing the jitterbug, the bop, the swing and the Rock 'n' Roll. Highly spirited, their spontaneous liveliness delighted us.

We loved to laugh about things like that. But nothing could arouse our curiosity and hold our attention better than the playful flirtation displayed by several boys and girls during a sentimental slow dance. Giving free rein to our romantic feelings, we conjectured all kinds of ideas about what was going to take place in Francois' bachelor quarters, which were appropriately named by him 'le Tripot' (the Bawdy Place). He had actually converted one of Grand-mere's former stables into a secret hide-out. But it was well understood that Nicole, Ghislaine and I were to stay away from his 'playroom.'

Naive we were, but somehow, we knew that Francois and his cronies were having more than just a little fun in there and that it was not just a figment of our imagination. The secrecy of it all was somewhat irritating. But when we stood there, looking down from the top of the stairs, at Francois dallying with the girls at his wonderful parties, I think that we were the happiest trio in the world.

Now our days in the mansion were coming to an end, and the estate was not going to be sold to an embassy, or to a movie star, as the family had hoped.

Unfortunately, rich developers purchased the mansion and the grounds to demolish them, and build a modern and very exclusive high-rise!

Dejected to think that Grand-mere's elegant mansion would be destroyed and no longer exist, I was already well aware that nothing would last forever. My days on Rue de la Faisanderie were over, and I would never see the mansion nor the grounds again.

CHAPTER 3

Adolescence - My Teen Years

I was fourteen years old when we made our big move to the Left Bank in Paris.

My parents, André and Sybil, bought an attractive and agreeable apartment on the second floor of a very nice 8-story building, erected in 1928. On one side, we were close to the Observatoire de Paris and within walking distance of the Jardins de l' Observatoire and the Jardin du Luxembourg. On the other side, we were close to the Place Denfert Rochereau, dominated by the monumental Lion De Belfort statue, a giant bronze sculpture, in the center of the square. The Catacombs, famed for their underground ossuaries, are also located on the square. Needless to say, I was never tempted to visit them. I definitely had enough exposure to some allegedly haunted crypts with my hazardous and risky ventures in the sewer, rue de la Faisanderie, with my cousin Francois!

Although more confining than the mansion, the apartment was spacious and beautiful. Unlike Grand-mere's mansion, the building had an elevator! When I entered the large foyer for the first time, I walked across the foyer to the double doors and discovered the lovely living room. I expressed my approval with smiles! The room was marvelous and wonderful, large enough to accommodate several pieces of Grand-mere's superb Napoleon III furniture. Back into the vestibule, from the entrance door on the right-hand side, a door gave way to a lengthy passage, along which you could access a good-sized kitchen, three spacious bedrooms and the bathrooms. The maid's room was on the first floor.

André and Sybil availed themselves of the bedroom next to the main bathroom, at the end of the passageway. Christian was given the back room, overlooking the courtyard. Along the passageway, on the left-hand side, across from the kitchen, a door opened to a short corridor. At the end of the short hallway, a second door afforded the entrance to the largest bedroom, which was allocated to Ghislaine and me. A small bathroom on the right side of the little corridor was ours as well. All the rooms had tall French windows. With the exception of the back room, every window had a view on the wide avenue. The chestnut trees with their rich foliage gave a brilliant green scope to the already attractive rooms. The living room and my parent's room had ashlar stone balconies, on which my mother had some of Grand-mere's beautifully shaped bowls, in which she planted red geraniums. The other bedrooms had wrought-iron balconies.

The new surroundings and the novelty of it all generated in me a strange mixture of excitement and a certain uneasiness. I was in the midst of my adolescent years and like most teenagers, I was struggling to find out who I was, and what I would become. At times, sharing a room with Ghislaine was difficult. She was allergic to neatness and my orderliness infuriated her. Her clothing, shoes and school books were all over the place. I disliked her untidiness so intensely that I would often pick up her belongings and put them away. That, of course, would cause more strife to break out. Keeping our room tidy was not the only cause of our friction; borrowing articles of clothing without asking the other's permission would also create disagreement between us. We would yell at each other. Our altercations were, when I think about it, extremely unattractive! Our parents were troubled by our quarrels. When they came into the room to give us a lecture, I thought that they would never stop talking. Their rebuke and scolding would annoy me to no end.

Preoccupied with my struggle for independence, I had at the time ambivalent feelings toward my parents. I loved and respected them, but I also resented having to live up to their expectations and I detested their criticism. Fighting for my opinions was important to me. I did not want their advice, yet I was often relieved by their sound recommendations. I was confused. The generation gap was there. I felt that my friends seemed to understand my fears and my hopes better than my parents and my teachers could.

I also tried to figure out how my friends could get away with so much! Filled with these thoughts, I argued that Michele and Monique had no curfew and that Anne could do this or do that! "Now look here! I don't care what your friends do," André insisted loud and clear. "Here, you are in my house and as long as you live under my roof, you do as I say."

There was no doubt that my striving for autonomy was difficult for both my parents and for me. I wanted to be treated like an adult, yet in many ways, I was still a child.

I had a marvelous closeness with Meme, my father's mother. I could confide in my grandmother. She understood me, she respected my opinions and my dreams. Meme came regularly to my parents' home for lunch. But I much preferred our outings together.

Meme cherished life and filled her existence by simply taking pleasures. She opened and uncovered a world that was totally different from my day-to-day routine.

Sitting in a Champs-Élysées café, watching the passers-by was always a source of pleasure for the both of us. We loved playing guessing games. Guessing games are engaging and make you think. As we observed people, we tried to figure out their nationality by their gait, their clothes and their shoes. Shoes were the number-one giveaway! However, the Americans were certainly the easiest ones to detect: they walked with their big radio hanging around the neck, to their belly!

Eating out with Meme was always a wonderful treat for me. She was a connoisseur of good foods. A gourmet, she delighted in eating with zest and gusto. If by chance she feasted her eyes on a sumptuous dessert on another table, she could easily indulge her craving for it by calling the waiter and ordering the truffle cake or the Peach Melba immediately. Meme could easily gratify her good appetite by eating four or five different deserts!

Meme was in every way a *bon vivant*. After the restaurant, she would invite me to go to the theatre or to the movies. I remember asking her to take me to see the movie *Irma la Douce*. She agreed, for she believed that if a teenager understands the story, he or she is ready for it. And if a young person doesn't understand it, it would just go over their head! I was absolutely enthralled that she would recognize my yearning for grown-up movies. Bound by mutual interests, loyalties and affection, I considered Meme to be one of my closest and dearest friends. Together, we talked about the complicated route that one travels to adulthood. Meme knew and understood the real me. She listened to me. I could speak freely to her about occurrences that were troublesome and bothersome to me, without the risk that my sentiments and concerns would be communicated to others. I could trust her.

Meme would also tell me stories about her youth. "As a young lady, I could never go out without my governess. No matter what, she would always be at my side!" Meme uttered, with a sigh. Then, with a smile on her face, Meme would also say that she could never forget her governess' sweet solicitude towards her when she said: "Therese, you are engaged, you may kiss your fiancé!" Meme paused for a moment and went on to say: "How could I ever forget the day when I was given the permission to kiss my fiancé for the first time! When I returned home to my mother, I told her that I had just lost half my virginity!" "Really," I asked with astonishment, "You were given the permission to kiss your fiancé, my grandfather Victor?" I was stunned and amazed by Meme's romantic anecdotes and reminiscences of her past. For sure, the rules and the practices of her generation were not the same as mine!

Meme always had so many unique experiences to relate to me. I was amused and loved her tales. I could tell by the expressions on her face that the emotions roused in her filled her with a certain nostalgia for the "good old days." The attitudes that prevailed in her youth tended to leave more to the imagination. I liked that. But now Meme's epoch was regarded as out of fashion and outdated. The conventions, the opulence, the polite society were all changing and were no longer compatible with the rapid strides forward of the new world.

****

The social and emotional changes that take place during the years of adolescence are certainly marked by a combination of environment, family, friends, teachers, peers, experiences and development.

I was discovering the painful self-consciousness a teenager experiences during adolescence. When I sat in the classroom before a rigid and severe schoolteacher, I was often concerned and affected by his or her judgment, and I would worry about my peers' reaction to my answers on a given subject.

I had high standards for myself, but with my lack of self-confidence and insecurities, I had doubts about my capabilities, competencies and knowledge.

Could my timidity have been the result of my father's belittling and denigrating me if I did not immediately have the right answer to his questions on history?

Could it be due to some professors' disparaging remarks in front of 30 students? Their critiques certainly affected me; they made me feel so stupid and foolish.

I will always remember Monsieur R, my Latin teacher, at the Lycée Janson de Sailly, a boys' secondary school with very few girls in each grade. I was about 12 years old, sitting quietly in class, when Monsieur R looked at me, shaking his head: "Mademoiselle Kiefe, you are not at the *Carnaval*, go home and take the ribbon out of your hair!" I was totally mortified. And in front of my fellow students! I could not even conjecture what Monsieur R would say about today's world, with students having tattoos, piercings and make-up, and wearing jeans with holes!

When I got a professor's criticisms, I would have a complete loss of self-assurance. Timid I was, but bored I was too. The unexciting routine and the depressingly dull classes, with the teacher's monotonous pitch, provided a rather poor stimulus to my imagination and would crush my inquisitiveness.

I needed a supportive atmosphere, yet so often I sat before a teacher, my arms folded, too scared to ask about something I did not understand. I thought that the mere fact that I had not grasped the lesson suggested a dense mind. The truth was that anxiety was building up inside of me, and the response to my inner tension was to simply withdraw.

I believe that the interaction between a teacher and a student is of great importance. Unfortunately, the method and practice of promulgating knowledge for some educators would often lack knowledge of people.

Of course, there are some incredible and remarkable teachers who will have a positive impact on a student. As I am thinking about school, Mademoiselle P, my French teacher, comes into my mind. I could never overlook her encouragement and uplifting inspiration. I can still hear her invigorating and meaningful words when she would compliment me on my homework. "Mademoiselle Kiefe, I need to read your essay to the class; it is outstanding." She would then pause for a moment and smile at me. Then, she went on to say: "Mademoiselle Kiefe, one day you must be a writer. Engage yourself in writing stories, in writing a book."

As I am writing now, Mademoiselle P comes vividly to my mind. I will never forget her. Her radiant and sparkling glance will always stay in my heart.

Indeed, I needed to communicate my feelings through creative and artistic work.

* * * * * * * * * * * * * * * * * *

Fortunately, my mother understood my predicament. She knew that, due to the highly structured environment of the French schools, I was performing below my capabilities. She also realized that my father's high expectations were not helping the situation. In addition, she recognized that during these awkward adolescent years, the rivalry between Ghislaine and me was at its peak. With a keen perspicacity and insight, my mother was able to persuade my father that I should sally forth and go to a boarding school. My father accepted my mother's recommendation and the decision was made. I would continue my studies abroad.

The excitement of having a big change in my life was, to say the least, intermingled with heavy concerns.

Grappling with separation anxiety, I pretended to be light-hearted and happy. Yet, I was despondent about having to say goodbye to all my friends and leave my family. Furthermore, my mother was expecting a baby and was going to give birth 3 or 4 weeks after my departure. Naturally, I was disheartened by the fact that I would not see the baby until my Christmas vacation!

I had strived so hard to become independent from my family. But now that the separation was imminent, I came to realize that the change would be a pivotal moment in my life. With some disquietude and apprehension, I realized that I was leaving the home and the familiar lifestyle that I had always known for a new and uncertain future. After all, I had just turned sixteen.

As I am reminiscing about my youth and thinking back to the day I left for England, I can still hear Papa's voice yelling out: "It's time to go!" Moments later, as the car pulled away from the curb, I had tears in my eyes. Still anxious and confused, I was on my way to a new place.

At the train station, filled with mixed emotions, the time had come for our goodbyes. With his candid and inspiring words of encouragement, Papa helped to subdue my fears. I was conscious of my father's support. But I also knew that it would take me a while to sort out and understand my abrupt shifts of moods.

We kissed and separated.

As the train slowly made its exit out of the station, I watched the scenery and the countryside quietly from my seat next to the window. I do not recall any unusual incidents during the voyage. I had so often crossed the English Channel, in both clement and tempestuous weather. But on this mid-September day, the waters were calm, the sun was out and the peaceful crossing permitted my thoughts to wander about. I tried innumerable times to picture myself arriving at the boarding school.

As soon as the ferry docked at the pier in Folkestone, the passengers disembarked and went through the usual formalities and customs. I simply followed the crowd.

Mr. H, the director of St. Margaret's, was there, waiting for me. Then, within minutes, we had reached our destination by car. St. Margaret's, an old, established school of academic excellence for girls, was located in the best residential part of Folkestone, within minutes of the sea.

I realized right away, that my way of life at St. Margaret's would have very little in common with the mode of living that I had in France. And that I would have to embrace the complexities of a totally different world and a complete change of routine.

Like most British schools, St. Margaret's had a dress code. The winter attire consisted of a navy jumper worn over a white Viyella cotton long-sleeve shirt and a navy blazer with the school's emblem. During the warmer months, the uniform was changed to a cool navy-and-white striped cotton dress with a round white collar. The clothes showed a definite, discreet refinement.

When it came to the evening, Mrs. H, our headmistress — a lady of high principles — suggested that her students change into mufti for dinner. She wanted, without any doubt, to instill in her young ladies the gentle manners and *savoir faire* often associated with breeding and culture.

Highly particular in taste and standards, Mrs. H knew how to provide and maintain for her students a tradition of courtesy and respect. At times, I wondered (and I was not the only one), how Mrs. H could be married to Mr. H. They were altogether so different. As quiet and dignified as she was, he was boisterous and somewhat rough. However, he had a certain *joie de vivre,* which did not prevail in her. Notwithstanding their differences, they both pledged a deep commitment to cultural pursuits. Their aim was to provide their students with a thoroughly sound education, and no effort was spared to develop in each girl a well-balanced individuality.

In no time at all, I was able to adjust myself to my new environment.

Cohabitation with six roommates was not difficult for me. We shared a large, airy dorm. The girls were friendly and easy to talk to. Penny, a delightful young British fair-skinned blond, was assigned the bed next to mine. She would make me laugh so much when she tried to impersonate Marilyn Monroe! Gohar, a relaxed and convivial student, came from Iran. Leila, a sweet, well-disposed young lady, came from Iran as well. Dora, born in Malaysia, was engaging and adorable. Sandra, a high-spirited British girl, was inclined to divulge bizarre stories to us. Yvonne was a reserved and quiet British girl who did not reveal much emotion or opinions.

The school had a large quota of overseas students. But I was the only French girl, and that in itself had a rather amazing effect among the pupils. There I was, a student straight from Paris who could speak English and converse with ease. The girls wanted to hear about the famous French fashions and the noted cuisine, or simply learn about the French way of life. Suddenly, I was the center of attraction. Their strong enthusiasm and curiosity for my country delighted me.

Adapting myself to the eating habits and to the food was probably the most difficult thing to do. The differences between French and British cuisine were enormous. Breakfast reached such proportions! I could rarely find the appetite to eat the herring or sardines, the fried potatoes or baked beans, the eggs or pancakes, the toast or muffins, which were served every morning with orange juice, tea and milk. Just the sight of all that nourishment so early in the morning aroused an intense aversion in me. I always had a strong abhorrence toward leaping out of bed and hastily swallowing down food before running off to school. I just preferred to do without it! But in St. Margaret's, breakfast was absolutely essential, for it was just about the most important meal of the day!

Lunch was quite ample, with poultry or stew, fresh vegetables from the school gardens and pudding or custard for dessert. The high tea, served at around five o'clock in the afternoon, was usually very light.

I remember my very first day when I asked flippantly about the dinner hour. "Oh! You ate it at five o'clock," Penelope exclaimed. Completely abashed by her retort, I stood there absolutely still for a minute, I simply could not imagine that I would not have anything more to eat until the next day! By eight o'clock I was totally famished for want of dinner!

Notwithstanding that all the classes were obviously taught in English, I followed most lessons with keen and energetic attention, and I was soon able to participate totally. Just as in France, the curriculum included all the academic subjects.

Languages and creative writing were always my forte; I enjoyed these classes very much. I was an enthusiastic student in Spanish. Miss M, an elderly unmarried woman, was our Spanish teacher.

When she spoke Spanish with a heavy British accent, the words out of her mouth sounded hilarious! She was a truly fascinating person with an extraordinary temperament that kept her teaching animated. A character, she was. Her classes seemed to run in jagged rhythms, both eccentric and conventional.

Actually, only a small group of students took part in the Romance language classes, but Miss M taught social studies as well. She had the capacity to combine the experience of an old head with the vitality of a young one. Her students loved her. Her pretty face was always alive with humor. But it was never easy to sit too close to her. Miss M and soap were not synonymous! Her clothes looked ancient and were frequently soiled. Yet one could readily overlook her foibles, as her endearing qualities and her concerted efforts toward her students always prevailed.

My French classes too had a certain dynamism. Miss R wanted to add a new dimension to the lessons and asked if I would participate in the teaching. My input did not only help to liven up the subject for the pupils, but it was unquestionably a wonderful boost for my ego as well.

I definitely had less affinity for mathematics, chemistry and physics. Not only they were not my favorite subjects, but I had to contend with both Miss C's and Miss K's strong Irish brogues. Whenever I crossed my sevens or reckoned my division by the customary method used in France, not only would Miss C take points off, but I would have to listen to her prolonged effusiveness! I could not understand her unfairness. After all, the correct answer should have been the only thing that counted!

I soon perceived that every school or college, whether in France or in England, proved to have a combination of some very lovely and inspiring teachers and some weird and eccentric ones.

Sports always had a cardinal place, in England. St. Margaret's was certainly no exception. When I recall the hockey games we played during the winter months, I can never forget the dreadful strong winds from the coastline and the incessant heavy rain we had at times. But these trying situations did not restrain our team's significant spirit from moving, with sprightly vigor, across the muddy or slippery frozen grassland. Gushing with abundant enthusiasm, we enjoyed the thrills and spills!

Beginning in April, St. Margaret's students would start engaging in games of cricket, one of Great Britain's most popular sports. Rain or shine, we played!

I could not conjecture why I was forced to participate, considering that I never mastered the game at the level of my peers. Furthermore, the slow pace of the sport exasperated me!

Indeed, I found that some sports were amusing, while others were kind of boring for me! But there is not a doubt in my mind that our team's loyalty, fighting spirit, enthusiasm, camaraderie and sprightly vigor in the matches we played at St. Margaret's were notable.

Music and art were not the only creative programs at St. Margaret's. The musical stage productions and choreography would attain the highest standards with Mr. H's exceptional talent as a producer. The lovely costumes, the elaborate scenery and the splendid staging were most impressive. The charm, the color and the gaiety of each scene, with their whimsical and imaginative stories, freely peppered with the liveliest of good fun, were absolutely enthralling.

Taking part in the singing, delightful dances and high humor was wonderful, but winning the hearts and applause of the audiences at the Pleasure Gardens thrilled the entire cast.

My life at St. Margaret's was assiduous and well organized. There was a time to attend classes, a time to study, a time for sports activities, a time for cultural pursuits, a time to eat and a time to sleep. Yet, there was still time to read a book or enjoy a movie on a dull winter weekend or, better still, time for good talks with friends. We shared our happiness, our fears, our dreams, our frustrations and our fun. We shared it all.

I missed my family, of course. But I liked my peers' spontaneous friendliness.

****

A couple of weeks after my arrival in St. Margaret's, I received Papa's telegram announcing Roxane's birth. I felt a sudden quiver of emotion. After all, having a new baby sister at the age of sixteen was kind of exceptional!

Roxane's birth electrified all kinds of feelings in me. On one hand, I was so thrilled and so delighted that I jumped up and down with excitement. On the other hand, I was somewhat distraught at the idea of being so far away and that I would have to wait until mid-December to see her!

My classmates understood my sentiments. Their perception was shown by their kindheartedness. I was so grateful to have friends with so much goodness and warmth in their hearts. I will never forget the day when I received the first photographs of Roxane. Penny was standing next to me. "Oh! She is adorable!" she exclaimed, as she laid eyes on the pictures. "You must show these beautiful snapshots to the girls in the dorm," she clamored with a huge smile across her face.

"Yes, let's make our way up the stairs," I whispered with delight. "She is exquisite" Leila exclaimed, as she stared at the photos. Then she turned to Gohar: "Look at Muriel's baby sister — she is darling!" When Sandra turned her eyes on the photos, her examination was so intense and concentrated, you would think that she had never seen a picture of an infant before!

I will never fail to recollect the persistent and endless ohs and ahs from my classmates. I was thrilled with my classmates' strong affinity and empathy, but I was longing to return to France to see Roxane.

Finally, the day for my return to Paris for the Christmas holiday arrived. My father picked me up at the train station. I was so excited and happy to see him.

As soon as Papa's car stopped in front of the building, I hurried up to the apartment and hastily entered Roxane's room, only to have my enthusiasm and eagerness crushed by Roxane's severe nanny who looked at me with a frown of disapproval. "She is sleeping. You may not enter the room until she wakes up," she said harshly. The tone of her voice was so belligerent, I could not believe her nastiness. How could she be so insensitive to my eagerness and longing to take a look at my baby sister? After all, I had traveled all the way from England and I was really anxious to see her!

At long last, a loud outcry was heard from Roxane's nursery. I did not wait for the nanny's invitation to rush into the room. I stretched myself up on tiptoe and stooped over the edge of the crib. In the dull light, I gazed at her with amazement. Her big blue eyes were wide open. She was so beautiful, with her shiny blond hair. She was most certainly an adorable two-and-a-half-month-old infant.

I barely had time to have a peep at Roxane when her ill-tempered nurse-maid requested that I leave right away. "I want no intrusion or interference while I feed the baby," she said in an outrageous and appalling pitch. I soon realized that the only thing to do was to let her tend to Roxane's needs, but I was annoyed and deeply disturbed that I had not even had a chance to pick up or hold my little sister! Disgusted by this woman's unwonted and unyielding firmness, I walked out of the room.

When I returned to St. Margaret's, the girls in the dorm wanted to know everything about Roxane.

"Roxane is a delightful and lovable infant, but the abominable nanny did not allow me near her," I cried out. Fortunately, the dragon had been hired for only a few months.

* * * * * * * * * * * * * * * * * *

The winters in Folkestone were viciously cold. I was not accustomed to such severe temperatures and could not believe that our dorms were not heated!

Every now and then, I would complain about the frigid temperature, but I was told repeatedly that the bone-chilling temperatures were much more favorable and conducive to our well-being than being in heated rooms. "It is healthier for you," they would insist. I did not arouse anyone's compassion. At times, the British lifestyle seemed rather rigorous and challenging to me!

I will never forget that freezing February morning when I discovered, to my horror, that the water that I had left in a glass under my bed the night before was frozen solid. I was truly astounded by the sight of the ice. "It's an outrage!" I uttered, shivering. But my outcry and shrieks bore little reaction; the girls were still sleeping. I had no other choice than to go back under my covers to try to keep as warm and snug as I could...that was until Mr. H's voice could be heard in the hallway. It was time to get up!

****

As I try to recall some of the most unusual happenings during my St. Margaret days, Halloween — a celebration observed in England and in several other countries on October 31st — comes to my mind. There was no such ritual in France. This ancient Celtic festival, when people would light bonfires and wear costumes to ward off ghosts, was totally unknown to me. In Catholic France, All Saints' Day, November 1st, with its traditional visit to the cemetery, was and still is an official day of mourning. Even though I did not partake in any observance, I always felt an air of sadness in Paris on that day.

To my great astonishment, I discovered that on the eve of All Saints' Day, children of all ages rejoice in wonderful masquerade parties. St. Margaret's was definitely not an exception. With much jubilation, the students engaged themselves in the festivities of Halloween. We all had to fashion our own costumes for the event. It goes without saying that we tried to be as original and as innovative as possible. After contemplating a few possibilities, I decided to use my heavy, plush dressing gown as a foundation for my imaginative and creative work. With care and determination, I sewed on it scissors of all sizes, several flamboyant spools of richly colored threads, bunches of shiny safety pins and several tape measures of various colors. And then to top it all, I fashioned a magnificent hat in the shape of a giant thimble made out of cardboard and multicolored construction paper.

To this day, I do not know why I opted to dress myself as a sewing kit! But I was happy with the result. I got lots of compliments for my uncommon choice of a costume to wear to the Halloween party.

The evening was full of joviality and holiday excitement. The conviviality, the small talk and the joking were, to say the least, beyond words. Everyone agreed that all of the costumes were beautifully imagined. The first prize was awarded to Sandra, who appeared as a tree. Built on an even grander scale than one could have imagined, she towered above everyone. As we admired her impressive efforts, we discovered that on one of her branches she had placed a darling little nest with two small birds made out of papier-mâché. Dazzled by her creation, we joined her in her triumph.

Once the party was over, we all returned to our dorms. But the strange and unexpected, was yet to come. The girls believed that we should try some clairvoyance at the witching hour of midnight. Their outlandish stories about sorcery and witchcraft fascinated me intensely and aroused my curiosity to no end. Thoroughly immersed in their supposed power, the girls believed that by eating an apple and combing their hair at the same time in front of a mirror in the dark, that the image of their future husband would appear in the mirror. Their vivid imagination gave way to whimsical ideas. Their bewitching magic amazed me and I decided to go along with it all.

Perhaps more than anything else, I, too, was hoping to see the man of my dreams! After all, girls our age already had romantic fantasies about love and marriage. We dreamed about the handsome and rich Prince Charming who would one day sweep us off our feet.

So, to further our quixotic hopes, we wrote down five names of boys we knew on five different pieces of paper and placed them under our pillow. Then, the next morning we picked one out at random — divulging, of course, the name of our future groom! I must admit that I was rather skeptical about it all. But the fun was real and our dreams were genuine, too. We all had a deep aspiration for a romantic future and were caught up in a serene reverie.

****

After I had completed my first year at St. Margaret's, my parents decided to send me to Spain for the entire month of August.

As the train rolled into the Malaga station in the late afternoon, I was met by Maria-Francesca (known as Kiska). She remembered me; we had met once in Paris when she visited my aunt, uncle and cousins.

I followed Kiska. We were greeted by her chauffeur, who was waiting for us, standing by his Chrysler automobile, a huge and fabulous car. As we drove through the narrow streets of Malaga, Kiska informed me that I was invited that evening to go with Raoul and Ramon, her two brothers, to a debutante ball in Torremolinos. I was ecstatic, for I had not anticipated such an extraordinary happening on the day of my arrival.

The car drove smoothly until it penetrated large gates and stopped in front of an immense and elegant mansion, surrounded by spacious and beautiful grounds with a large swimming pool.

Swiftly ushered through the door, I was dazed by the sumptuous residence, with its magnificent high ceilings, marble floors and glorious rooms, all furnished in a refined and harmonious Spanish style.

I was then promptly introduced to Kiska's parents, to her six brothers and to her little sister. In her early twenties, Kiska was the eldest. The boys followed and then there was little Maria, who was four years old.

The entire family was delightful. They radiated such friendliness that I felt right away a special quiver in my heart for these charming people.

After a light meal, I was taken upstairs to my bedroom. I was very impressed by the grandiosity of the accommodations. Just like the rooms downstairs, the chamber had the Spanish flair, which I adore.

I was ready to unpack, but I could not find my suitcase! As I stood perplexed, the nursemaid came in and advised me that my suitcase had been emptied out and that all of my dresses and clothes had been pressed and put away in the closet and in the chest of drawers. I was obviously taken by surprise.

"Señorita, vuestro baño esta listo," (your bath is ready) the nursemaid exclaimed, as she pointed the way to the bathroom. I thanked her and she left the room. But the unexpected was yet to come.

I was stepping into the bathtub totally naked when, to my amazement, the nursemaid reappeared with a bunch of thick towels. She placed the towels on the little table near the bathtub and, without a word out of her mouth, took the liberty of washing me! I could hardly believe what was happening to me.

I was absolutely stupefied by the service and the care I was experiencing. I was definitely not accustomed to such attention and deference by the maids in France.

It seemed that in Spain, domestics and nursemaids were easy to find and to employ at low pay. So many people were very poor and homeless, and they needed lodging and nourishment so badly, that they were ready to put their shoulder to the wheel and take a job, no matter what!

In addition to a multitude of servants, each member of the R family had their own governess, who would tend to their slightest needs! Indeed, the lifestyle of the wealthy in Spain was still present in families who could still enjoy their important social and economic status. I must admit that I could have easily adhered to their comfortable and elegant mode of existence.

As was arranged, the chauffeured automobile was waiting for Raoul, Ramon and me, to take us to Torremolinos, to the debutante ball. In a short time, we had reached our journey's end. Strolling up the cobblestone path to a ravishing villa, sitting on top of a hill overlooking the Mediterranean Sea, I was practically walking on the pavements of heaven. The party was taking place on the grounds surrounding the majestic estate. The diverse, cultivated collection of magnificent plants and trees in the garden created the perfect and ideal setting for the event. The colorful illuminations attached to the branches of the trees were glittering under the celestial roof. It was an extraordinary scene of opulence. The picturesque setting was ideal. The atmosphere had an exotic charm, blended with the sensuous beauty of an exquisite summer night. Overpowered by this loveliness, I felt caught up in a reverie and I was transported into a dream world.

I was greeted with open arms by Marina, a young debutante from high society. Then Raoul and Ramon introduced me to their friends. They all lived in Madrid and would travel down to Andalusia, in Southern Spain, to spend their summer vacations in their families' villas along the Mediterranean Sea. And to my amazement, I had precipitated a certain curiosity among these high-spirited, elegant young men and women. Notwithstanding the fact that their French was far from perfect and that my Spanish was by no means perfect, a marvelous warmth emanated from our exchanges. Their friendliness towards "la Senorita Francescita" (the French *demoiselle*), as they called me, was utterly delightful. Never in my life had I seen such hospitality.

As the elegant and impressively beautiful dinner was served to us, we had the pleasure of listening to some astounding musician instrumentalists, dressed in their typical black Spanish outfits, strumming their guitars. They were absolutely enthralling. Then, to my delight, a group of graceful dancers, all dressed in rich and flamboyant attire, executed a wonderful Flamenco performance with their castanets. I was positively enchanted by the gaiety and the marvelous atmosphere surrounding me. Rapturous, I joined the enthusiastic audience by clapping my hands in a sprightly manner.

After the folkloric show, the orchestra played a myriad of tangos, waltzes, foxtrots and slow dances. Raoul, Ramon and some of their friends invited me to dance.

And then Juan asked me to waltz. I was by no means a good waltzer. But at his insistence, I accepted. We twirled and we whirled around and around the dance floor. Then, somewhat dizzy, I nearly fell, but Juan's strong hold kept me from slipping! "Would you like to take a stroll in the garden?" Juan whispered in my ear. Without a doubt, I accepted.

In his early twenties, fastidious in dress and style, Juan, with his exceptionally good looks, could easily have fit in the category of the classic tall, dark and handsome young man. Leisurely walking hand in hand through the lovely grounds and the sweet aromatic vegetation, we talked. It was not all that easy. Juan did not speak French and my Spanish was only scholastic, but somehow, we were able to communicate. As we looked to the sea, we admired the gleam of the small, lighted yachts gently moving in the darkness of the night. A sense of well-being overtook me. I was genuinely happy. When the guitarists began to sing a famous serenade, we walked over and sat on a large terrace to listen to them. They were so enchanting and inspiring.

That unforgettable and exquisite evening was far from over. Juan took my hand and invited me to amble along the path, down to the waterfall. On our way there, we stopped and looked up to the picturesque sky with its brilliant display of a shining moon and bright stars. We were exhilarated. It was all so wonderful and peaceful. Then, Juan's seductive eyes fastened themselves upon my eyes. I soon realized that Juan was adopting a decidedly flirtatious manner and that his behavior showed a romantic interest in me. Juan embraced me tightly in his arms and kissed me. To this day, I remember the jubilation and the great joy I felt in my heart.

We continued admiring the lovely surroundings until we decided to slowly make it back to the party. By the time we returned to the reception, Raoul and Ramon were waiting for me. It was time to leave. My bedtime had certainly passed hours ago! I had journeyed a long way to Malaga, but I was not tired.

When I found myself alone, I began to fidget about the room. Looking through the open window at the sunrise, I reflected on my first encounter with Juan. He danced rather nicely, I thought. And then, happy and electric, I started to dance on my own. One two three, One two three. I was overpowered by a strange feeling. I wanted to have a boyfriend and Juan fit the mental image of the young man conjured so often in my dreams.

Upon this happy thought, I closed my eyes and I fantasized that Juan was sweeping me off my feet. Dancing on the clouds, in the realm of my vivid and romantic imagination, I was soon able to lose myself completely in a deep sleep.

Refreshed by a few hours of rest, I was excited and ready to start a new day. I knew that I would meet Juan in a few hours, at another debutante party, and I was really looking forward to seeing him again.

Late in the morning, I went downstairs and entered the vast dining room where the breakfast table was set. "*Hola, buenos dias*" I said, with a smile. Ramon stood up and invited me to sit down. "Where is everyone?" I asked. "There are no family gatherings for breakfast. Everyone has their own time and clock." But then *Abuelo* — the grandfather — walked into the room. As I got up to shake hands with him, the distinguished silver-haired gentleman approached me and with a big smile, he extended a few polite words of welcome to me. I was warmly touched.

Ramon told me that his *abuelo* came down to Malaga every summer to be with his family. But unlike Ramon's parents, who led a very active social life, Abuelo wanted to have a tranquil and peaceful life.

"Really!" I interjected. "You don't seem to realize that my father has a very important function in the government of Spain," Ramon blurted out. Unquestionably, I was spending my summer vacation among some notably dignified people! *Abuelo* rang the buzzer for the kitchen maid to serve us.

We stayed for quite some time at the table, getting better acquainted while we ate sweet watermelon and some delicious Spanish tortillas with our coffee.

****

Meanwhile, the chauffeured car was ready and waiting for Raoul, Ramon and me to take us to the *playa* — the beach — where all their friends were going to join us.

For sure, these Madrilenians knew how to have an epicurean lifestyle. They had a life filled with all the pleasures of existence. Their luxurious habits and their tastes in eating and drinking were continuous sources of enjoyment.

As I looked at them, basking in the hot and brilliant sunshine, I thought of the Italian idioms *dolce vita* and *dolce far niente*, expressions that certainly fit their sweet and nonchalant lifestyle.

With the searing temperature, we placed ourselves on the soft and warm sand, close to the water so that we could splash ourselves from time to time in the waves or swim in the blue crystal waters of the Mediterranean Sea.

It was just splendid to just lie there, on the fine sand under the azure sky with my eyes closed, listening to the rhythm of the tides. The steady and smooth movement of the waves was not only music to my ears, but its harmonious and appeasing cadence removed me far from Raoul, Ramon and their friends. Their voices were already growing faint, as if in a distance. I gave heed to the melodious music of the sea ebbing and flowing around the edges of the coastline. There I was on a crowded beach. Yet, I was alone with my thoughts, in close contact with nature. I felt a profound reverence for our creator.

Hours had elapsed. Coming back from an imagined and unrealistically ideal world, I woke up and noticed that the tidal waters had receded. Then, I turned my eyes upon the beach. I discerned Raoul, Ramon and their friends. They were busy scrutinizing the shapely young women who were strolling leisurely along the sea and the half-naked bathers.

But it was time for Raoul, Ramon and me to return for lunch at the family's mansion. At around four o'clock in the afternoon, excellent and refined Spanish cuisine was served. Most of the family, including *Abuelo*, was there. They would always eat lunch together. The exchanges at the table were animated and full of joy. After lunch, we all retired to our rooms. It was time for a nice long *siesta*. Even though I had slept on the beach, I was happy to retire and read in my cool bedroom.

In the late afternoon, Kiska suggested that we take a short trip into town. As the car approached the main thoroughfare, she ordered the chauffeur to stop at the shoemaker's boutique. As we entered, Kiska tapped me on my shoulder and asked me if I would like to have a pair of made-to-order shoes. "Oh, what a great idea!" I exclaimed, without giving it a second thought. It was an easy decision to make; shoes were always my passion and having a pair specially designed for me filled me with joy. The artisan had an enormous assemblage of varicolored leathers, a huge supply of Variform heels of every height and size, and an immense quantity of materials for his craftsmanship.

With Kiska's advice, I chose a low-cut, pointed, high-heeled sandal in a black patent leather. The old man took his time to measure my feet. I was ecstatic. I was buying my first high-fashion, made-to-order shoes.

Little did I know that these gorgeous sandals would turn out to be a disaster! The heels were so high that I twisted my ankle every time I tried to wear them and the narrow thin straps crippled my feet and hampered my toes. In short, my custom-made shoes were a total fiasco! Needless to say, I have never ordered another pair of made-to-order shoes again.

After our stop at the shoemaker's, Kiska asked me if I would like to have a picture taken of me as a "Spanish Lady." "Of course, I would love to have a picture taken of me as a 'Spanish Lady,' what an original and fabulous idea!" Soon we arrived at the photo studio, where we were greeted by Señor Garcia, a short, feisty, middle-aged man. As I walked around, I could only admire the gentleman's magnificent photographs and portraits hanging on the walls of his studio. His subjects were presented with such accuracy and fidelity to detail. His proficiency and mastery were definitely apparent. "I am impressed by his work," I said enthusiastically.

"Señor Garcia can take pictures of you right now," Kiska uttered softly. This was so fortuitous and unexpected that I jumped with joy.

"Would you like to go as a Spanish señorita?" Kiska wanted to know.

"Oh absolutely! I would love to have Señor Garcia work on me."

Like a makeup artist, Señor Garcia applied the cosmetics on me. The subtle effects wrought by the additional makeup gave me a new visage. He continued his work by pulling my hair to the back, into a chignon and kept on going by crowning the bun with a magnificent large decorative *peineta*, a high tortoise-shell comb. Then, he secured an exquisite red hibiscus on the left side of my head and he put long golden earrings on my ears. Lastly, he added at the top of the *peineta* a graceful black lace mantilla, which flowed onto my shoulders. As I looked at myself in the mirror, I smiled. I was amazed at my transformation. Señor Garcia was silent as he studied my face. "All is well, follow me," he said with a grin. He directed me to an area of pronounced illumination.

"Look up, look down, smile — but not too much, turn to the left, turn a little more to the right," he commanded until I was finally sitting in the desired position. "Good, do not move, hold your posture until I am finished," he called out with authority. Without complaints, though not necessarily without annoyance, I agreed to put up with his directions. "Well, señorita, your photo session is finished," he uttered as he rubbed his hands together, a smile curving at the corners of his mouth.

"Señor Garcia is certainly very meticulous," I whispered in Kiska's ear. There was not a doubt that Señor Garcia took his métier to heart and devoted his full attention to the mastery of photography. His portrait of me as a "Spanish Lady" was no exception. I was enthralled and enchanted by the photograph.

For decades, my parents had the framed picture in the living room. Now, I have it in my home and when I look at it, it brings back sweet memories. No matter what happens, some memories can never be replaced.

After leaving the studio, both Kiska and I agreed that we needed a little respite before returning to the house and to ready ourselves for the evening's social events.

We stopped at a café and sat there, watching the people strolling. I laughed seeing Kiska tapping a spoon against a glass, which had been left at the table, to attract the waiter's attention. When the *camarero* appeared, she ordered two orange juices.

The waiter took his time, but we were in no rush. Kiska and I were having a lively conversation about the Spanish way of life. I had a strong desire to learn more about the culture and the social customs of the country.

An hour later, satiated and relaxed, the chauffeur drove us back to the mansion.

As I was preparing myself for Carmen's debutante ball, Juan came to my mind and these questions appeared: Will he ask me to dance? Will he take a stroll with me, as he did last night or will he ignore me? I just did not know what to expect.

Dressed in a long, white-and-blue strapless evening gown, with my lovely dark curls hanging over my shoulders, I glanced in the mirror to powder my nose and add a touch of lipstick. I gazed for a moment at the image reflected. I was beaming with happiness. I was having such a great time in Malaga and I loved every moment of it.

Escorted by Raoul and Ramon, I was ready to leave.

The chauffeur drove us to Carmen's palatial villa overlooking the blue Mediterranean Sea. The tempo and the magnificence, once characteristic of Spanish civilization, were again evident in this superb event. The tasteful opulence of the premises and the refinement and grace of the hostess and her guests unfurled a continuous scene of elegance and beauty before my eyes. It was enchantingly perfect. I was completely enraptured by it all.

The setting sun over the sea appeared effulgent and resplendent, and the sky was flushed with crimson, but it was already very late and the sun soon disappeared completely. But the small colorful lights attached to the walls of the villa and to the trees were scintillating in the dark of the night.

I was having a fabulous time with Raoul, Ramon and their friends when Juan joined our group. Pretending to be surprised to see him, I exclaimed with strong emotion, "Juan, I was not sure I'd see you here tonight!"

"Oh, but I hoped to see you at all the parties," he said spontaneously. Juan's fervent warmth and friendly disposition filled me with happiness.

Clustered closely together and elegantly attired, the sophisticated and aristocratic young men and women were dancing.

"Muriel, would you like to dance?" Juan asked me, with glittering eyes.

"Yes, I would love to dance," I answered with a keen sentiment.

We danced for a little while. Then, hand in hand, we withdrew, sauntering at a leisurely pace on a little walk to the rose garden. A mantle of dust over the gravel path clouded its surface, but the full moon and twinkling stars were wonderfully romantic. The atmosphere was electric with emotion. The noises of the crowd grew faint and only the soothing rustling sound of leaves was noticeable.

At first, I blushed as Juan cast his bright brown eyes upon mine.

"You look so pretty tonight," he said softly. His remark would have made me self-conscious, but my awkwardness was soon alleviated by his chivalrous assurance and courteous manners. When he put his arms around me, I was enveloped in a sort of fantasy dream world. Then, after fixedly looking at me for a few moments, he held my face in his gentle hands, caressed my lips with his and kissed me. I felt an extreme happiness surging through my entire body. Neither of us spoke for a while. I was trying to reconcile my feelings with the social mores of the fifties. Unlike today's tolerance of boy-girl relationships, yesterday's society frowned upon any sexual intimacy before marriage. And I could hear my mother's message: "Do not forget who you are." That said it all.

As I was deliberating for a moment, Juan's keen brown eyes met mine. I smiled. He stared at me and kissed me again. Overpowered by sudden and disarming sentiments, I was conscious that I was falling in love for the very first time. I mulled these thoughts over for a minute or two, but then Juan asked me if I would like to dance.

"Yes, of course I would like to dance," I answered with a smile.

"Good, let's go and join our friends."

Leaning on his arm, we started to walk back to the party.

In addition of enjoying the beach, the strolls, the car rides along the picturesque *riviera*, the numerous debutante balls, the fiestas and the parties, there was also the bullfighting — known as *corrida*.

When Señor de R told me that he had purchased seven tickets for me to see seven bullfights, seven days in a row, I nearly flipped.

"You will enjoy the *corridas* as much as the Spaniards do," he exclaimed, with a twinkle in his eyes.

I was actually afraid of going to see one bullfight, let alone seven! But I could not refuse his invitation.

The first performance was at night. Señor and Señora de R were attending the *corrida* with their children, their friends and me. As we approached the coliseum, the traffic was unreal, the bustling horse-drawn carriages arrived there in profusion. Soon, the elegant ladies and gentlemen, dressed in their Andalusian attire, stepped down from their coaches. The women, in particular, with their richly colored shawls, mantillas and high combs, were a feast for the eyes. I was stunned by the scene and stopped a moment to look around. Thousands of people were making their way into the arena. Getting through the crowd was very difficult, but due to Señor de R's important position in the government, his special pass allowed us to have immediate access to the presidential tribune.

As soon as the matadors, the toreadors, the picadors and the banderilleros made their entrance into the arena, the crowd acclaimed them with enthusiastic and loud applause. They walked around, saluting the audience. The cheers were abundant. The *corrida* started with the matador attempting to irritate and overpower the bull with the movements of his cape as he whipped it around. As I was watching him, trying to subdue the poor animal, my heart was pounding. What was more dramatically shocking to me was seeing the picadors on their horses, armed with spears, repeatedly puncturing the bull.

As I saw the blood gushing out from the spots where the poor animal was struck, I sat there perplexed by the incomprehensible cruelty. Finally, dressed in his magnificent embroidered costume, the banderillero walked into the arena. As he pulled out his shining blade, the spectators followed his every gesture with extreme passion, shouting "Ole! Ole! Ole!"

Their high spirits were unrestrained, their involvement unbelievable. The conclusion of the *corrida* is always the same: the matador kills the bull. The bullfighter's success was hailed enthusiastically with a triumphal ovation. The spectators were impressed by the matador's power — completely carried away, they tossed lots of flowers and hats to the proud victor, who was also given the ears and tail of the bull as an award for a well-done job.

The cumulative impact of the three slaughtered bulls that night was hard for me to accept. Bewildered, I asked Raoul, "How can people take pleasure in such a wicked sport?"

"Let me explain the rules to you," Ramon said calmly as we walked out. "Don't worry; the bull does not have time to suffer. The time of combat is measured for the matadors, the toreadors, the picadors and the banderilleros. Each is limited to a certain number of minutes. They have to follow a set of rules and guidelines."

I stared at him a moment, but I remained silent. I couldn't stop visualizing the brutality of it all. Noticing my dismay, he stroked my cheek and questioned me about my feelings regarding hunting and fishing. I did not answer.

"Let's join our friends," he suggested with a smile.

Soon afterward, we were all sitting in a café, drinking cold beverages. Juan was there too. Their ardent advocacy of bullfighting was strong, but soon our conversation turned to other cultural interests, activities and hobbies.

However, there was another *corrida* the next afternoon! I was invited to sit on the shady side of the arena, between Juan and Raoul. "Relax and make an attempt to understand and enjoy the bullfight," Juan implored desperately as he put his arm around me. I could not believe that I had surrendered and that I had returned with the boys to the coliseum. In the arena, the crowd gave an ebullient cheer. The burst of voices with "Ole! Ole!" was incredible. Well, I must say that as I grew more accustomed to the various steps culminating in the matador's ceremonial execution of the bull, I became more absorbed and I was soon participating in the boundless enthusiasm of the audience.

By the seventh bullfight, I had gained a total understanding of the most popular diversion in Spain.

As I reminiscence about my sojourn in Malaga, a multitude of recollections and anecdotes are still crystal clear in my mind.

I could never forget the cordiality of the de R family and the amity of their friends. They were all so warm and welcoming. The de R family was definitely amused by Juan's romantic courting of me. Raoul and Ramon had apparently disclosed to them my affinity with Juan. It made me laugh when the *abuelo* would address me as *la Novia* (the fiancée!) In a genteel manner, he would constantly query me about my fondness for Juan.

The numerous debutante balls and parties I attended are unforgettable. Through the mists of my memory, I remember these parties with a certain nostalgia. It was that summer in Malaga, that I experienced, for the first time, a tender emotion for a young man. On the eve of my departure, the soirée in Anna's villa was in full swing. The music was soft and sentimental.

How could I ever forget the sensuous beauty of that evening! On our way back to the chauffeured automobile, Juan slackened his pace and murmured, "I will always remember the happy times we spent together. I love you."

I was in my room alone, lying on my bed fully awake. I could not help thinking of Juan. Consciously, I felt the impact of my infatuation. But with a quivering heart, I suddenly realized that I was leaving the next day for France.

The conflict was overwhelming me. On one hand, I was reflecting on the wonderful flashes of innocent mirth between us; then, on the other hand, I realized that I might never see Juan again. I tried to suppress the idea, but torn between opposing reflections in my mind, I started to sob un-controllably and cried myself to sleep.

The morning sun slanted obliquely and brilliantly, through the cracks of the shutters. I emerged from my reveries and stretched out my arms vigorously until I was wide awake. As I got up to open the windows, I caught sight of the beautiful trees and the colorful flowers in the garden, and then, completely wrapped up in my thoughts about my incredible and wonderful stay in Malaga, I heard someone knocking at the door.

I opened the door. Kiska was there. She put her arms around me and said, "We loved having you with us, but you must get yourself ready."

The maid came into the room to pack my bags and I finished dressing myself. I strived to free my mind during those final hours in Malaga, but a strong feeling of nostalgia overcame me.

As Kiska and I reached the platform in the Malaga station, I suddenly felt someone walking behind me. When I turned around, Juan was there! I felt a strange change in my pulse as he held me tightly in his arms.

"The train is rolling in," Juan cried out, as he picked up my suitcase. As I got onto the train, my heart was precipitously pulsating, after Juan had kissed me goodbye, farewell, *adieu*... I hated goodbyes. I could not help looking at him from my window seat. His eyes, too, seemed to be fixed on me. Kiska was in the background waving. She was discreet and understood everything.

I am on my way home now, I thought as the train moved away at a slow speed. I did not speak to anyone in the compartment for a long while. I needed to reminisce. I was overwhelmed by so many feelings. My vacation in Malaga had been so special. After all, my very first romance was certainly a matter of no small importance to me.

After a couple of weeks in Paris, I was on my way to St. Margaret's in England.

Of course, everyone in the dorm had all kinds of unusual stories to relate to about their summer vacation. They simply liked to brag and tell tales of their conquests — real or not, they clung to them, whispering secrets of their so-called amusing discoveries with young men, if only to impress their classmates.

Now that the summer was over, I had to work seriously to prepare for my Oxford exams. However, once in a while, I became distracted as my thoughts returned to Spain. After all, it was one of the most significant and noteworthy events of my adolescent years. I had met my first Prince Charming.

Juan and I exchanged a number of letters. My fantasies were about him and my dreams at night were inspired by him. But as sentimental as I was inside, outside, the reality was there, with classes, damp grey skies and exams.

No doubt about it, Malaga was like another world!

CHAPTER 4

To Live and to Work

After completing my two years in England, I returned to my parents' home in Paris with a happy feeling of satisfaction from the good results of my exams. The achievement attained had a significant impact on me. The positive experiences that I shared with my teachers and classmates were, to say the least, very important as well.

When I had to study for my finals, the good exchanges of handwritten letters in Spanish between Juan and me stopped. But my summer vacation in Malaga was still vivid in my mind. Different from the milieu that I had known during the first 16 years of my life, my lengthy sojourn abroad had exposed me to a totally new way of life.

Now I was back under my parent's roof, realizing that I was no longer yesterday's little girl. My two years in England had been a turning point, marking my transition from childhood to adulthood. I was determined to achieve my own identity and become my own person. I had the urge to work. I wanted to earn money and get some independence. I craved a job involving human contact. I loved to talk to people more than anything. I was eager to meet people from all walks of life and from all parts of the globe. I wanted to widen my horizons and satisfy my thirst for traveling the world.

But my parents enrolled me in accounting and business law classes. I wanted to be an air hostess. Being a flight attendant would be a perfect fit for me; it would open the world for me and I could discover and explore its beauty with my own eyes. I had conjured so many images in my mind and had so many dreams. When I was told what I had fantasied about was not possible — that I could not become an air hostess until the age of twenty-one! — I was so disappointed. Furthermore, I had not realized that it would not have been possible for me to be an air hostess at twenty-one. In the 1950s, an air hostess had to be tall and I have always had the stature of a petite woman!

A few weeks later, through a friend of my parents, I was offered a job in the foreign exchange department of a well-known British bank. I was only eighteen years old, with absolutely no work experience, but I knew that I wanted, in addition to my courses, some practical training and hands-on experience. I will always remember the day when my father left me in front of the bank — a grandiose and beautiful edifice close to the magnificent Tuileries Gardens, a sort of haven in the bustling heart of Paris. I did not know exactly what to expect on my very first day, nor what I was supposed to do in the Foreign Exchange department. But when Mr. C, the director of the department, noticed my awkward predicament, he quietly came over to me. Smiling pleasantly, he whispered in my ear, "I, too, felt odd on the first day of my first job!"

His gentle and tranquil voice reassured me. Mr. C was a cordial, easygoing middle-aged British gentleman. His prematurely white hair made him look older than he was, but his handsome dark eyes contrasted splendidly with his short white hair. Sedate in manner, he bore a pensive expression. Yet one of his most appealing features was the gallantry with which he treated his employees. "Let me introduce you to your co-workers," he said eagerly. I followed him from desk to desk. There were, of course, plenty of handshakes and good words.

Looking back, I believe that the position I was assigned to was very good on-the-job training for me. I did my best to always be polite and pleasant by bestowing stellar customer service. Above all, I needed to be highly organized and socially confident to deal directly with customers.

When I think of my co-workers, Madame D comes to my mind, with her natural impulses toward venomous retribution and vindicatory reprisals when she did not approve of others' performance. At times, she would become genuinely abrasive and harsh with her colleagues. Justine, who sat across from Madame D, was always extremely punctilious in her work. Unusually absorbed by her occupation, she never divulged anything about herself. Then there was Mr. Roger, our departmental manager, who had an entanglement with Michele, the young lady who sat across from me. Michele's beautiful figure would show through her tight dresses as she walked back and forth in the department, swaying her little behind. Her blonde hair, freckled complexion and pearly eyes would have hardly attracted attention, had she not fluttered her long eyelashes as quickly as butterfly wings every time she saw a person of the opposite sex.

Was Mr. Roger amused by Michele's flirtatious allure, given that her affectation and mannerisms were so extremely artificial, or was she, in his eyes, an object of ridicule? I could not say. She certainly made her attempts to impress Mr. Roger, and I often wondered how many false promises he had made to twenty-year-old Michele! The whole situation was kind of comical to me.

I had a good relationship with my boss and colleagues, but I never socialized with any of them. After a speedy appearance for lunch in the cafeteria, I would disappear and take a walk along the crowded streets in the neighborhood. I still remember when, shortly after my start at the bank, I discovered the best bakery and patisserie. The large window display had an array of deliciously rich cakes. It was easy for me to succumb to their succulent and sweet moistness, especially after the light and often taste-less repasts in the bank's luncheonette. Naughty me, I indulged myself, satisfying my palate with a fine delight almost every day!

At my parent's insistence, I attended evening courses in business and accounting. The classes were quite interesting. But I had to take a typing and stenography program as well. What a punishment that was! Typing reminded of the piano lessons, which I loathed. I could never forget the instructor's strong voice: "Typing involves placing eight fingers on the keyboard." Perplexing and annoying it certainly was for me. I wished I could put my fingers on the pulse of something human and not on a machine! To this day, I have never been able to master typing with more than one or two fingers!

I soon discovered that living at home with my parents and siblings was really different after my return from England. There was so much less criticism on the part of my parents. I believe that they understood that I needed to be my own person.

After being abroad two years, family became all the more important to me. Sharing a room with my sixteen-year-old sister Ghislaine seemed like a good deal after sharing a dorm with six other students! Just like most girls her age, Ghislaine would occasionally appear glum and dejected, and then at other times she would be a marvelously giddy teenager, full of the heady zest of adolescence. Despite her changeable moods and her critical attitude toward my imperfections, we loved each other. Since she enjoyed the culinary arts, she would cook, and because I favored a well-kept home and the subtle effect wrought by a personal touch, I would clean. We vowed to remain single and share our lives together! We thought that we would be the perfect pair. Ha! Ha!

When I think of Ghislaine during her teenage years, a pretty girl she was, petite and slender. She had fine, smooth blonde hair, a little nose, a cute mouth in the shape of a heart and bright eyes. I remember catching frequent glimpses of her dainty silhouette as she danced the rock 'n' roll and boogie-woogie at parties or at Le Caveau de la Huchette in Paris, where one could immerse oneself in the world of the popular music of the 1950s and dance. Extremely quick and gracious, she was very popular among the young men who loved to show off their proficiency with someone who could follow their quick steps and share their enthusiasm.

I rocked 'n' rolled, but I still preferred the waltz, the tango and the slow! She liked the boys her age; I preferred older men. There was a great deal of communication between Ghislaine and me, but when it came right down to it, our social spheres were widely different and our opinions often differed as well. As I open the door to my feelings, I recall a host of little incidents, arguments, exuberance, gay laughter and tears that enlivened our childhood. They seemed to be of little consequence at the time, yet they mattered and did not vanish from my memory. When I think of the emotions shared in our childhood, I say to myself that they are not dreams — they are memories.

The seven-year age difference that I had with my brother was obviously quite noticeable. Of average height for his age, with a light complexion, soft brown hair and expressive blue eyes, he was a good-looking lad. Reserved around people, he seemed to live in a happy world of his own. Christian preferred to retire to his room to do his homework or read a good book. *The Adventures of Tintin* by Herge, the famous cartoonist, was among his favored and treasured series. He enjoyed jigsaw puzzles, easy or hard, in a variety of themes. Labelling and organizing, in a logical order, his stamp collection excited his curiosity and attention as well. Rather than putting up with his sisters' shenanigans and high-spirited behavior, he favored his solo activities and hobbies!

Once in a while, I would quickly open the door of his room and slip in. Christian would show me the most recent model boats and planes he had built. I admired the dexterity with which he assembled them. Not only did he have an accumulation of noteworthy structures around his room, but next to them he piled up a formidable assortment of hideous objects that he acquired as prizes for his remarkable adroitness in rifle and archery practice at the Jardin d' Acclimatation in the Bois de Boulogne or at a street fair. When I would comment on his achievement at aiming accurately at a distant object, he would look at me with an air of pride, saying, "There is some room for more!"

My younger sister Roxane, a marvelous two-year-old toddler at the time, was living in her own little world of toys and mischief. Ravishing and exquisite, she certainly was. I loved her dearly. However, the big age difference between us was there; she was a little kid and I had reached the stage of a young adult, working and studying.

When I think of my parents, Andre and Sybil, it could not have been easy for them to bring up four children from infancy to adulthood with such a large age gap between the siblings. The intricacies and complexities of promoting the emotional, social and intellectual growth of children who are at entirely different stages in their development is certainly very challenging for mothers and fathers. Notwithstanding the disparity of our ages and the variance in our temperaments, interrelation in our family life was of utmost importance to our parents. I loved my family dearly. I loved having my little confidential chats with my mother.

The tranquility of the long winter months aroused a feeling of quiescence in me. The realization that I needed a change of scenery burned within me. I needed to get away. I had asserted my independence through my job. I should go forward and plan my next escape, I thought. I went to the office of a popular travel bureau on the Avenue de l'Opera.

"Can I help you?" the agent called out amiably.

Pensive, I kept quiet. In my mind, there was suddenly crystalizing a vivid picture. I was seeing myself lying in the sun, on a beach by the blue sea, delighting in an enchanting existence among lovely surroundings.

"What kind of trip are you interested in?" the agent inquired, observing me, as I stood silently in front of the counter.

"I am actually not sure."

"How long do you plan to stay away?"

"The entire month of August," I said smilingly.

"Would you like to travel alone or in a group?"

"Traveling with a group sounds like a great idea. I have no desire to travel alone," I exclaimed.

"What types of trip do you prefer?"

"I would very much like to relax on a warm and sunny beach, but I am also longing to explore a civilization at its very source as well. What do you suggest?"

"How about Greece?" he retorted.

"Greece! What a marvelous idea. That's it. I'll go to Greece." And without delay, the travel agent gave me several brochures. After examining carefully, the various pamphlets and brochures, a sojourn in Lambiri on the Gulf of Corinth, which included numerous sightseeing trips, had the power of an irresistible attraction for me.

"This vacation package in Greece seems too alluring to resist," I said to the agent as I returned the brochure. He nodded his head in a gesture of acknowledgment and without a word had acknowledged that I made a good choice. Right away, the full-service trip planning was completed; my vacation in Greece was scheduled and organized. Jubilant, I was. I had mastered another important step in my fight for independence. Instead of having my parents determine what I should do during my vacation and where I should go, I was now able to make plans of my own and get them off the ground, exactly as I wished!

In the couple of weeks until the day of my departure, I would frequently dream about the extraordinary sights I was going to discover. Yet, on the eve of my departure, I felt a certain apprehension grabbing hold of me. I realized that I had known the tranquility of a sheltered life, whether it was under the vigilant eyes of my parents or those within the walls of St. Margaret's. Now that the outside world was waiting for me, I could not imagine what to expect. Should I really travel so far away and find myself in such a completely different environment where I would not know a soul and where I would not speak the language, or should I stay home? With my conflicting emotions, I had difficulty sleeping: on the one side there was my curiosity about discovering new, enchanting places and meeting interesting people, and on the other side there was the challenge of the unknown and the unfamiliar situations that could occur. Struggling with my ambivalent feelings, I realized that all situations have positive and negative aspects and that one should always try to be positive and get on with life. Finally, I was able to suppress my unwanted feelings and get a little sleep.

I had an appointment for registration at a cafe, across from the Gare de Lyon Station, the following evening. As I approached the meeting place, I saw a large banner bearing the words "Lambiri Greece." I did not thrust myself forward. I remained a few steps back and gazed at the people standing close to a round table, where our escort was sitting. Their youthful countenances seemed to express an amicable sociability.

As I was watching them, my thoughts were suddenly interrupted by Papa's voice: "Go ahead, you must register and fill a tag for your suitcase."

"I was waiting for you, Papa. Were you able to park your car easily?"

"Yes, yes," he mumbled, hastening up to our escort.

After a time, the formalities were completed. Then, leaving my tagged luggage in the registration area, I followed my father's quick step to the station. Soon we were able to find the track and the train heading to Brindisi, Italy, for my ferry connection to the port of Patras in Greece. When we reached the eleventh carriage, Papa got onto the train with me and escorted me along the crowded corridor. When he realized that we had missed my compartment, he turned around, irritated, and uttered with exasperation, "We must retrace our steps! We missed your compartment!"

A few seconds later, Papa opened a sliding door and slipped into the empty compartment. "Look you have a corner seat near the door," he sighed, with a slight frown on his face. "For such a long train ride, I would have preferred a window seat, but there is no sense in getting flustered."

Soon a couple entered. "*Bonjour! Bonjour!*" they both exclaimed.

"*Bonjour!*" We echoed in perfect harmony. Then, without further exchanges, my father suggested that I give my fellow travelers an opportunity to install themselves.

Wedging ourselves down the narrow corridor through passengers and bags was, to say the least, difficult. But we made it to the platform.

"You still have a full twenty-five minutes before the departure of your train," Andre ascertained, looking at his watch.

My father and I loved the electrifying atmosphere of a railroad station and felt that the hurry-scurry and the hurly-burly were all part of the excitement. As we walked back and forth at a slow pace, we watched the hurried travelers with their awkward bundles trying to make their way between the loaded chariots transporting mail and packages or squeezing themselves through the space between the train and the beverage and newspaper vendors. Some voyagers were speedily zig-zagging around people; however, occasionally one would stumble on a young child trailing after his or her mother and father, while others were slowed down by an elderly woman or man, walking unsteadily.

The conductor was helping a few lost souls to find their carriage. Busy, busy, it was. Many were saying their goodbyes to family or friends with a broad smile on their face, while for others the farewell brought tears to their eyes and a heavy heart. In the thick of it all, lovers, completely oblivious to the myriad passersby, were holding each other and kissing. Observing their passion as they were saying their *au-revoir*, a curious sensation flickered within me. Stirred by a certain emotion, the *adieu* with Juan was suddenly haunting my reverie!

The ambiance around us breathed such an extraordinary tempo that time elapsed rapidly. "The mechanics who check the bolts of the links connecting the cars are almost done; you must get back on the train," Papa said softly.

I smiled and came forward to kiss him. Papa hugged me. As he realized a shadow of uneasiness on my part, he whispered, "Don't worry, you will have a good time."

I looked up at his face, which was as convincing as ever. I embraced him and stepped onto the train.

Making headway along the crowded narrow passage, I stopped to open the window across from my compartment. Papa was standing exactly under that window. "Is your compartment full?" he asked.

"Yes, the carriage is full, with the couple and three young ladies."

"Really!" he exclaimed simply.

Then, as silence fell between us, a clamorous voice over the loudspeaker announcing the departure of the train echoed through the entire length of the platform. My father glanced at his watch and looked up at me. "Your train is leaving on time," he pointed out enthusiastically.

"Yes, there we go!" I called out as the train started to move slowly.

As I stood at the window waving my hand, I spotted Papa from a distance, his hand moving back and forth, but as the train followed the curved rails out of the station, he was soon out of sight.

I turned around and sat down in the compartment. I could feel the air of camaraderie emanating from the little group. We had instant communication with one another. I have always enjoyed conversing with my traveling companions and getting to know them. We all talked at length about ourselves and about our trip. Nic and Michou, a married couple, were sitting across from each other by the window. Tall, blond, much older than his wife, well into his thirties and dead calm, Nic stared at Michou while she was discoursing emphatically on their lifestyle. A petite brunette with dark sparkling eyes and a dark complexion, Michou was wearing a lightweight designer sports outfit. Beautifully dressed, she looked stunning. Michou wanted everyone in the compartment to know that their trip was exceptional.

"What makes it exceptional?" I queried.

"My husband and I do not usually take our vacations together," Michou affirmed, in a rather resolute manner.

We were all somewhat surprised by her explicit response.

"But you do live together?" Louise interjected.

"To a moderate extent, we do." Michou answered, emphatically. "Nic is a good man, but he insists on his freedom," she added with a sigh.

"Do you have children?" Louise asked.

"No, Nic does not want children," she replied.

I could not help glancing at Nic. Listening to his wife's superfluous and expansive verbiage, he seemed lonely in his corner seat.

We all remained quiet for a moment. Then Louise, a perky little woman in her late twenties, blonde with green eyes and long eyelashes, looked at everyone. "Yes, there are different lifestyles." Louise paused to catch her breath. "I am not married, but I do have love affairs."

I took umbrage at her honesty and did not respond. I remember how strange it was for me to listen to Michou and Louise sharing their private matters. I was somewhat astonished by Nic and Michou's casual lifestyle.

I had never heard of an open marriage before. These people were definitely ahead of their time!

The two sisters, Francine and Colette, kept quiet during our exchange. Francine's tall and broad figure stretched as she murmured in a barely audible voice, "Flaunting concubinage is futile. The value of good judgement is of utmost importance; it is crucial and imperative that one comes to terms with oneself. Don't misunderstand me: I like uncomplicated relationships and without pretending to be wise, I defy libertinism and leave it to others."

"Well, it's your prerogative," Louise retorted ardently.

"Let's change the subject — we are arriving in Dijon!" Colette cried out.

As the train reached its first stop, we stood up to look out of the window. "There is not much activity on the station's platform. We can all step off the train and stand together outside," Michou suggested.

But unexpectedly, Paul, our escort opened the door. "How is everyone?" he asked jovially. He did not wait for an answer and politely requested that we hand him our tickets and passports. "I will take care of the customs and the frontier formalities for all of you so that you can get some rest." After he finished collecting the important documents, he assured us that we would be served breakfast trays early in the morning.

As we journeyed out of Dijon, for some moments we sat there in silence. I was gazing in awe at the night. Like a ghost on the windowpane, the moon was shimmering, while the darkness of the night flooded the outside world. But when Nic clapped his hands for attention, my poetic reverie was abruptly interrupted.

"It is time for us to get some sleep!" he said loudly.

"Yes!" we echoed.

Nic suggested that two persons sleep in the luggage nets above, two lie down on the seats, and two sleep on the floor. Harmoniously, it was decided that the petites, Louise and myself, would sleep in the nets, that the tall sisters would take the seats and that the couple would share the floor. The luggage was piled up at the end of the outer corridor. "Louise, Muriel, let me help you to get up there." Nic offered his strong, tightly intertwined fingers as a secure footing for us to reach our respective luggage nets. At first, I felt a little insecure looking down from my unconventional hammock, but I was soon able to comfortably arrange my makeshift berth by placing my handbag and my sweater under my head as a pillow and spreading out my summer raincoat over my body as a blanket. In the meantime, the others, too, had rapidly installed themselves. Louise had disappeared under her big shawl. Walling themselves along the entire length of the seats, Francine and Colette seemed very tranquil and cozy. Lying on the floor, on spread-out newspapers, Nic had his arms around Michou. Notwithstanding their open marriage, they really seemed to care for each other.

I was asked to turn the light off. For a little while, I let my mind wander about, but not for long because the gentle rocking of the train soon lulled me to sleep.

A few hours later, the rising sun struck my face with its heat and woke me up. When our escort appeared at the door, everyone else was still sleeping, surprised he was, when he saw the very unusual sleeping arrangements. "*Buon giorno!*" he exclaimed with a definite Italian accent.

"*Buon giorno!*" we echoed in sleepy voices.

"I need to serve the coffee before it gets cold," he said softly.

"That is certainly a great idea," Michou retorted.

Slowly waking up from our torpor, we realized that we had reached Italy's beautiful east coast and that our train was moving along the Adriatic Sea, stopping along the way in the resorts of Ravenna, Rimini, Ancona and Bari. Looking out of the window, the spectacular scenery enchanted us. The atmosphere of camaraderie within our small group, with the incessant chatter and wonderful laughter, was considerable.

Late that evening, we arrived in Brindisi for our ferryboat connection to Greece. We had now reached the second stage of our journey. Once on board, we went straight to the upper deck where we spent most of the night talking and laughing in the cool breeze of the open sea.

When we arrived the next morning in Corfu, we were told that we would have a couple of hours on shore. Eager to see something of the island, Louise, Francine, Colette and I decided to hire a horse and buggy for a jolting ride through Corfu, enchanted by our surroundings. Light-hearted and happy, we admired it all.

When we returned, the sailors were getting ready to continue the four-and-a-half-hour trip on the Ionian Sea, which is south of the Adriatic Sea and part of the Mediterranean. Soon after our vessel left Corfu, I leaned back on my deck chair and I closed my eyes, enjoying the gentle rocking of the boat and the smooth, warm, salty air. I was thoroughly enjoying the peaceful crossing. But the strong voice of our escort giving out his instructions brought me back to reality: "We are arriving in Patras. I'll meet you all downstairs." I grabbed my hand luggage from under my seat and headed for the narrow stairs to go down to the lower deck. We all gathered and departed from the ferryboat to the chauffeured transit vehicle waiting for us.

After a few miles drive from the bustling port of Patras, we arrived in the village of Lambiri, nestled among the soft hills of the Peloponnese region. The hosts at the reception office were very welcoming. They invited us for a light meal in the main pavilion, a lovely building with huge bays. The restaurant, serving typical and traditional Greek cuisine, had stunning views overlooking the sea. Then, with a carefree spirit, under a beautiful blue sky, our guide gave us a complete tour of the resort. As we walked around the resort, he pointed out the little store, the hairdresser, the bank, the game room. Further away was the discotheque across from the beach. Here he stopped to talk to us: "You can satisfy your athletic desires with volleyball, ping-pong, pétanque, golf, underwater sports and water sports. Furthermore, if you want to go fishing or cross over the Gulf of Corinth to unknown horizons, caique boats are at your disposal." It all sounded good, but I already knew that my major sport would be relaxation and carefree idleness on the beach! As our guide pointed to the dance floor, he said with a grin ear to ear, "You will have an amazing choice of nocturnal events. Every evening there will be a theatrical show or singers on the stage or a variety show or folkloric dances or masquerades or games — we have it all."

In a frame of olive and coniferous trees, the bungalows, surrounded by flowers, were spread out. Louise and I shared simple and adequate accommodations. As soon as our hostess left us, we threw our suitcases over the beds and unpacked. It did not take us long to get fully installed. We were ready to start our vacation. "Louise, would you like to come to the beach and go swimming with me?" I called out.

"With pleasure. Let's go!"

We followed the little path down to the sun-kissed beach and went for a dive in the blue-green sea. Overtaken by happiness, we remained under the warm blue sky for a long while. I listened to the ebbing of the waves. Then, with the evening tide's change of sound and color upon us,

I realized that it was time to leave the beach and return to our room to ready ourselves for the evening activities.

After drifting off in careful consideration, Louise turned to me: "Muriel, we are roommates, but we must give each other complete freedom to come and go as we please."

"Absolutely," I responded brightly. I am in total agreement with you. Why should we be hampered or restrained to follow our impulses?"

Elegant in her lovely printed dress, Louise looked at me and said, "Muriel, I love your blue-and-white striped dress. It is charming and your hair is easy on the eyes. I wish I had long hair like yours. Mine is so fine that I have to keep it very short."

"Louise, your golden hair is smooth and pretty. I really like your short hair."

"Well, thank you. Shall we go?"

"Of course. We did not come all the way to Greece to waste our precious vacation satisfying our little vanities."

Lambiri throbbed with a pulse of its own, but frequently I slipped out of our resort to visit the majestic ruins, with their fascinating myths and legends. I remember climbing the winding road to the summit of the Acropolis. Rich in history, the marble Parthenon, with its remarkable sense of harmony and balance, was simply amazing to see. With an overwhelming feeling of reverence, I walked around the rocky and slippery ground. Captivated by the spectacular views of the Greek capital, I almost lost my group. They had already made their way down!

All's well that ends well. I found my group.

Our sightseeing was far from over. After enjoying the prodigious panoramic view of Athens from the top of the Acropolis, we were now discovering the bright and beautiful city of Athens. Then, ending our tour at the National Archaeological Museum, we ambled around the fabulous marble figures and well-preserved paintings. The collection of Greek antiquity transported me into another world.

Fascinated by the ancient world of Greece, I joined my group for a visit to Delphi. With its splendid panoramic views from Mount Parnassus's slopes, Delphi's archaeological site is certainly a wonderful tourist destination. For sure, we were not alone!

We discovered the breathtaking view from the high road above the Gulf of Corinth. The incredible vista exerted an appreciable effect on all of us. Gazing at the long, landlocked portion of the Ionian Sea (which looked like a gigantic serpent), almost too narrow for ships to pass through, I stood there speechless for a moment. I was stunned by the deep inlet of the Ionian, separating the Peloponnese from mainland Greece. It was, to say the least, a unique experience for me.

Different, but equally fascinating was our donkey ride up the tortuous paths of the rugged Mount Hymettus to the old monastery of Kaisariani. I felt sorry for the poor burros carrying tourists up and down the hill, stamping their feet at a very slow pace on the burning, rough terrain. As we cast our eyes on the Bay of Aegina and on the Cyclades Archipelago from the towering plateau, we were all enraptured by the beauty of the abundant views. We frequently stopped to admire the picturesque sights. Amid the laurels and cypresses, we encountered a delightful Byzantine church and monastery.

I could certainly ascertain the fondness that our guide had for his country. We were on our sightseeing tour bus, traveling back to Lambiri, when our guide got up and reflected with pride and veneration on his country's history and beauty. He finished his little speech by adding, "I do not need to tell you how much my country means to me and I do want to thank you for being here."

Beyond a doubt, Greece is an enthralling and a spellbinding land to visit. I could never forget the spectacular, enchanting sights.

As I muse upon my recollections of this extraordinary country of legend, Pedro comes to my mind with an eruption of emotions.

I could never forget the moment when Pedro, in a lighthearted manner, breezed into the resort wearing navy pants and a white sport shirt, the whiteness of his shirt contrasted beautifully with his dark complexion and his bright brown eyes. His countenance expressed real determination. Very tall and magnificently built, he had a certain virile grace.

While I was finishing my dinner on my first evening in Lambiri, he approached my table and with a smile, asked amiably: "Mademoiselle, would you like to dance?"

"Of course, I would love to dance," I uttered as I rose. Because he towered over me so much, it must have been almost comical to see us together, gliding all over the dance floor.

Pedro spoke English fairly well and could also occasionally throw a few words of French into our conversation. Since my Greek was totally non-existent, I must admit that I was relieved that he could speak English. We continued to dance for a while. Then suddenly, in a most cheery tone, he invited me for a drink. "You must try some ouzo," he insisted at the bar, as he ordered a glass of the anise-flavored Greek liqueur for me.

Pedro watched me take my first sip. Then, full of curiosity, he asked, "Do you like it?"

"Yes, it is very good. Although different, it reminds me of my great-grand-mother's anisette."

Pedro laughed. Raising his glass, he wished me the very best for my stay in Greece.

Desiring to make me acquainted with the person he was, and wanting to know more about my cultural background, our exchanges were natural and genuine. "Lambiri is a wonderful place," Pedro said softly. "I come here every day and enjoy the warm and lovely summer nights."

"Do you live near here?" I asked.

"I spend the summers in Patras, where my parents and five sisters live, but I study in Italy. My university is in Rome," he said calmly.

"What do you study?" I queried.

"My courses include political science, cultural anthropology, sociology, foreign policy and more. I am pursuing these subjects to become a diplomat and live abroad as an ambassador," he answered with a cheerful expression.

"How wonderful! I am impressed."

Looking at me with a certain air of nobility, crowned by a tender regard, Pedro bent over and whispered, "It would please me intensely to spend time with you and get to know you. Nightlife here is festive and offers fun and gaiety until the wee hours of the morning. I would very much like to invite you to a variety of ethnic restaurants, cafes and clubs during your stay in Greece."

Glowing with happiness, I smiled. Then, taking my hand, Pedro invited me again to the dance floor.

Giving way to a certain irrepressible exuberance, Pedro suggested that we make our way to a tavern nearby, to listen to some Greek folk songs accompanied by a bouzouki orchestra. Delighted to see the "real" Greek scene, I followed Pedro to the colorful little village of Lambiri. The small group of dwellings on the quaint market square was vibrant with life and animated by all kinds of lights, sounds and motion.

In one of the exotic open-air cafes, the chairs on the terrace were, to a large extent, empty. The men had left their old-fashioned tables and chairs to dance. Dancing in a line, with their hands placed on their neighbors' shoulders, they alternated slow and fast steps. Thrilled with their choreography, I watched them with delight. But then, somewhat perplexed, I turned to Pedro and asked inquisitively "Where are the women?"

"Women mostly stay home, while men meet up, drink wine and dance this typical country Greek dance, called the *sirtaki.*"

Looking at my confused facial expression, Pedro paused for a moment. "Would you like to stay here for a while? We can order some popular Greek seafood and watch the men dance."

"Yes, I would like that very much." I answered, contemplating the pleasant ambience.

While I was gazing with fascination at the enchanting steps of the *sirtaki,* Pedro was conversing with the cafe owner. "I should introduce you to my French friend, from Paris," Pedro cried out.

"We love French people very much," the cafe owner asserted kindly. "A cordial welcome to you. Let's open a bottle of wine to applaud your visit to Greece." Pedro chuckled softly and lit a cigarette.

"With their charm and gracious courtesy, I definitely think that the Greek people are great ambassadors for their country," I remarked with conviction.

Giving me a triumphant look, Pedro said, "I can see by the way you look, there is genuine merriment in your face. I am glad that you like it here." Holding my hand for a few minutes, he added, "We are having a good time together. Let's eat, drink and see each other as much as we can during your vacation."

After that first evening, I saw Pedro almost every day. At the start, it was a purely friendly relationship. Pedro was very proud and happy to take me around the beautiful surroundings. Whether it was to the cities of

Patras or Athens or to the charming countryside or simply to villages like Lambiri, it was always a marvelous adventure filled with joy.

Recalling my adventures in Greece, I could never forget that afternoon when I was to meet Pedro and his friend Alexandros at the bus station in Patras. Louise, my roommate, was heading for Patras as well. We decided to leave together and take the bus.

"Oh drat! We missed the bus," said Louise with an incredulous stare and an expression of annoyance. "Look, it's turning left at the next crossing."

"What can we do?" I sighed in disbelief. "The next bus is scheduled to arrive in two hours and we need to get to Patras."

Putting her arm around me, she said, "Don't be so pessimistic. We will find a way to get there."

"How?" I asked in despair.

"We are going to hitchhike," Louise declared.

"Hitchhike? Do you really want to hitchhike?" I retorted, somewhat baffled.

"You bet! My eye is on the road. For the purpose of getting us to our destination as soon as possible, I am paying close attention to any car or truck going our way. It's past two o'clock — will you do it?"

"Okay, I have no choice. I'll be daring and go with you," I answered softly.

"Look here! A truck is coming, a truck is coming!" Louise cried out, as she frantically tried to catch the attention of the driver with her handkerchief.

As the truck slowed down and came to a halt, the driver opened his door. "Patras — the bus terminal," we echoed loud and clear.

The driver nodded, and the man sitting next to him grunted his approval with a big toothless smile in our direction. Our chauffeur stepped down from his seat and walked to the back of his truck to release the latches of the trailer. Then, with his help, Louise and I pulled ourselves up onto the platform and sat across from each other on the hard surface of large containers. As soon as the metal-hinged door of the trailer was shut, the driver went back to his wheel and we were on our way to Patras.

Then, unexpectedly, Louise and I heard creepy sounds coming from the back of the trailer. Not able to discern what was going on, we were greatly puzzled. Suddenly we saw two hefty men staring at each other in a suspicious duplicity, sauntering closer and closer to us. Right away, I sensed that they were up to no good. Their countenances betrayed their turpitude. Staring at us in a lecherous manner, they exchanged a few words in Greek.

My heart was pounding, I was paralyzed with fright when one of the men kneeled down at my side. I do not remember what he looked like. Yet I cannot ever forget his clammy hand squeezing my knee, nor the fact that he tried to kiss me. Our screams could not be heard by anyone. I felt helpless and frightfully scared. However, my despondency suddenly vanished and turned into an unknown strength. Thus, I managed to wiggle out of his clutch and kick him in the right place. A few feet away, Louise, who was experiencing almost the same kind of sordid encounter as I, was able to turn on him vehemently and scratch his face in retaliation. Finally, with guilt on their faces, the two men moved away from us.

Trying to catch our breath and calm our uneasiness, Louise and I huddled together. Notwithstanding the sun's heat, which pierced the coarsely woven mesh of the trailer, we were shivering. It was unbearable to be there, locked up in a moving vehicle with two men who had tried to fondle us. While we were waiting anxiously for our safe arrival in Patras, there was an uncomfortable silence.

It was almost three o'clock when we finally reached our destination.

A clatter followed by another clatter struck the metal-hinged door. The sound of the rattling chains was like soft music to our ears. As the driver helped us to jump down from the platform, we muttered a couple of words of thanks and went off.

Pedro was there, waiting for me. As soon as he laid his eyes on me, he said, uneasily, "What is it, Muriel? You look faint and pale."

"Yes, you do," Louise asserted.

Without hesitation, I cried out, "Louise, you look rather shaky as well."

After catching our breath, we divulged the monstrous happenings during our ride to Patras.

"I was very concerned whether we would be able to pull ourselves out of that difficult situation," I said, "but notwithstanding the horror of it all, our determination to fight them off saved us."

"The two men were simply having their thrills at our expense," Louise added indignantly.

Stunned by the obscenity of our disclosure, Pedro repeated, "It's unbelievable, it's unbelievable."

"Hitchhiking was my idea. I am guilty," Louise asserted with tears running down her face.

"But I consented to go with you!" I exclaimed without hesitation.

"Yes, that's true," she sighed, showing a certain relief.

Then, remembering that she had an appointment, Louise was able to compose herself and bid us "*au revoir.*"

Wanting to relieve my distress, Pedro wrapped his arms around me and, in a heartfelt way, hugged me. He kissed me gently and in an amazingly short time, I was able to reconcile myself to the thought that someone like Pedro was there for me.

Then, looking at his watch and shaking his head, Pedro said that Alexandros was waiting for us and that we were late for our appointment.

"Come on, let's go! I want you to meet Alexandros. He has been my friend as long as I can remember. We just love doing things together — talking, playing sports or going places. I am sure that you will really like him."

"Without a doubt, It will be a pleasure to meet Alexandros," I acknowledged immediately.

Pedro held my hand and squeezed it affectionately as we walked across the square to a little cafe.

Indeed, it was a great pleasure for me to meet Alexandros. I found him congenial and easygoing, amusing and very friendly. Just like Pedro, Alexandros loved the enchanting ambiance of the resort of Lambiri. Immersing themselves among the foreign vacationers was very appealing to them. They took great delight in going there every day during the summer months.

I will never forget Pedro's soothing solicitude that afternoon in Patras. Nor could I ever forget his extraordinary personality. He was not only a charming young man, but I was particularly impressed by his manners and warmth as he escorted me almost every day, here and there, doing things that pleased me. In the evening, we would often go for a walk along the beach. With the clear, warm nights and the moon giving enough light for us to see each other, we kept our heart-to-heart conversation going. Although at times, lost in our thoughts, we remained silent.

As I am reminiscing and indulging in the noteworthy recollections of my youth, I remember vividly the evening when Pedro suddenly stopped walking to convey his feelings to me. "Muriel, I delight in your company, I have never met someone like you. You are unique and very special," he uttered with a twinkle in his eyes.

Smitten by his flattering comments, I was deeply moved.

"Yes, I am crazy about you and I am falling in love with you," he admitted as he lifted my face up, kissing me gently on the lips.

Mesmerized by sheer happiness, I was aware that I was equally smitten with Pedro. I was also falling in love.

I could never forget my last evening in Lambiri. Pedro invited to a lovely restaurant. Sitting outdoors with a soft breeze from the Ionian Sea, we were engaged in conversation when a photographer asked Pedro if he could take a picture of us. Accepting with an irresistible elan, Pedro suggested that I sit on his lap so that the photographer could take a picture of the two love birds. I smiled, but I was unhappily conscious that my vacation in Greece was coming to an end.

After our wonderful Greek dinner, Pedro invited me to dance. But as soon as the music stopped, he requested, with resolute determination, that we leave the tavern and take a walk along the beach. The moon was shining even brighter than before. Silent for a while, we walked.

Then Pedro halted and whispered into my ear: "You are definitely the kind of girl I would like to have as my bride. Will you marry me?"

My heart started to throb rapidly. As I was trying to appraise his words, Pedro was lovingly stroking my face, and prognosticating that with his formidable future as a diplomat, I would have nothing to worry about.

There was a moment of absolute stillness. Was I losing myself in a dream?

Sharing my life with Pedro, a future diplomat, would probably be a momentous, life-changing decision. I didn't know what to make of it. I was trying to appraise the situation. Could I possibly imagine myself, with all the necessary diplomatic protocol and international courtesy etiquette, as an ambassador's wife? In addition, I would definitely need to speak Greek. I felt uncertain. It occurred to me that love is complicated.

We continued walking along the beach. Pedro stopped and lifted my face to apprise me that he would not be able to walk down the aisle until his four sisters were married! He went on: "This comes from a family tradition. My parents are committed to perpetuating this custom from generation to generation." Filled with astonishment, I was blown away. I could not find words to express my surprise. I had never heard anything like that before.

Unhappily conscious, I realized that my month in Greece was coming to an end.

Before boarding the ship in Patras, the next day, holding me closely in his arms, Pedro uttered. "Muriel, I do not know how to convey to you the deep sadness I feel that you are about to leave Greece, my country. I hope that you will soon come back to me." Pedro embraced me and whispered almost inaudibly, "Have a wonderful journey." Goodbyes are never easy, but I knew that I would never lose the memories of the wonderful times we shared together.

Standing back on the quay, Pedro was watching me while I boarded the ship. As the boat was leaving the harbor, I was looking at Pedro from the deck. Expressing tenderness, we waved at each other and we tried to smile. That is until I realized that I could no longer see him. I turned around and discovered an empty seat. I sat there, caressed by a gentle wind. I had had a wonderful summer vacation. But I was also over-whelmed with emotion, having left Pedro.

Just being outside on the deck was a soothing solace for me. Instead of joining my group of travelers for dinner, I sat there pensive, pondering over my four wonderful weeks in Greece. As the moon appeared and stripped the darkness from the sea, I saw a young woman walking on the deck. With her downcast face, she seemed to be as dejected as I was. We looked at each other and we both simultaneously smiled. Denise sat at my side and we talked. We soon realized that we had both left our hearts in Greece! After engaging in conversation, we remained quiet for a moment. Then, directing her eyes at me, Denise suggested that we drink away our sorrows with a glass of ouzo! Commiserating and supporting each other in our difficult situation, we sipped our ouzo and we chattered all night. It was such a relief to talk to her.

The next day, we reached the Port of Brindisi and boarded the train for our next stop, Milano. Denise and I wanted to continue our journey together. The timing was propitious for us: the lady who had a window seat across from me wanted to switch compartments. Denise was ecstatic to take her place.

The gentleman sitting next to Denise was eying me attentively with his big, dark, yearning eyes. At first, I ignored him, but when Denise got up to take a walk down the corridor, he introduced himself by taking my right hand in his own for a moment. His name was Jacques. "I am so glad to see you here. I really wanted to get to know you, but every time I caught sight of you in Lambiri, you were in the company of a tall young man."

With consternation, I dropped my sunglasses on the floor and did not know what to say. I almost felt sorry for Jacques. After all, watching a woman you are interested in in the arms of another man must be somewhat troublesome!

Thinking about Jacques's confession, I observed him as he sat there, trying to quench his thirst with orange juice. He was of short stature and in his middle thirties, and his countenance and demeanor imparted a definite intelligence. With the exception of his very thin lips, he had no finely chiseled features. His fair complexion, burnt by the sun, had a fiery reddish color, which seemed to be accentuated by his dark brown hair. Ignoring my half-dazed condition from a lack of sleep, Jacques kept expounding his views and impressions of his sojourn in Greece.

At long last, he stopped talking and there was a stillness in the compartment. I stared at the white beaches along the Adriatic Sea. I could see myself walking, running, bouncing, happy and free, hand in hand with Pedro, on the warm sand. But I was soon aroused from my reverie by Denise. She broke the silence with her soft voice: "Your friends Colette and Francine in the next compartment would love to see you."

"So are you going to run away from us?" Jacques asked regretfully.

I rose and smiled. "Don't worry, I'll be back," I retorted as I hurried along to see my friends.

After having a pleasant chit-chat with Colette and Francine, I returned to my compartment. Denise and Jacques were waiting for me. We talked some more, reminiscing with a tinge of sadness and nostalgia that our holiday in Greece had ended and that we were going back to Paris to continue our daily routine. I realized that after this sublime and awe-inspiring interruption, I would have to return to the reality of working at the bank and continuing my studies.

As soon as we arrived in Milano, the escort assembled our group of travelers and called for our attention: "With the two hours to spare before the departure of our train to Paris, you have the choice of staying in a cafe here or leaving the train station and taking a walk. It is up to you."

"But we don't want to drag our luggage!" Denise yelled out.

"No problem. The luggage will stay with me, but be conscious of the fact that you have to arrive in time to pick up your luggage. Be punctual — you cannot afford lateness!"

Denise and I emerged from the station sharing the same idea. We both wanted the experience of buying shoes in Italy. It did not take us long to find a very engaging and appealing shoe store. The realm of possibilities in that boutique was beyond our expectations. We tried on several pairs of high-quality, fashionable leather shoes. We quietly contemplated several styles with careful consideration. Denise and I were unable to resist the impulse to purchase our very first high-heeled shoes. In addition to our highfalutin' fancy new shoes, Denise and I decided to indulge in our largesse and give ourselves another special pleasure by acquiring elegant, extra-long umbrellas. Animated and joyful with our purchases, Denise and I left the boutique. Our melancholy and despondency had invariably lightened up.

We hurried back to the platform in the train station, where our group was congregating together for the train to Paris. We did not have a long wait. The loud din of the locomotive rose and soon the whole train stopped. Crawling one by one into our reserved car, we claimed our seats. Denise and Jacques were once again sitting across from me. By the time the train left Milano, Jacques had closed his eyes and fallen into a deep sleep. Whereas, Denise and I, thrilled with excitement, kept ecstatically admiring our new high-heeled shoes. Our unhappiness had been somewhat alleviated with our newfound treasures. And more importantly, it was the beginning of a lasting friendship with Denise.

A short time before our arrival in the French capital, with an appraising look and consideration, Jacques asked me politely for a date: "I genuinely want to see you and get to know you," he emphasized, as he handed over his calling card to me. When I caught sight of it, I was impressed, I never expected Jacques to be a deputy of the Assemblee Nationale and a member of the Cabinet.

The sound of the brakes was heard. We had reached Paris. My father was on the platform, waiting to pick me up.

The next day, after breakfast with the entire family, I returned to the bank and began to work!

CHAPTER 5

Reminiscences and Anecdotes

Almost immediately after my return from Greece, Jacques telephoned and expressed his desire to see me again. I accepted his cordial solicitation with pleasure. I wanted to know more about him and his position as a member of the Cabinet at the Assemblée Générale.

A couple of days after his phone call, we convened our rendezvous in an upscale restaurant on the left bank of the Seine. Our succulent five-course and mouthwatering dinner was wonderful.

Jacques had a style of gentlemanly behavior that I naturally liked very much. He seemed to be interested in everything, but he chose not to discuss politics with me and ignored the topic of Greece completely. He definitely preferred discussing art, music, theater and film. But when I spoke about my family ties, the expression of impatience in his countenance was noticeable. Seemingly, his thoughts flashed back to the turbulent path of his adolescence caused by his parents' divorce and being an only child. Then, pushing back his empty coffee cup and dessert plate, he added, with an attitude of conceited confidence, that he really had more important things to contemplate than his youth.

We stopped talking for a short while, but the restaurant was filled with echoes of voices, Jacques was there, sitting quietly in a dark navy suit, with a starched white shirt which was adorned by a meticulously arranged red bow tie.

After a few moments of reflection and careful consideration, he looked at me attentively and invited me to accompany him to the theater the following Saturday. I liked the idea. I was always thrilled to see stage performances, whether they were comedies, dramas or musicals.

Without any hesitation, I succumbed to the idea of going with Jacques to the Comedie Francaise to see "Tartuffe," one of Moliere's famous theatrical comedies. I could not push my temptation away. My thirst for that kind of entertainment was always there.

In retrospect, Jacques and I had an undeniable friendly connection. He always claimed to have a strong emotional attachment to me. I was, at times, bothered by his romantic overtures. I really, truly did not know what to do. On one hand, I remember being flattered and gratified that a man of his caliber would take such interest in me. Yet, on the other hand, there were things about his behavior I detested. He could sometimes be pompous and supercilious with taxi drivers or waiters. And that was not all. Like any politician, he needed an audience. Even if it was an audience of one!

As I disclosed earlier in my memoirs, I always had wonderful conversations with Meme, my darling grandmother. I could always confide in private matters. I would never have to worry about her divulging anything to anybody.

I remember describing to her, in the same breath, Jacques' accomplishments and deploring the unfortunate wavelengths between us. Meme paid attention to all the details. She was always fascinated and thoroughly amused by the whole course of the experiences I encountered in my youth. Evidently, Meme was entertained by my earnest verbiage about "Papillon's" eccentricities and peculiarities. Since Jacques wore a bow tie every day, we called him 'Papillon' when we talked about him. It was actually a very fitting nickname, since the French word for a bow tie is "noeud-papillon." With the exception of formal occasions, bow ties were really outdated in the late fifties.

I craved to untangle my ambivalent and uncertain sentiments in respect to Jacques, the positive versus the negative aspects of my relationship with him. Trying to sort out it all, I talked about it with Meme. Leaning back in her armchair, she directed her eyes at me and uttered, in a soft voice, "I don't think that I have to persuade you to go out with him. Papillon seems to have several appealing and attractive plans for you."

"Yes, it is quite true, I enjoy the variety of our outings and I do appreciate the time we spend together. But I am definitely not going to compromise my liberty."

Conveying to Meme my determination for autonomy and my choice to meet and go out with other individuals was a relief.

Nodding, Meme responded, "Truly my darling, the years have gone by so rapidly. You were not long ago a little girl, and suddenly, you are now a young demoiselle!"

I smiled broadly and thanked her for her patience and understanding regarding my predicament. Then, looking down at my watch, dimly illuminated by the small table lamp, I realize how much time had elapsed. "Meme, I am sorry if I seem rushed, but I must go home and change, Papillon is taking me out this evening to see a show," I whispered.

"Enjoy your soiree at the theater with Jacques," Meme uttered sweetly, as she managed to raise herself from her seat to give me a warm hug.

I definitely wanted to continue having a relaxed friendship with Jacques. But I had the desire to meet other people and not wallow in nostalgia about past infatuations.

As I am divulging some of my never-forgotten yesterdays, I can still see Sybil, my mother, entering my room to give me a letter. With a twinkle in her eyes, she handed it to me and sat down. To my complete astonishment, the two-page missive was from Alexandros, Pedro's close friend. His letter was, to say the least, unexpected.

When I finished reading it, my mother's wandering gaze met my face. "Muriel, is everything okay?" she inquired softly.

"Maman, this is crazy!" I muttered.

"What is it darling?" she asked as she put her arm around me.

"Maman, this letter is from Alexandros. I met him in Greece. He is a close friend of Pedro, the young man who had a strong interest in me."

"That is very unusual. Usually, it is the person who has a penchant for you who will contact you, not his buddy," Maman remarked, with a grin from ear to ear.

"Maman, please read it," I insisted.

Patras, 20 September 1957

My dear Muriel,

Of course you remember Pedro's friend from Patras. As you see I write you first... I am so busy in the Bank, in the exchange department. I have to deal with the tourists who have not stopped coming yet, though the weather in Greece has changed a little...

I do not go to dance in Lambiri, because there is no interest. There are very few people from France and the orchestra has left fifteen days ago. The bar which was full of life and joy is now empty... But I'll always remember the charming nights I had spent there among the polite people of France dancing or laughing or speaking for love... Of course you remember now my hobby to speak about love with you. I am not a bad boy like some other boys of Greece who wanted more things from the French girls. I only wanted to know, as I have explained to you, the way of thinking of the French girls about this subject. Really I have done much progress in my mind about this.

Do not think that I am doing always this job when I meet a girl. In contrary, I try to amuse them as much as I can. My girl here in Greece loves me very much because, as she says, when she is with me, everything is different. Another time, I'll write you more about us.

I know you had a good journey from Greece to Paris and you have spent very well your 'vacances' in our country. My friend Pedro informed me, he showed me your letter and that's why I know something from its contents. But instead of Pedro's answer, you have mine.

Never wait for any letter from him. He just left Patras for Italy yesterday. He really told me that he will never write to you, because as he explained, he dislikes correspondence with people who he will never see again. I just tell you the truth and please do not write to him anything about this, if you write to him.

Dear Muriel, do not think that he is a bad boy, writing is not his hobby, my hobby is to write.

I am expecting now your answer soon. Write to me if you do not mind about your family, about your plans for the future and everything else you think is interesting for me.

You will have soon my answer with everything you will ask me to write about.

Yours sincerely,
Alexandros

"He sounds like a nice young man," my mother murmured quietly.

I looked at her, but I remained silent for a moment. Then, overwhelmed by a strange sensation, I began to laugh hysterically.

"Maman, this is ridiculous! In my wildest imagination, I could not have dreamt that Alexandros would be the one to write to me and tell me that it was all over with Pedro." With a momentary stupor, I stood there, gazing at Alexandro's penmanship. Then, listening to my mother's soothing talk, I was able to pull myself together.

I assumed, without any evidence, that Pedro told Alexandros that his crush on me was over and done with. But I did give credence to Alexandros' aspiration, to allow himself to believe that my attention might be drawn to a fortunate rival! I know it was presumptuous of me to assume that, but I could imagine the anguish in Alexandros' heart each time he saw me with Pedro!

I resisted the urge to write to Pedro, and I resolved to write the following day to Alexandros.

I will share with you segments from the multiple missives I received, and still have, from Alexandros. It will help you to understand some of the traditions of Greek society in the 1950s.

Due to their past and different traditions, the customs, practices and lifestyle in every country are often very different, which makes traveling abroad and meeting people who are poles apart from all the more meaningful and electrifying.

Patras 30 September 1957

My dear Muriel,

Thanks a lot for your nice letter. Indeed you are an excellent girl and it was very kind of you to have so soon your answer. So I do the same and I hope to have a good friendship with you, though you are so far away. Someday I may meet you again.

Many things happen day by day. In our country we use to say: "The mountains only cannot approach each other, but the people someday meet again."

I am very proud because I have a friend from Paris, the best Capital city in Europe... I am jealous because you live in a more civilized world than me, full of beauty.

Alexandros' long letters were a treat. He always expressed his feelings in an extraordinary manner. I could depend on his analytical abilities, his earnestness and warmth. Apparently, his banking career took precedence over his political aspirations and his community activities. But above all, he always placed a high value on the human side of things, on family ties and friendship. I must interject that I shared, and still share, the same viewpoint pertaining to relationships.

Far from being inconsequential and insignificant, our written exchanges revealed many enlightening observations about society.

Patras 28 October 1957

My dear Muriel,

Thank you very much for your long nice letter. Everything was interesting and you have given me a clean picture of your life in "gay" Paris, which is always my dream... Something like this will happen after the two years of my service, in the army...

Today, we celebrated in whole Greece a great national feast... We defeated the Germans and Italians who came to conquer Greece during the second world war. All the houses were decorated with Greek flags and in the morning, we had a parade of school children, scouts, army, navy and air force...

I do remember the historical "Oxi Day," It was 28th of October 1940. I was 5 years old. The day when the first Italian and German airplanes bombed Patras. Too many buildings were destroyed and too many people were killed. My father was invited as soldier. Me, my mother and my little brother went to save ourselves in shelters. Then we went to a village where we suffered too much, until the war finished. I must have much paper to write you all these adventures during the second world war...

Looking at your hobbies, I saw that I have the same ones. All represent the joy of life... I went to two parties where I had a very pleasant time with girls dancing the "rock and roll" and of course the tango, the dance of love, with the lights switched-off...

And now my dear good friend, I finished my letter, waiting for yours. Write me about everything you think is interesting for us...

Heartily yours,
Alexandros

Patras 27 January 1958

My dear Muriel,

I received your fine letter and I thank you very much for it. You are really a good girl and you never forget your duties...

I have spent very well Christmas and New Year...I went to many dances and parties. I danced the rock and roll and 'calypso'. Do you know this dance?... Harry Belafonte is a good singer of calypso' dances. I like 'Day-O,' 'The Banana Boat Song.'

In Patras now we have Carnival days... People come from all over Greece, especially from Athens. There are many music halls here with orchestras from Athens. You can go everywhere and dance till morning. If you have good company and money you can enjoy yourself very much...

Do you have any boy friend now? Excuse me for this question. I simply would like to know more about you. As for me I have a nice girl friend and I go to many dances with her.

Yesterday I went on an excursion to Olympia... I have gone there many times before but I went because I had very good company.

I wait soon a letter of you. Write me everything about you. You must trust me.

I have no news from Pedro. His sister told me that he is well...

Yours sincerely,
Alexandros

Patras 2 April 1958

My dear Muriel,

It is a long time since I received your nice letter. Please excuse this delay... But it is very important to have every news from my best friend from wonderful Paris. Thank you very much for any information about your boy friends in Paris. You really are a girl who knows about life and try to enjoy it as much as possible. Paris is a city where joy and gaiety are in the daily program of *people. I have written you many times that my dream is a visit there. So I'll have the opportunity to meet my best friend Muriel...*

There is a month since the Carnival days. It is true that Patras holds the best Carnival in Greece. For two weeks the city looked like Rio de Janeiro. Everything was celebrated and a parade of coaches were passing under the sounds a gay music. Disguised in costumes, people were dancing with the best orchestras from Athens. People came from all over Greece. Now everything has finished and Patras is back to quiet and calm...

As you know I play the guitar. I belong in a music organization of amateur musicians. We play good music...

In Patras we have good weather. I hope to visit Lambiri very soon...

I end my letter wishing you a happy and joyful Easter to you and all your family. My greetings to your sisters.

> *Yours sincerely,*
> *Alexandros*

Alexandros and I were never romantically involved, but our exchange of letters continued for several months, at irregular intervals. I was simply charmed and fascinated by his sincerity and candidness. Sharing our views about our work, our countries and our way of life were definitely delightful and enriching.

Sometimes I would read entire passages from his letters to my mother, adoring his polite and courteous manner.

One way or the other, either in Paris or in Patras, Alexandros and I wanted to meet again.

But I guess that it was not meant to be! He never crossed my path. Yet, I will not ever forget the chivalrous consideration that he had for his Parisian friend.

****

As I am reminiscing, I remember an evening as though it was yesterday. I went with a group of friends to the Caveau de la Huchette, located in the Latin Quarter, close to La Fontaine St Michel and Notre Dame. The building dates back to the 16th century. But it was only after the Second World War that the medieval cellar was turned into a lively nightclub.

The atmosphere in the Caveau de la Huchette could not have been more exhilarating and animated. The lighthearted ambiance was filled with merrymaking, dancing to the great music of the '50s.

Intently staring at me, a young man approached me. With friendliness in his hazel eyes, he asked me to dance. I accepted with pleasure. For quite some time, we frolicked energetically to the rock' n' roll and boogie-woogie music. Then, we naturally started talking, but the noisy crowd and the very loud music prevented us from catching most of our chitchat.

"I would like to introduce myself to you and get to know you. We should exit," the young man said almost inaudibly in my ear. I followed him outside.

Fully revealed by the streetlights, Serge looked like a typical upper-middle-class Frenchman in his twenties, of average height, with a smooth, fair complexion and light brown hair. He was wearing an expensive suede jacket over his narrow pants. Absorbed by his countenance, I did not hear Serge's request. Gently tapping me on my arm, he repeated that he wanted to take a little walk.

As we strolled along the animated streets near the nightclub, Serge was telling me about his engineering studies. Then, letting out a deep, audible sigh, he stopped talking.

"What's wrong? You look troubled," I said softly.

"Well, due to the fact that I am compelled to do my military service, I will have to put the application of my profession on hold."

"I sympathize with you, but this is the prospective fate of the boys!" I exclaimed.

"I don't see why I should destroy my immediate future with this harrowing experience," he said with a pang of bitterness.

Well, I could understand his predicament. After all, he had not enlisted of his free will. Military service in France was required by law.

Suppressing a smile and fixing my eyes upon him, I tried to soothe and reassure him. "The fact remains that you have been appointed, and acknowledging it will help you to come to terms with it and bring yourself to bear it!"

Serge seemed to be surprised and pleased by my response. He nodded in agreement and, resisting the impulse to kiss me, invited me to return to the nightclub.

When we got back, it was like a furnace. I wasn't in the mood to stay. But Serge seized my hand and bid me to dance. Fortunately, his anger at the military service seemed to have elapsed, at least for the rest of the evening.

After a few bobs and twirls dancing "le rock," we left the club. Holding hands, we walked over to a nice cafe in the neighborhood. There, we had a lovely tete-a-tete.

"Are you a regular at the Caveau de la Huchette?" Serge wanted to know.

I told him that I seldom went to discotheques or cabarets, and that I preferred the atmosphere of a private party, rather than the ambiance of a nightclub.

We were having so much fun together that we paid no attention to the time. It was past midnight! Serge decided to escort me home.

Leaving the cafe, we sauntered up the Boulevard St Michel, passed the Luxembourg Gardens, and headed to my building. When we arrived at the doorstep, he said that he wanted to see me again very soon. He jotted down my telephone number, gave me a little kiss and walked away.

I saw Serge several times before his departure for his military service.

We went for beautiful walks through the Luxembourg Gardens, winding up at his favorite cafes. Needless to say, we returned a couple of times to the Caveau de la Huchette to rock 'n' roll and boogie-woogie! We laughed, we talked, we danced, we flirted. We invariably had a good time together.

On the eve of his departure, Serge made some advances that I did not anticipate. Half-amused, half-appalled by his forwardness, I protested his attempt to disrupt our friendship. I was finally able to dissuade him from his apparent romantic strategy.

"I do not want you to get the wrong idea about me," Serge whispered as he caressed my hair. "But, my little doe, you must understand how much I want you and how much I want you to belong to me!" ("My little doe" is the translation for "Ma petite biche.")

Serge was not happy, but he was not as deeply distraught as I feared. And despite my refusal, the amity between us did not noticeably change.

Serge left Paris for a military station in Compiegne, in northern France, where he was drafted for his compulsory enlistment in the national service.

For the next couple of months, I received a large number of letters from him. He never shied away from writing truthfully about living in the army, and how much he missed me. I am now sharing with you the translation of some of his first letters:

I really miss you, my little doe. Before I fall asleep, I want to tell you something about my life here.

The men for the most part are likable — deferred conscripts, they all have a high intellectual level which I appreciate immensely — many are married and have children….Yet, the lieutenant who is in charge of my platoon is barely twenty-five years old!

You should have seen my battalion marching in a column through the forest to the cadence of the sergeant's strident orders: "Left, right, left, right, turn, etc…etc…" We strode vigorously until we had completed our twenty kilometers. I was tired, so very tired.

The next afternoon I had to grasp the hilt of the bayonet. The officer seemed horrified at the spectacle I made of myself. Looking at me with beady eyes, he mused awhile and then became so loquacious, he just did not stop talking. Admittedly, I felt pretty dumb….

Naturally, in the army, one has to also face duty in the kitchen. Can you imagine me in the kitchen, peeling potatoes? There were of course some other irksome tasks, but I will spare you the details….

In the evenings, I sit down in the conference room to study and prepare for the entrance examination to become an officer. The room is not heated. I have never had such cold hands….

Now, my little doe, I have summed up my activities for you. But I ought to tell you that I look very different with my shorn scalp and I doubt that you could possibly imagine what I look like in my uniform. You would probably agree with me that my army gear leaves much to be desired. Theoretically one must be impeccable. I have tried three uniforms, but the jackets are far too large on me and the pants are ten centimeters too short! Don't laugh! I can see you smile. Don't worry, I won't embarrass you by taking you out in this marvelous attire!

I am looking at my watch — it is midnight! At this hour last Sunday, we were together and what a great evening it was. It's difficult for me to believe that I am actually here. I miss you, my little doe. Time and again my thoughts travel across the miles to you.

I leave you for now with a passionate kiss.

> *Your poor little soldier,*
> *Serge*

Serge's letters were truly enchanting. We continued to correspond for quite some time.

However, Serge's delicate sensitivity put him in an emotional state when he received my lengthy missive, advising him that I had made plans for a journey to Italy and Yugoslavia during the Easter holidays.

Infuriated by my decision, he responded angrily, "Something does not jibe with what I know about your character. I am coming home on leave and you are on your way to Italy and Yugoslavia! Is that possible?"

Wishing to avoid any misunderstanding, I replied immediately. This is the translation of my letter:

My dear Serge,

With an apology for disappointing you, I would like to assure you that I did not intentionally mean to offend you.

There was no indication in your letters that you were going to have an off-duty break on the long Easter weekend and that you were intending to return to Paris.

Honestly, I am torn between two alternatives. In truth, I really would love to see you again, but I am also in great need of breathing space from the routine of my job in the bank and my studies… Furthermore, I have already paid in full for my sightseeing tour of Italy and Yugoslavia.

Admitting that I have always had the strong desire to widen my horizons and experience the world, I will go for it. I apologize profusely and beg your pardon.

With all my affection, I am asking for your forgiveness, and I am already looking forward to your next visit to Paris.

Your little doe

Serge wrote back that he was upset and that he hoped to see me after my trip. But that was not the case. He stopped writing and I never saw him again.

Looking back at the friendship and laughter we shared, I will always remember our good times together.

****

It's fun to reminisce about the past. Of course, it is easier to revel in the good memories, rather than the distressing recollections that one might have. But I want to emphasize that my memories are full of the meaningful people and events that have touched my life and made me the person I am.

****

Now, I will share with you some of my thoughts and feelings about my trip to Italy and Yugoslavia, which is bringing images and memories to my mind.

As soon as we arrived in Venice, our tour guide led the way to a little "albergo," where we were going to lodge for a few days. Situated near the famous Rialto Bridge and a couple of minutes away from the splendid Piazza San Marco, our hotel was located in well-chosen surroundings.

My young traveling companions were as amused as I was by our tour guide when he revealed that our hotel was actually on the small square where Casanova, the Italian writer, used to meet his young lovers!

Immediately after we entered the albergo, our guide was busy allocating rooms. I soon found out that I was going to share my accommodations with Michele for the entire journey. Of the same age as me, petite with flaming red hair, a pale complexion and a freckled face, Michele was a friendly girl and a pleasant roommate.

Reflecting on my first trip to Venice, I could not ever forget the wonderful wave of excitement I sensed as I was ambling leisurely along the canals with my group, admiring the marble facades mirrored in the water and the countless bridges crossing the canals. We were all simply mesmerized by the unique architecture of some of the bridges.

Watching the gondoliers, dressed in their black pants and striped shirts, steering their gondolas with one oar was absolutely enchanting.

"Oh! It is all so captivating and charming!" I mumbled, half-hypnotized by the beauty of it all. Everyone in my group agreed with me. Enthralled and fascinated we were.

The Grand Canal, seen from the Piazza San Marco with the reflection of the palaces, the churches and the monuments, was even more extraordinary.

As we walked across the Piazza, I stopped for a moment and listened to the cooing pigeons. I was so amused to see a myriad of them perched on the heads and shoulders of the tourists!

After visiting Saint Mark's Basilica, the Doge's Palace and more, our escort suggested that we take a vaporetto to the picturesque island of Murano, known for its refined, handcrafted glassware — chandeliers, sculptures and figurines. We stopped in a couple of factories and watched the crafters. We were all amazed by the skill of the glass blowers.

Without a doubt, discovering the romantic city of Venice was, for me, a fabulous and captivating experience.

On our way to Yugoslavia, we stopped in Trieste, a seaport on the Adriatic. We stayed in a hotel in the center of the town and we were able to enjoy walking around.

The following day, we reached the magnificent Palace Hotel in Portoroz, near Piran in northwestern Yugoslavia, which used to be part of Trieste.

When we were told by our escort that we would have a couple of days there to enjoy the pretty resort and the beautiful coast of the Adriatic Sea before our sightseeing excursions began, there was enthusiastic applause from our group.

We all needed a pause! The sunny beach, the clear sea, the relaxing walks, the calm and the beauty of it all, gave us a superb break. Yet, as nice as it was, I had the thirst to see new sights and take the opportunity to discover the region and experience the culture and the way of life of the people living in Slovenia.

Michele and I decided to take a day trip on our own, with a private guide. Minutes before 6 a.m., we left with our escort and travelled a good hour by bus to Ljubljana, where we stopped for breakfast in an ordinary eating house. Men and women were sitting on benches around scattered tables. Their cheerless expressions and dingy apparel said much about their tough existence. As I saw them, I thought of the women paving the highway along the route we had driven through. I stood dazed for a moment. But not for long. Our escort waved his hand in my direction and asked me to sit down.

We ate our breakfast, which was simple, but copious. Then, to our greatest surprise, our escort poured some slivovitz, a strong plum brandy, into our glasses. "Try it — this is the most popular Yugoslavian drink," he said, leaning back on his chair.

"Thank you, but I don't go for that sort of drink, let alone early in the morning." I retorted.

Looking at me doubtfully, he asked, "Do you really mean that?"

"Yes, I do not care for alcoholic beverages."

"Oh no, no, that's impossible — you and your friend must join me, for at least a sip," he cried out anxiously.

"Well since you insist, I will make an exception and try it," I sighed.

A few minutes later our glasses were empty and we left for the airport.

I am sure that the slivovitz had had a numbing effect on me, because if I had been totally conscious, never would I have boarded the four-seater propeller plane from Ljubljana to the bustling city of Zagreb! I will not even attempt to describe the motion of the plane. Moving in every direction at a rapid speed, I thought that I was in the midst of a nightmare! Fortunately, the flight was short.

We spent the day walking around Zagreb, Yugoslavia's ancient capital. I liked the picturesque town and its friendly people, but I immediately realized that, under Marshal Tito, who was the supreme commander at that time, life for the Yugoslavian people was extremely arduous. No matter where you looked, that feeling was everywhere. The people were definitely oppressed under his dictatorship.

Tito's image was posted everywhere: on the street corners, the buildings, the buses, in a flowerbed, absolutely everywhere. Our guide told us about the propaganda in the newspapers. It was abundantly clear to Michele and me that we were suddenly transported into a whole different world. Nonetheless, we were able to indulge in the scenic beauty of Zagreb. To discover the lovely medieval edifices, the Gothic cathedral, the Baroque church, the main square with its 17th-century buildings, the pleasing landscape of the park and the narrow and colorful streets of this attractive town was very enriching for us.

On another day, Michele and I decided to leave Portoroz and take a tour to the enthralling cave of Postojna, some 40 miles away from Ljubljana. Discovering the gorgeous formations of this spectacular subterranean cave from the little underground train was an incredible and captivating experience. Awe-inspiring, it was!

Another unforgettable and unusual event was the day Michele and I spent at the Lipica Stud Farm, known for its white horses. Amazingly, the place was open to tourists. We were charmed by this unique estate, and watching the dressage of the saddled horses was definitely an unexpected encounter for me.

As I recall the magnificence of Venice and the enchanting coast and towns of Yugoslavia, I realize how enthralling my two weeks were.

****

When I returned to Paris, my daily life continued with my work, studies, and outings with family and friends. But, whenever possible, I would take the opportunity to travel. Trips always spanned the chasm between the routine and my restlessness.

Thinking about my adventures and escapades during the year of 1958, the Brussels World's Fair comes to my mind. I went there with my friends, Lilian and Bernard.

We attempted to visit as many pavilions as we could. The architecture of these structures was, for the most part, in the Art Nouveau style — striking and spectacular, they were. But I should definitely not forget to mention the eye-catching relic of this major event, the towering and iconic "Atomium" (spheres made out of steel), which is still, after all these years, a landmark in Brussels.

The huge crowds of visitors did not faze me, although I was somewhat concerned that I would lose sight of Lilian and Bernard and get lost! I was beguiled and fascinated by the international ambiance; one could hear every language. All in all, the vibrant and sprightly atmosphere of our day there was electrifying and unforgettable.

After our visit to the Brussels World's Fair, we continued our journey to the exquisite medieval city of Bruges, where we had a wonderful time wandering around the scenic historical center and the lovely canals. Bruges, with its crisscross canals mirroring the pretty medieval houses, reminded me of Venice.

When we had finished admiring the picturesque town, Lilian and Bernard suggested that we go to Ostend, a fashionable resort on the North Sea coast, for dinner. It was a divine place to stop at for a scrumptious repast and enjoy the local specialties, such as fresh-caught shrimp, mussels, and fish. After a long day, nothing could have given us more pleasure than to savor a delicious meal with a beautiful sea view. We ended our day with an easygoing promenade.

The few days spent in Belgian with my dear friends were most certainly eventful and significant.

Whenever I could take a break from my routine and broaden my horizons, I would go away. I would take advantage of the opportunity to spend a long weekend in Holland — the country of windmills and tulips — or take a delightful visit to London to see family and friends and enjoy the great theater performances, or simply enjoy some "Dolce Vita" on a beach in Deauville.

Soon the year of 1958 was coming to an end. Up to then, I had always wanted to spend Christmas and New Year's with my family. But spurred by my need for adventure, I joined a group with my sister, Ghislaine, and went to the skiing resort of Meribel, in the French Alps.

When I opened the bedroom shutters the morning after our arrival, I caught sight of the snow-topped hills and the bright sunshine — enchanting it was! As soon as I finished having my breakfast, I left the hotel and headed to the ski rental place.

I was very excited to put on skis for the very first time. But when I saw them on my feet, my joy turned to dismay. They looked so lengthy and impractical. Furthermore, I realized that I could hardly keep my balance on the slippery white blanket of snow!

Cautiously, I made my way to the beginner's ski class. Not that I expected to be able to ski down the gentle, smooth slope right away, but I did not anticipate that for several days, the coach was only going to teach us the appropriate way to fall! I already had an inadvertent tendency to fall on my behind, so I wondered why I would have to pay to practice this!

Although it was at times challenging for a beginner like me, the beautiful resort of Meribel will always be remembered as a charming village. Additionally, the ski lifts were not only a great way for skiers to reach some of the highest points, but they allowed people like me to set foot on the lovely terrace of a restaurant to have a relaxed lunch in a wonderful setting.

After spending the day skiing, social activities would take place.

I remember a wintry afternoon when I was sitting by the brick fireplace, sipping my hot chocolate, when Jeanne emerged from behind. "This is a delightful spot," she uttered with a smile as she sat down in the armchair beside me.

I couldn't have agreed more with her; the soft warmth of the fire and the relaxed ambiance were definitely inviting. In a moment, our conversation turned friendly. There was something genuine about Jeanne. I saw immediately her inner natural beauty. I esteemed and valued the wholesome individual she was.

As I am writing about our strong friendship and how we met, I have just heard that a few days ago, Jeanne passed away. For over sixty-two years, Jeanne was a wonderful friend and will always remain in my heart.

Jeanne's life had not been easy. She was a teenager when she had to face, during the Second World War, the untimely death of her father, who suffered a heart attack. This loss had a profound effect on her.

She lived with her mother, her younger sister and her two younger brothers on a large estate, an hour away from Bordeaux. She was eager to leave home and immerse herself in her studies at the University of Bordeaux. There, she fell in love with a fellow student, but her mother did not accept their liaison. This broke her heart; the bruise was deep and had a significant impact on her destiny. Jeanne never married and she devoted her life to teaching English.

She was assigned to a lycée in Paris. Then, wanting to broaden her horizons, she decided to teach English in Africa. She enjoyed living for several years in the dynamic metropolis of Dakar; then she was sent further into the interior of West Africa. She loved her life there. But when she contracted a serious case of hepatitis, she had to be repatriated.

It took her several months to get back on her feet. Yet, Africa remained etched on her mind.

She missed the colorful and exotic beauty of Senegal, the thrilling excursions along the banks of the Senegal River, where she had discovered the huge baobab trees alive with red monkeys. She loved the picturesque villages, the African people in their multicolored cottons, extravagant jewelry and fantastic headdress. She missed her young students, she missed it all, but she could not return to the tropical climate.

So, she settled for Tunisia. It was in Africa, with many fabulous fascinating places to explore, but it was not the same. After a couple of years there, she returned to Paris, where she taught in a lycée until she retired.

As she grew older, Jeanne decided to return to her family estate and live with her mother. When her mother died, she bought her siblings' shares of the property. Amazingly, she enjoyed a solo life, with a view of the vines, in the middle of nowhere.

Meribel was not only scenically beautiful, but the atmosphere of camaraderie there was delightful. With the laughter, the socializing, the dancing in the local discotheques, the evenings were always filled with joviality.

As I reminisce, a masquerade party comes to my mind. Everyone had to wear a costume that evening. At first, my sister Ghislaine balked somewhat at the idea — she saw nothing fun in this — but soon she decided to go along with the frolic. She left the room and returned promptly with a sizable empty potato bag.

"Where are the scissors?" she asked.

"I will fetch them for you," I replied with a puzzled frown. I went to my sewing kit and returned a minute later with them.

"I have to make three cuts — one on the bottom and two on the sides," she said. Minutes later, Ghislaine was triumphant, staring at herself in the mirror. "This is 'la robe sac,' designed by Yves Saint

Laurent!" she boasted, as she posed in her loose-fitting dress, copying the gestures of a model.

"Ghislaine you are, without a doubt, 'a la mode.' 'La robe sac,' in today's fashion world is 'le denier cri'! You are dressed to kill. I applaud you heartily."

She smiled and continued twirling around the room.

"No one can make a dress made from the jute fiber of a potato bag look as sophisticated as you!" I blurted out.

We both giggled.

"Listen, Ghislaine," I said, "I love your sense of originality and your wonderful wit. But now I have to try on the costume I concocted this afternoon."

After contemplating what to create, I had decided to go as a newspaper saleslady. I fashioned a pleated skirt from newspapers. Then, I selected a black sweater, upon which I taped several small newspaper articles and advertisements. Finally, I constructed a unique hat by covering a square box with newspapers. I made certain that the name of the newspaper, *France Soir*, would be in front, for everyone to see.

When I walked into the party room, I was startled to see such an amazing variety of colorful costumes. The place was bursting with hysterical laughter.

I wanted to play the role of the person I was impersonating. I stood up high on my toes, holding a stack of newspapers, and called out in a loud voice: "France Soir," "France Soir."

A tall fellow, dressed as a pirate, admired my attire. "I really like your costume, but how can you dance with me with that bunch of newspapers in your arms? No one dances with such a load!"

I needed no further urging to promptly put down the encumbering load and hit the dance floor.

****

CHAPTER 6

The Summer Meme Died

During the first months of 1959, everything was moving smoothly forward along its course. That was before I was told in early July that Meme was close to dying. I knew that she had had cancer, but with her *joie de vivre* she was able to combat her cancerous growth for nine long years. However, her inexhaustible strength was not able to suppress the malignancy when it metastasized from her kidneys to her lungs.

I was bewildered by the dreadful news. I shed bitter tears, while my mother gently stroked the hair off my forehead and kissed me. Trying to console me, she held me in her arms. It was summer and yet I had the shivers! I was so totally destroyed at the thought of losing my precious grandmother.

In the afternoon, my mother accompanied me to the hospital. But I remember asking her to leave me alone with Meme. My mother understood that I needed some time with Meme.

I pulled up a chair beside Meme's bed. "Meme, I am here, I am here," I whispered, reaching out to hold her weakened hand. What could I possibly say to someone so dear to me who was dying? For a while I was silent.

Aware of the truth of her situation, Meme opened her eyes and uttered, gently, "We are born for a purely ephemeral existence, but remember to live your life fully, each day."

I nodded.

"I have always wanted nothing less than the best for you, my darling."

"Meme, you have always displayed your warm-hearted loving kindness and concern for me."

There was a moment of silence. Then Meme expressed clearly her aspiration for me: "I want you to meet someone very special, someone who can give you all the love you deserve."

Holding my hand, Meme continued to speak. Her tenderness warmed my heart.

Death-pale, with her eyes half-closed, Meme murmured, "I am tired of feeling so much pain. I don't want to live anymore."

Fear and sadness were penetrating me. I was almost numb with despair.

Withdrawing her hand from mine, in a hushed tone, she murmured, "Darling, I am so exhausted. You should go now."

My heart was very heavy. It was an awful moment. I was losing my Meme, my best friend and confidant. I kissed her and left her bedside.

Standing in the doorway, I looked once more at her and walked away.

Knowing that the malignant enemy was winning and was going to cheat me out of additional years with my Meme was very painful.

When I returned home, my mother was there, waiting for me. Lovingly, she wrapped her arms around me and did not utter a word.

After we entered my bedroom, my mother and I sat down. Staring at her troubled eyes, I wanted to know what Maman had on her mind. For a moment, the stillness in the room remained. Then, my mother spoke. "Muriel, you cannot even conjecture how difficult it is for me to keep Roxane in the heat of the city. Do you agree with me that your little sister should be taken away for a few days from the sweltering and oppressive heat?"

"Yes, Maman. I appreciate your concern."

"Muriel, I am seriously encouraging you to schedule your departure with Roxane for tomorrow."

I definitely had not anticipated my mother's sending Roxane and me, for some breathing space and respite to Normandy. Be that as it may, my mother's determination was such that I agreed.

The next day, Roxane and I left Paris for Mesnil-Val, a small hamlet in the heart of Normandy. We sojourned in a charming little inn surrounded by beautiful grounds. The bedroom was comfortable, with a pleasant view on the flower garden. The dining room was very appealing. Roxane enjoyed the playground. Full of energy, she would bounce around from the swings to the seesaw or the slides. I could not sit for a moment!

The next day we were having our dinner when my mother telephoned to let me know that Meme had passed away. "Believe me darling, she had endured more than she could bear," Maman said in a subdued tone.

Even so, I could not imagine that she had left our world. I was shattered by the painful news. My mother tried to console me, but I had a difficult time keeping my grief from exploding.

"With the funeral arrangements, we have to take measures that we deem necessary to protect your little sister. So, it is essential that you keep Roxane in the countryside for a couple more days."

I promised to take good care of my little sister. But I believed that my mother was trying to, first and foremost, shield *me* from going to the funeral.

Again, my eyes were filled with tears, but I had to put myself back together and pick up Roxane from the manager's office, where I had left her during the telephone conversation with my mother.

I hugged my little sister. I held her in my arms and I gave her a big kiss. Then, she looked at me with her big, blue, sparkling eyes, busting with vitality: "Mumu, tell me a story."

How could I say no to my precious little sister? I knew many fairy tales. I opted to select the story of "Goldilocks and the Three Bears." Sharing these moments with her was an escape from the heaviness that filled my mind and my heart with sorrow. When I saw that Roxane's eyes were closing, I hugged her, kissed her and tucked her in bed.

I was still in disbelief that I would never see Meme again and that I had lost such a solid and reassuring friend. She was always there to comfort me, to encourage me, to support me and to cheer me on.

As Roxane's playmate, I was fully engaged in a wide variety of merrymaking for the next couple days.

A day after Meme's funeral, Roxane and I returned to Paris.

My mother thanked me profusely for taking care of Roxane.

I was conscious that she had a slight pang of guilt about sending me away. She pulled herself together, determined to give me her reasons. "Let me now assure you that I had nothing but your best interest in mind. I felt somehow that the funeral would have been an agonizing experience for you. I knew how much you adored your grandma and I wanted you to remember her as she was."

There was a pause, then my mother went on to say, "Furthermore, in keeping with the Jewish tradition, you should not go to a cemetery as long as your parents are alive."

I stared at my mother with a mixture of curiosity and consternation.

"The funeral was held in the Montparnasse Cemetery before a small group of family and friends. Meme is now buried with her parents, in the same Mausoleum," my mother said.

"It's going to be tough to adjust ourselves to life without her," I murmured.

"My mother nodded. "It's sad, it's sad, but life has to go on."

"I guess so," I answered automatically, but I was not quite reassured, although I knew she was right.

I spent the rest of the afternoon sitting on the sofa in the living room, talking to my mother. My father came in, looking tired. I could imagine that he was badly hurt by his mother's death. I threw myself into his arms. I wanted to say something, but I kept quiet.

Our common distress was inexpressibly painful. Suddenly, Maman got up and with her warmth and kindness, and said, "It is time for dinner!"

****

Dejected by Meme's agonizing death and feeling the disarray creeping through me, I yearned desperately to escape. I wanted to get away, move on and take a new path. I deemed it necessary to make an immediate plan of action as soon as possible.

A few days later, I was alone at the dinner table with my parents. My siblings were abroad. Ghislaine was in Germany improving her German and

Christian was perfecting his English in England. Roxane was tucked in bed, sleeping soundly.

When I told my parents that I was resigning from the bank and that I had decided to leave Paris and spend a couple of months in Spain, to improve my Spanish, they were surprised.

"Oh! Do you really intend to stop working at the bank!" my father exclaimed, somewhat aghast.

"Yes, Papa, as soon as possible." I was twirling my napkin ring on my fingers, proclaiming that I was very close to my twenty-first birthday and that from now on, I should be able to make my own choices.

Notwithstanding her feeling of anxiety, my mother looked at me with an amused little smile: "Where are you thinking of going?"

I leaned back on my chair and told my parents that I was planning to sojourn in the port city of Santander, on the north coast of Spain — between the Asturias to the west and the Basque Country to the east.

"Where will you lodge in Santander?" my mother asked.

"Conchita, my Spanish friend, is making all the arrangements for me."

There was an awkward silence. "I thought that you would hold your position at the bank much longer," said my father, disenchanted.

My father still wanted to control me. I protested against my father's authority. And having given my notice to the bank, it was obvious, in my mind, that I was going to imminently be on my way. I needed to move on.

My sojourn in Santander, though, was not quite what I had bargained for.

Conchita was not going back to Santander. "I want to spend the entire summer in Paris and I have chosen to take courses at la Sorbonne. Furthermore, I must tell you that you won't be able to stay in my parents' home."

I asked the reason for this last-minute change of plans.

"Well, after 23 years of marriage, my father is leaving my mother for another women, one of his patients," she cried out in dismay. Recounting the emotionally challenging news from her mother, Conchita needed to catch her breath. Then, looking at me, she said that with the help of a friend, she found another place of residence for me.

I certainly did not anticipate this and I was somewhat troubled by the shuffling of my plans. But that is life! *Mais, c'est la vie!*

****

My journey by train to Santander was long, but easy.

When I arrived in Santander, I grabbed a taxi and gave the driver the address. After a fairly short drive, the car stopped in front of a nice old building adorned with ornate wrought iron. When I reached the fourth floor and rang the doorbell, I was greeted by la Señora Virgo. Tall, in a loose black dress, she had the appearance of being in her middle fifties. Her black hair was tied into a chignon at the back of her head, her complexion was dark, and her reddened eyes told the story of her shattered life. Devastated by her husband's recent death, she had, seemingly, cried a great deal.

I stepped into the small dark vestibule of the apartment. I could not believe how cluttered it was, a jumble of disorganized memorabilia. Somewhat perplexed by the disorder of it all, I stood there until I was summoned by la Señora, to follow her into the dining room. When I caught sight of the smears and the stains on the tablecloth, I was totally shocked.

By nature, I always liked order and cleanliness.

Seized by a sudden uneasiness, I asked myself, "What the heck am I doing here?" I remembered that I wanted to leave Paris as quickly as possible and that I had a strong desire to go to Spain. But I was probably dreaming of another Malaga experience! Perhaps I assumed that all the Spanish people had the same style and standard of living as the de R family.

Señora Virgo invited me to sit down with her. Since her French was nonexistent, we spoke in Spanish. Even at my intermediate level of proficiency, I was able to keep the conversation going.

After a few exchanges, it was clear to me that we had little in common, but I listened courteously to her endless monologue of piteous torment, owing to the death of her husband Julio, and that she was now alone.

Furthermore, her relationship with her daughter had deteriorated in the last months, and last but not least, she was suffering from a bad heart.

The grief was deep inside her. I could detect it in the tone of her voice. Her emotional outburst was real.

Her manner of speaking was loud and hurried. I sat still, but it was far from easy for me to listen to so much rigmarole and whimpering after the pain I went through with my Meme's demise.

But I understood her predicaments, and notwithstanding that I was hot and tired, I wanted to provide her with some support by letting her know that I was sorry and that I understood the suffering that she was enduring.

Señora Virgo got up and embraced me. Then, without any warning, the maid stepped into the dining room. She looked at us, sitting across the table. "Buenas tardes, quieres un jugo de naranja?"

I responded with relief: "Si, por favor, muchas gracias." I needed so badly, a beverage to cool off!

The maid stepped out of the room; Señora Virgo followed her.

Pensive, with the sun shining through the windows, I tried to reassure myself about the disenchanting atmosphere.

Moments later, Señora Virgo returned quietly. I was expecting another outburst, but all she said was, "Te gustaria ver tu habitacion?" (Would you like to see your bedroom?)

"Si, me gustaría verlo y desempacar." (Yes, I would like to see it and unpack.)

I followed Señora Virgo down the lengthy dark corridor to what was going to be my abode for the next eight weeks.

As we reached the last door, on the right-hand side of the narrow passageway, Señora Virgo stopped and whispered, "Ahi esta su dormitorio." (Here is your bedroom.)

When she opened the door, I caught sight of an overcrowded room filled with outworn and obsolete furnishings. Nothing went together and the creepy decor gave me the heebie-jeebies, but I tried not to show the despondency caused by the dreary and dingy stuff around.

When Señora Virgo left the room, the first thing that occurred to me was to open the windows and let some fresh air come in. The view from the window was actually pleasant. After unpacking my suitcase, taking a shower and changing my clothes, I rushed off to the Sardinaro beach, set in a wide, sweeping bay bordered with flowers and tamarisk trees. Feasting my eyes on the long stretch of golden sand and the beautiful turquoise sea was such a relief and consolation for me, after the loss of Meme and the disappointment of not staying with Conchita in her parent's home.

I had enrolled in a college to improve my Spanish, but at times the classes seemed endless. The room had no air conditioning and my impatience to get to the beach was often acute and intense.

Fortunately, I met a wonderful group of foreign students. They came from all over Europe: France, Germany, England, Holland and other countries. We would go to the beaches together and enjoy sunbathing, swimming, walking and talking, either in Spanish, English or French.

Sharing facts and opinions about our country was awesome, and at times, astonishing!

Meeting people from all walks of life has always been an eye-opening experience for me, and respecting cultural differences without imposing my own values, was, and still is, of utmost importance for me.

Santander had a great assortment of beaches. We could choose to go to the Playa Matalenas, the Playa de Los Molinucos, the Playa de Magdalena and more, but we usually opted to take ourselves to the Playa Sardinero, where we could enjoy the very wide sandy beach.

A few days after my arrival in Santander, I met Franz, a tall, dark and handsome Austrian from Vienna. As I was sitting on the beach, watching the sun going down over the sea, Franz introduced himself and sat down beside me. He looked at me with his beautiful green eyes; his curly brown hair gave his face a soft appearance. He spoke French with a delightful accent and, without a doubt, was a talented charmer. I found him to be a very nice and friendly fellow.

After some small talk, he asked me whether I would like to join him and his friends for dinner that evening.

Without hesitation, I responded, "Yes, I would very much like to, but I do have to go back to my room to shower and dress."

"No problem — give me your address and I will pick you up at nine o'clock."

Two hours later, on the doorstep of the Vigo residence, Franz was waiting for me. I must admit that he appeared a lot different from the man I had seen, nestled on the warm sand, which offered the advantage of his harmonious body in a bathing suit. Nevertheless, he was still a remarkably handsome young man.

As we walked over to the very popular cellar El Delphin Verde, Franz entertained me with all kinds of statistics. Being a mathematician, he was a compiler of statistical data and he had all of the latest at his fingertips! I looked at him, surprised.

"It's not really complicated," he said with a grin from ear to ear.

"I am sorry, but this is really a foreign science to me."

Franz burst out laughing and asserted, in a confident manner, "I know that mathematics and statistics are not for everyone."

I nodded approvingly.

He smiled and murmured in a conciliatory tone, "I am so sorry — I do statistical data every day and I get carried away!"

A few moments later, we entered the restaurant and walked down the steps to a long and narrow, whitewashed cellar. Dozens of young men and women were sitting at the lengthy wooden tables, on long wooden benches. Our new friends were there. They moved closer together and invited Franz and me to sit down.

The whole rhythm of that evening was most pleasant. The lively spirits of the guitarists stimulated everyone with exotic songs, while the restaurant owner prepared for us one of his favorite dishes: sopa al cuarto de hora, a delicious seafood soup, and some tasty Basque country appetizers.

When the dinner was over, Franz took me on a delightful walk along the bay. The slow rising and heaving of the waves was music to my ears. As we watched the lights of the boats moving slowly on the horizon, we talked about ourselves, our aspirations and more. It was actually almost one o'clock in the morning when Franz walked me back to the Vigo residence!

"I know that you have some classes tomorrow, but would you like to have lunch with me? We could meet at 2 p.m. Are you available?" Without hesitation, I agreed to meet Franz the next day, at the Beach Cafe for lunch.

And for a happy and congenial two weeks, we appreciated each other's company at the beach, in restaurants and on our walks, with flirtatious jokes and kisses.

I knew that my so-called friend, Anna, had her eye on Franz. I recognized a sort of competitiveness in her, as she played a coaxing game with incessant seducing glances. So naturally, Franz read in her intense expressions, a sort of appeal. After all, he could probably get from her the very thing that I refused to give him.

Franz knew my stand on the subject of making love. However, just like most young men, Franz's objective was to avail himself of all the benefits!

Just as I expected, Franz and Anna soon had something going on, which was more than a simple exchange of glances. One day I spotted Franz on the Magdalena Beach with his arms around Anna. Overwhelmed, I did not utter a word and went home, somewhat dejected.

My heart was now clouded with disappointment and unhappiness. I had the feeling that everything was closing in on me. I was destroyed by Meme's passing, pulverized by Franz's behavior. And then, to add to my malaise, I was living in an unkempt home that always smelled of olive oil and fried fish!

A couple of days later, I took myself in the afternoon to a Santander dance club, where I was going to join some of my friends. There, I met Rita, a German young lady from Hanover. Rita was actually studying Spanish at the same college that I was. Standing in the shadow of trees, we talked for a while. She was loquacious and fluent in English. We were able to exchange some thoughts on a few topics. She made a couple of suggestions of places to explore together. Enchanted, I was. I had found a new friend. From that day on, we met every day.

But I will always bear in mind the afternoon on the beach when Rita poured out her heartbreak concerning her father. "My father was a Gestapo officer. He was killed in 1942." Rita needed to take a moment to catch her breath. "I have no intention of excusing my father, and I will always condemn the Nazi horror." With a heavy sigh, she stopped again for a minute, and with wrenching guilt on her face, she declared: "Muriel, I am sure that you understand how ashamed I am of being a German citizen."

"Rita, I fully understand. The Holocaust was absolutely hideous and despicable, but you are in no way responsible for your father's pitiful and deplorable infamy. You were just a kid during that dreadful episode. How old were you when your father died?"

"I was seven years old. I was an only child. My mother never remarried."

When Rita spoke about the anguish that marked her childhood and teenage years, I could see her distress and her torturing grief.

Due to the atrocities committed during World War II, I always had certain indignation and resentment of the Germans. But in all fairness, Rita was just a young child. She is absolutely not to be blamed for Nazi crimes.

Rita and I spent hours on the beach, talking.

"Don't worry Rita; it is important for us to go forward. I know that with a steady radiance of light in our hearts, we are capable of sallying forth and being friends," I said with a beaming smile.

There was something real and fascinating about Rita. I liked her fiery wit and her sound logic. Tall and beautiful, with a smooth and fair complexion, short blond hair and pale blue eyes, she was an endless source of interest.

For my 21st birthday, Rita invited me to come on the rooftop of her building to celebrate my "coming of age" with her. I thought that it was a delightful gesture on her part, to want to express her kind wishes to me *en tete a tete*.

When I arrived on the rooftop, I surely did not expect to see all the foreign students with whom I had connected. More than a dozen young men and women, dressed in their Sunday best were there, waiting for me. I was so very touched by Rita's thoughtfulness and her adroitness and *savior-faire* — she excluded Franz and Anna from the party.

Nothing was lacking. The buffet, the wine and the music, the cheerful energy and the enthusiastic tempo of my ebullient friends.

I still have a lovely decorative miniature of a fisherman given to me by Rita.

Shortly after my birthday, my group of friends disintegrated — they were all going back to their countries. In early October, I boarded the train for my return to Paris.

CHAPTER 7

A Difficult Autumn

The morning after my return to Paris, I woke up on a chilly and damp October day. Staying put for a while, I reflected on my sojourn in Santander and Rita and my classmates' kindness. Yet, I was unhappily aware that when they all left for their respective countries, just a few days after the celebration of my twenty-first birthday, I had to cope with loneliness.

With the lack of attention of Señora Virgo, my uninteresting host, the last few weeks of my stay in Santander were, to say the least, somewhat grueling. But somehow, I was able to appease my solitude with some tasty gazpacho and wonderful Spanish paella!

As I was lying on my bed, trying to decompress and stop ruminating about past disappointments, like Franz and Anna's behavior, my mother came into my bedroom with some hot coffee and croissants. Noticing my troubled expression, she sat down on the edge of my bed.

"What's wrong?" she queried. She really wanted to know what was eating me up.

Sharing my feelings of excitement, joy, sadness or nostalgia with my mother was habitual and easy. With her indulgence, her perspective, and her attitude, Maman could judge my sentiments well and fairly. She always had an astonishing understanding of a situation. Her viewpoint would guide me to have a distinct perspective on things.

I divulged to my mother the unpleasant doldrums I felt during my last weeks in Santander and my despondency about Franz. She kept quiet for a moment and, acknowledging my disappointments, gave me her thoughts.

I listened to her with a certain passivity as she insisted that I should not dwell upon my peck of troubles and my somewhat challenging two months in Spain.

There was a pause, after which she added softly, "Anyway, I think that the best thing for you, darling, would be for you to stop feeling sorry for yourself."

"Yes, Maman, you are right. I must leave the summer behind me and get on with my life."

My mother smiled triumphantly. "Good, that's my girl!"

I sat up and gave vent to a tremendous sigh. Then I reached for my tray and took a sip of coffee.

****

I was now ready to set my heart on my yearning to research, with determination, the avenues for some possible employment opportunities in the travel industry.

Eager to check the classified ads for the job of my dreams, I bought the *Figaro* and the *Monde* newspapers. But unfortunately, the positions available were not exactly what I had in mind — they involved engineering or secretarial work.

Every morning, I spent time writing letters to all the major airlines and travel offices in the city. I included my *curriculum vitae*, emphasizing my ability to speak three languages, and a short personal anecdote regarding my job at the bank. But my attempt to achieve my goal was utterly fruitless — they simply did not hire staff in the fall.

Demoralizing, it was! In despondency, I sunk down into an armchair. I sat with my head bent, brooding, recalling the conversation with my father about leaving the bank. Decision-making is never an easy thing to do.

As I was trying to consider a possible interim job, my father walked into the living room. When he caught sight of my pensive mood, he kept quiet for a moment. Papa knew my strong desire for a position in the travel business and that despite all my efforts, my attempts were in vain!

Wanting to reassure me, he told me that there was no rush to get a job.

****

After some more deliberation, I decided to respond to an ad from a dentist who was looking to hire an assistant.

Wondering what to wear for my meeting with the dentist, I was trying on all kinds of suits and dresses when my mother walked into my room.

"Do I look ridiculous in this suit?" I asked.

Maman laughed, taking it for a joke.

"Do not laugh, Maman. I am going for an interview tomorrow!"

"Well, my darling, you are not going to a cocktail party. You do not need such a dressy outfit. Stay classic. You ought to try on your royal blue dress," Maman suggested without hesitation.

"Are you telling me that I should wear that simple frock?" I exclaimed, throwing my hands into the air.

"Sure, why not? It fits you well and the color is becoming on you. Please put it on."

I tried it on. As I glanced at myself in the mirror, I laughed.

"Ha! Ha! You are right, Maman. It looks like it was custom-designed for me!"

"Honestly, Muriel, you look lovely in it."

"Okay, my predicament is solved! Now I ought to tidy my mess," I said with a grin.

As my mother was watching me, the door opened suddenly. It was my father, letting us know that dinner was ready and that we should make our way to the dining room table.

****

Notwithstanding the apprehension I felt about working as a dentist assistant — a job that was not really appealing to me — I braced myself and kept my appointment.

The dentist's office was near the Rond-Point des Champs-Élysées, on the second floor of a very nice limestone building. As I looked up for the small doorbell button, my heart was pounding. "Here you are, making every effort to get a job," I muttered to myself. "You should not stand at the door — you should just go in." Courageously and unflinchingly, I pressed the doorbell button.

The secretary, a woman in her late thirties, opened the door.

"Bonjour! I am here for an interview with Doctor L," I said with determination.

The young lady escorted me into the waiting room. I was there for only a few minutes when Doctor L crossed the threshold and introduced himself. Without hesitation, he requested that I follow him to his office.

"You are interested in the dental assistant job?" he queried.

"Yes, doctor."

"Do you have any experience or practical knowledge? Do you have any idea what it's like to work in a dental office?"

"No, Doctor." Yet I remembered well my experiences as a patient, sitting in a dentist's chair, and I could easily imagine what could take place in his "torture chamber."

Doctor L leaned forward and repeated the question: "Do you have any idea what it's like to work in a dental office?"

"I have a slight understanding, and I am ready and willing to learn more," I answered straight away.

"Well, I am going to elucidate for you the general tasks: preparing patients for their dental work, setting up the trays with the materials needed for the procedures, sterilizing and disinfecting the instruments and helping with the X-rays. It may also be incumbent upon you to lend a hand to the secretary with the telephone and dealing with the making and the confirming of appointments."

There was a pause for a moment. The quietness of the room was almost tangible. I was uncomfortably aware that I was being scrutinized by

Doctor L, but I pretended that it did not matter and I responded with a shy smile.

Unexpectedly, Doctor L broke the silence: "I am going to give you a chance. Come in early tomorrow. Isabelle will be here to teach you the appropriate skills and coach you."

Expressing my gratitude, I gave him a good handshake.

"Goodbye Mademoiselle, until we meet again tomorrow," he imparted with a certain gallantry.

The interview was short, and I soon realized that the rushed exchange with Doctor L did not lend itself to deliberation on my part.

When I arrived at Doctor L's office the next morning, I was eager to take on my new duties. But I was totally unprepared for what followed.

As soon as I was introduced to Mademoiselle Isabelle, the dental assistant who was going to show me the ropes, I felt a surge of social malaise vis-á-vis of me. Her aversion towards me was definitely apparent.

With foolish pride, she told me that Doctor L had a crush on her and that rumors were flying that he and his wife were going to divorce. She was so obsessed with him that she was totally oblivious to the fact that he looked at every woman like a sex symbol!

Doctor L was a good-looking gentleman in his forties, tall with a mature face and blond hair. He thought nothing of flirting openly and making unguarded comments to the ladies while he was working on them.

At times, his personality and his behavior were impossible to understand.

Within a short period of dull drudgery, I realized that I had had a warped sense of reality when I accepted the job.

On one side, I had Doctor L, who was constantly ordering me around, and on the other side, I had Mademoiselle Isabelle, who resented me and was determined to make her views known!

I will never forget the afternoon when Doctor L and Mademoiselle Isabelle were so excited about the arrival of the Countess, an elderly patient. They greeted this enigmatic high society figure with such reverence that I was somewhat curious to see her.

As soon as I approached the dental chair where the noblewoman was sitting, with her mouth wide open, I jumped back instinctively and held my nose — her foul-smelling breath was not to be believed! Doctor L witnessed my reaction. I knew right away that I was in trouble.

For a moment he stood there, and then he proceeded to pull out the Countess' infected tooth. As soon as he was finished with the procedure, he invited me to follow him into his office.

"Do you really intend to come tomorrow?" he asked sarcastically, in a raspy voice.

Bewilderment and awkwardness were my first reactions. Cautiously, I replied, "I don't understand."

"I believe that I made my point, Mademoiselle. You do not have the required skills for an acceptable level of performance at this job."

I realized that there was no sense in arguing with him. Expressing my timid agreement, I bent my head as a sign of respect and left his office.

As I walked slowly down the street, with tears filling my eyes, I kept replaying the incident in my mind. My wrought nerves could not stand the affront that I had sustained from the doctor. Yet, as distressed as I was, the truth was that I had no desire to continue my irksome tasks in that unpleasant atmosphere.

My thoughts flashed back to the pathetic agony of looking for a job, and my father's reaction when I told him that I was giving up my job at the bank. What will Papa say now, I wondered!

I tried to gather my thoughts and called my parents from a café. As I shared with them my unpleasant discharge, I perceived their enormous kindheartedness. Of course, I had no doubts about my mother's understanding of the matter, but my father's quiet and reassuring acknowledgment was music to my ears.

After a few days of nonchalance, I took a temporary assignment in a public relations agency. The job involved filing documents and researching them. But I soon realized that I did not have the temperament to waste the so-called best years of my youth behind an old desk in an isolated, small room!

Just as I returned home one December evening, utterly exhausted from another boring day at work, my sister Ghislaine surprised me with a question. "Would you like to go abroad?" she whispered.

I looked at her with a quizzical expression on my face and raised my eyebrows. "Yes, I would love to go abroad, but at the moment, I do not have the money for it," I admitted sadly.

Ghislaine snuggled back against the large leather armchair and assembled her newspaper neatly. "Read this," she said with a twinkle in her eyes. I seated myself and read the classified advertisement.

"The agency Voir et Connaître is looking for someone to accompany a group to Austria during the Christmas-New Year two-weeks recess," I asserted, looking up from the newspaper.

"Yes, they are," Ghislaine confirmed softly.

"Oh! Ghislaine, you are an angel. This is exactly what I have been craving!"

Our mother was taking her coat off. Her ears perked up when she heard us talking in the living room. Astonished by my sprightliness, Maman whispered, "Muriel, what are you so excited about?"

"Ghislaine saw a classified ad in the newspaper. A travel agency is in search of an escort to take a group to the ski slopes in Austria."

"That's great, but what about your job?"

I told her I had decided to resign from the boring office job. I wanted more excitement. My wistful longing had to end. "I have set my heart on pursuing my ambition for broader and meaningful experiences, with human contact, which I could achieve with a career in travel," I stated categorically.

Maman looked at Ghislaine. "What is going on here?"

Ghislaine smiled. "I gather that Muriel liked the ad I showed her. It does suggest that after a two-month pause in hiring in the travel business, they are now beginning to hire staff again."

"Maman," I said, "you know that vacation planning, globetrotting, and learning about life and people fascinate me."

My mother stared at me with a warm understanding. "Go for it!" she affirmed, gazing appreciatively at Ghislaine. "I cannot tell you how pleased I am that the travel market is hiring again." Then, looking at her watch, she declared, "Girls, it is time to get ourselves ready for dinner."

****

After a good night's sleep and a phone call to the travel bureau, I rushed over for my appointment with the manager.

I was given an oral examination which included questions about my experiences, my opinions, and more.

Inquisitive, he was, and straight up, I was.

Yet, to this day, I am somewhat abashed by what happened when the gentleman asked, "Do you speak German?"

"Of course," I burst out. "Ja, ich spreche deutsch." (Yes, I speak German.) "Ja, ich verstehe alles." (Yes, I understand everything.)

He looked at me with a silent assessment. "Very good, Mademoiselle. You will be in charge of a group going to the small mountain village of Partenen in Austria."

I was ecstatic and yet surprised by the impulse I had to spontaneously take advantage of the few German words I knew. The more one bluffs, the more one impresses!

****

With the triumph, I brought my jubilant news to my family. A thought came to me that I should invite some of them, and my friends, to go to Partenen. My brother, Christian, and my two dear friends, Jeanne and Denise, signed up for the ski trip.

To my delight, they were part of the large group of young men and young women I was in charge of. And there we were together, on our way…

As soon as we boarded the train, one could feel the congenial atmophere of camaraderie. The train ride from Paris to Innsbruck, in Austria, was way over twelve hours. The next morning, we arrived in Innsbruck where we had to awkwardly descend from the train with our luggage and skis and catch another train to Partenen.

Unlike some of Austria's well-known, fashionable ski resorts, Partenen was an out-of-the-way farming village with an appealing, onion-domed mini-church at its center.

Quiet and somewhat isolated, the little hamlet in the Alps counted no more than two or three hotels and a few small houses with plenty of slopes and ski-lifts, offering skiers several impressive descents and cross-country trails.

When I entered the small hotel with my group of travelers, a lovely young lady was standing behind the reception desk.

As I approached her to hand over the thirty vouchers for my vacationers, I said, "Guten Tag!" ("Good day!"), with a French accent, of course!

Then, looking at me, she clearly and distinctly asked for the passports: "Bitte, die Pässe."

When I handed over the passports to her, she said, with a courteous manner and a friendly smile, "Danke!" (Thank you). But I soon realized that she only spoke Austrian-German. Challenging, it would be for me! I thought.

I stood back and waited for her to give me the keys to the rooms. Sweet-natured, she got hold of my suitcase and ushered me to a rather simple room on the first floor.

There, she gave me a bunch of keys for rooms on the first and second floors, for me to decide the best way to assign the rooms to my fellow travelers. She smiled, said nothing, and left.

Somewhat worried and confused, I had to face the dilemma of who was going to share a room with whom? Each and every traveler was single, and just a few had come with a sister, a brother, a cousin or a friend.

I naturally and humorously announced that the girls should lodge on the first floor and the boys should occupy the rooms on the second floor. Ready to oblige, the group simply smiled and seemed favorably disposed to my suggestion.

I thought that it was all settled. That was until some pangs of desire on the part of a few suddenly changed the supposed order of things. I had, perhaps, an exaggerated idea of morality and I simply didn't know what was expected of me, but I could hardly cage these young men and women! So, I decided to simply ignore the hanky-panky and enjoy the unsophisticated pleasures of this unassuming and yet wonderful spot in the heart of the Tyrol.

The well-groomed practice slopes were a pleasure. The panoramic views above Partenen and the neighboring villages were beautiful. With a happy and easygoing attitude, everyone went skiing every day.

That was until two skiers collided. Paul was speedily heading down a slippery slope when he hit his friend Pierre, who had fallen down. I was obviously troubled by the unforeseen occurrence, but I was the one in charge to watch over Paul and make the right decisions about his care. A doctor examined him and assessed that he had no broken bones. Nevertheless, he had some bleeding from the abrasions on his legs.

After the medical examination, I had to fill in all the blank spaces on the insurance claim forms. With just a little help, I was able to complete my task in German!

The evenings in Partenen were very pleasant and welcoming. The fireplaces, combined with the Christmas decorations in the lounges and the restaurant, blended perfectly to create a wonderfully relaxing and enchanting, cozy ambiance.

The dinners were simple but enjoyable. The soft lighting, the endearing exchanges, and the laughter gave everyone such a wonderful escape from their routine.

My venture to the Austrian Alps turned out to be an amazing experence. I was so grateful to Ghislaine for alleviating my distress that day by showing me the ad in the newspaper.

With an optimistic frame of mind, I was able to wave my hand at discouragement and look forward to a new year filled with excitement and satisfaction.

CHAPTER 8

Unexpected and Astonishing Events

A few days after my return to Paris from the Austrian Alps, I started to look seriously for job opportunities. The airlines, the travel agents and many other companies were all hiring!

During the third season of the past year, when the leaves were falling from the trees, I was going through dilemmas and difficult choices. I understood that I was, in fact, underestimating myself. I had capitulated to an unconscious, gradual, subtle form of self-disparagement. That was, of course, until the day I was hired to chaperone a group abroad. I then understood what I could possibly achieve. The seed of exuberance germinated to produce a new me!

With these thoughts in mind, I responded to the ads and submitted my curriculum vitae, along with completed applications, to Air France, to the Kellogg Company and to American Express — three totally different businesses!

Upon receiving invitations for an interview from the three companies, I scheduled my appointments for the next couple of days.

As soon as I showed up for the cross-examination, I realized that I was not the only candidate seeking an assignment for the position! When I saw lots of contenders waiting for their turn, I was somewhat overwhelmed by an unpleasant emotion, but fortunately, the despondency lasted for only a short while.

To my amazement, the vivid recollection of my interview with the manager of the agency Voir et Connaitre crossed my mind like an unexpected jolt. I certainly did not profess to be "Miss Know-it-all" with my interviewers, but I did try to generate enthusiasm and communicate my eagerness to work with people and put to use the English and Spanish that I had studied diligently. Furthermore, I perceived that a calm and collected demeanor would definitely prevail over self-conscious distress.

The lengthy question-and-answer sessions with the interviewers of the three different companies were basically the same. I would have liked to have seen a reassuring smile, but the crafty professionals would always sit sternly at their desks and give me evasive utterances such as: "We will let you know, Mademoiselle. We will get back to you."

Considering that I had completed the three challenging tests given by the interviewers of Air France, Kellogg Company and American Express, all I could do now was to wait to hear back from them, get their assessments and ascertain the end result.

I was having lunch the following day with my parents when the phone rang. A dignified voice was asking to speak with me. It was Mr. G from American Express. He did not say much, but the clarity of his words was like music to my ears: "I was greatly impressed by your attitude and your demeanor, Mademoiselle. The job is yours. Would you please come and see me tomorrow?"

There was a silence in the room. As soon as I got off the phone, I looked at my parents and I declared, emphatically, "I think that I might have a job!" Little did I know that by that evening I would have three job opportunities! The ball was definitely in my court!

The outcome exceeded my expectations. Spiritually elevated and inspired by hope, I was feeling wonderful and determined to succeed.

Alone in my bedroom, filled with awe and trepidation, I tried to figure out the most desirable course of action to take. Should I go for the job as a ground hostess for Air France, or Kellogg's public relations job, or choose to be a hostess and interpreter for American Express, I asked myself.

As I was contemplating the three possibilities, my mother came into my bedroom. "Muriel, how are you doing? What do you intend to do with the options you have? Do you have a preference?" my mother asked with curiosity.

"Well, due to the irregular hours at the airport required by the Air France job, I would not be able to register for lectures and classes as a part-time student; juggling my schedule would complicate my life in every way."

"Yes, you are right," Maman retorted.

"I would certainly gain experience working for Kellogg and possibly get the opportunity of becoming a professionally savvy female in the business world!" I exclaimed with a grin from ear to ear.

"Yes, my darling, I am sure that you would have the ability to successfully accomplish your objective."

"However, Maman, after reflecting on my interest in meeting and interacting with people from different parts of the globe and discovering their diverse ways of life, I am definitely drawn to the appointment offered by American Express — being a hostess and interpreter for them."

"Bravo! I know, my darling, that you had your heart set on a job in the tourism business. This is a marvelous choice. I am so happy for you," my mother uttered endearingly, with a smile across her face.

"Eureka! Eureka!" I cried, jumping up and down with joy. "I found the job I was looking for! The nasty, dreary doldrums are over! Hurrah! Hurrah!"

"Listen, sweetheart, let's apprise your papa and your siblings of your firm decision."

Beaming from ear to ear, I followed Maman to the living room.

****

After having accepted my assignment with American Express, I was conscious of the sense of contentment and satisfaction I felt. With pleasure and without a hitch or stress, I adapted immediately to my new surroundings. The air of the premises seemed to palpitate with an effusive and continuous world of surprise.

As I sit at my desk today reminiscing, I can still visualize the adventure and the excitement I experienced each and every day, with people from all walks of life, coming and going through the revolving doors of American Express.

There was something stimulating about the mood around our Information Desk. Furthermore, working side by side with Odile was a privilege. Odile was an engaging and attractive young married lady, tall and slender, with ravishing brown eyes and a dark complexion. Her capability and efficiency generated customer satisfaction. I felt very fortunate in having her as a colleague. Her forthcoming display of affability brought about a real, friendly relationship between us.

Whenever it was needed, our minds joined in a concentrated spark. We knew quite well how to handle any question addressed to us and help our customers.

There were, of course, some never-to-be-forgotten weird remarks on the part of some tourists.

It seems only yesterday that a middle-aged woman from Texas was standing before me, non-stop coughing and sneezing. After blowing her nose loudly, she asked, with a thick Texan accent, "Where is the nearest park?"

"The Tuileries Garden is between the Louvre and the Place de la Concorde, within walking distance." I brought out a map to show her the route. "Take la Rue de la Paix, continue on Rue de Castiglione and you will arrive at the Tuileries Garden."

My directions must have conveyed to her a slight distaste.

Raising her eyebrows with exaggerated surprise, she looked at me and said, "How do you explain that the names of the streets are not in English?"

I could not stop myself. I replied, "Madame, you are not in America, you are in France, and the names of the streets are in French."

She did not acknowledge that I was right; she just continued protesting the inconvenience, caused by the fact that it was a foreign language.

I was kind of astonished by some unfamiliar requests on the part of American tourists. They would wander into American Express and would always ask: "Where is the water fountain?" This was new to me; I had never heard of anyone, at home or abroad, drinking water from a fountain.

I was also amazed by the astonishing number of tourists from the United States who approached my desk for information about the restaurants in the area. I would always give them a few good addresses of bistros and brasseries where they could taste and savor outstanding French cuisine. Yet, I would often hear: "Do they serve hamburgers?" "Do they serve hot dogs?" "Where can I get cottage cheese and Jello?"

I could not imagine that one could visit the capital of French gastronomy and want to eat hamburgers, hot dogs or cottage cheese and Jello. But I soon realized that some people are set in their ways and are not about to change!

Notwithstanding all of this, the post I was assigned to was an unbelievable and enthralling experience for me.

I had so many great days, busy days, thrilling days, eventful days. I was engrossed by the attention I was giving to all the visitors asking for directions, advice and information concerning their stay in Paris. Many wanted to know where they could purchase "Made in France" goods such as Limoges porcelain, cosmetics, perfumes, etc. But it goes without saying that the majority were inclined to buy French gourmet foods — namely foie gras, cheeses, mustard, wines and more.

As the summer months approached, the tourists were coming in droves to enjoy the French capital.

****

When I indulge in these reminiscences of some of my unforgettable encounters with travelers, I still feel exhilarated.

I will never forget Vera, a lovely lady in her late sixties from Tennessee. With a smile, she pressed forward to my desk with an inquiry: "Mademoiselle, would you know of someone who speaks English who could chaperone me around Paris?"

"Yes, Madame, my friend Lilian would certainly be a very responsible companion and translator for you. I will call her right away." Without delay, an appointment was scheduled for Lilian to perform the service the following day.

Vera showed her gratitude and appreciation by inviting us and Bernard, Lilian's husband, to join her and her friend, Ashley, for a dinner at Chez Maxim's, one of the most famous and fashionable restaurants in the world. With its Art Nouveau decor, elegance and superb cuisine, it was without a doubt a sensational evening.

I still have the original and fabulous menu, with the date of our dinner party — July 13th, 1960 — and four little notes signed by Vera, Ashley, Lilian and Bernard: "To one of the sweetest little girls I have ever met. Lovingly, Vera Wilson." I was very moved by Vera's touching words. I am so glad that I kept these memorabilia and I wonder if the others still have theirs.

****

Going forward in my recollections, I can still see Al and Steve, two medical students from Yale, hurrying over to my information desk on a July afternoon.

"Paris is such a wonderful city," Al blurted out.

"Steve and I are absolutely impressed by the beauty of it all. We really love exploring the fabulous metropolis by strolling along the wide avenues, visiting the museums, wandering around the stunning gardens. They are all such a pleasure to discover. However, we both recognize that going from place to place is not enough and that we are missing something important."

"Such as?" I interjected.

"Well, to our regret, we haven't mingled with the French people," said Steve.

"Could you possibly recommend and introduce us to a French family?" Al asked, smiling at me.

"Oh, yes, you must meet my family," I simply replied. Both Al and Steve were surprised by my quick riposte. "I will give my mother a call right away."

A few hours later, Al and Steve were warmly welcomed by my family. My mother's well-known hospitality and kindness were shown when she invited the boys, in a very enchanting way, to stay for dinner. Without a moment's hesitation, our two newfound friends readily accepted and joined the family table.

The two students were, at that point in time, in their early twenties. Tall in stature, with thick brown curly hair and brown eyes, there was something solid and reassuring about Al. Steve, a short and slender young man with straight light brown hair and brown eyes, was, with his collegiate appearance, a contrast to the seriousness of his friend Al.

The following day, my sister Ghislaine and I agreed to do some sightseeing with Al and Steve. Bouncing with vitality and enthusiasm around the Latin Quarter and the banks of the Seine, we walked, we talked, we laughed. Suddenly, Al stopped for a moment and, with a guiding spirit, he suggested, "Let's all take our weight off our feet and stop in a French Bistro."

After pondering the menu, Al mumbled, "Muriel, do you have a suggestion?"

"In France, tournedos and French fries are very popular," I suggested.

I do not recall what we ate that evening, but I do remember that over dinner, we exchanged views about our preferences, our opportunities and our choices. We got along incredibly well.

Before their departure for Italy, where they were hoping to discover some more beauty, Ghislaine and I were able to squeeze in a couple of evening outings and home visits with Al and Steve.

Our farewell took place in a most gracious way. Al and Steve were wholeheartedly convinced that they had just spent the most pleasurable two weeks of their life. "We had the advantages that many tourists strive desperately to get," Steve said.

Al looked at me, nodding in agreement. "Your family is the best!" he said as he bent over and kissed me on the cheek.

We were just good friends, with no romance to jeopardize our wonderful camaraderie.

Al told us that he would be returning alone to Paris at the end of August and that Steve would have to fly back to New York at the end of their Italian sojourn.

****

As I am reminiscing, the image of Bob comes into my mind. Unexpectedly, he approached my desk at American Express and proceeded to ask me questions about my job. As he was in the filming industry, he wanted to take pictures of me. But I guess that I was not photogenic enough to be a star. Ha ha! Nevertheless, we ended up going out together.

He would always take me to the top restaurants in Paris, where we would always enjoy gastronomic foods in a romantic atmosphere — just to name a couple of them, Lasserre, located close to the Champs-Elysees and known for its crystal-clear roof, and La Tour d'Argent, a historic restaurant, which was absolutely delightful as well.

Wherever we dined, it was always sumptuous and extravagant. But as everyone knows, there are exceptions to the rule.

Knowing that I was not working the following Saturday, Bob called me to invite me out for lunch. He chose to go up to Montmartre. I liked the idea and accepted his request with pleasure.

I will never forget our lunch in the charming restaurant, La Mère Catherine. There we were, seated on a terrace in the heart of Montmartre when a gypsy came over to us and asked me to give her my left hand. My first reaction was to say no. She insisted.

In a high-pitched tone, Bob encouraged me to accept the palm-reading and not turn her down. After some hesitation, I surrendered.

Immediately, the "clairvoyant" prognosticated clearly the following: "I see you going over the seas. You will be married before the end of the year. You will have three children, however, you will have a lamentable tragedy. You will have a long life."

It did not take her a long time to foretell my future. Without further ado, she concluded my palm-reading. Bob paid her and she left.

I looked at Bob and told him, "This is a scam. This woman sees me with an American and makes up a story for money!"

Little did I know! I will come back to this in my future chapters...

Shortly after that, I stopped seeing Bob. He wanted more from me than I was willing to give him!

* * * * * * * * * * * * * * * * * *

Meanwhile my relationship with Jacques had reached the stage where he was regarding me as a desirable match.

I could never forget the day when he sent a chauffeured Cadillac to pick me up for a drive to the countryside. Wrapped in a fantasy discourse, Jacques carried on about the subject of marriage.

I responded by saying that in my reasonable opinion, I was too young to consider marriage and that I was simply not ready to get married. Jacques gave no heed to my excuses and simply said that he could wait.

Two days later, Jacques insisted that I should meet him for lunch at the Café des Ministères. It was Jacques's favorite traditional French restaurant for lunch on workdays. Firm and resolute, Jacques said that it was very important for me to show up and that he absolutely counted on me.

Somewhat startled, I glanced at him. What possible rationale motivated him to invite me, with such insistence? But I finally agreed to join him.

As soon as I entered the restaurant, the maitre d' hotel greeted me and asked for the name on the reservation. Without delay, he escorted me to a table. I looked at him with amazement and said, "This is not Monsieur K's table. This table is set up for three guests."

"Oui, Madame," he simply acknowledged, and left.

Resisting the urge to run out, I sat down quietly and waited. The restaurant was totally packed with men.

A gentleman showed up and with a gesture of respect, he acknowledged that he was Monsieur K senior, Jacques's father.

I was speechless. I could not believe that Jacques's father would be intruding with no warning from Jacques.

The resemblance between father and son was amazing. Jacques was an absolute carbon-copy of his father, with the same appearances and the same features.

As I was having a little chat with Monsieur K, I knew that his eyes were on me and that I was under close scrutiny.

I just tried to make the best of an uncomfortable situation.

At long last, Jacques arrived. He looked at us and with an exuberant attitude and blurted out: "How great to see you both together."

I stared at him and murmured, "I am sure that you are thrilled to bits! This was certainly an overwhelming surprise for me!"

Monsieur K clapped his hands and called for the waiter. "We are ready to order!" he gestured, giving back the menus.

For the next two hours I sat with Jacques and his father, trying to keep my mind off the shockwave I had sustained. I *was* able to take part in the conversation.

Just before we withdrew from the table, Monsieur K said that he was going with his son for a rendezvous.

Actually, I was kind of happy to put an end to this unexpected introduction and be on my way to meet a friend with whom I had an appointment.

However, as soon as I returned home, I picked up the telephone to call Jacques.

"Jacques, I was thunderstruck to see your father at the restaurant today."

"Of course you were astonished and somewhat dismayed, but it turned out very well. My father was enchanted to meet you."

"I felt ridiculously inadequate when you were discussing politics."

"Muriel, rest assured, my father was greatly impressed by you," Jacques persisted.

"I just was not prepared for this."

"I suppose so, but you were perfectly fine."

"Jacques, why did you put me through this?"

"Because I wanted my father to meet you. I am very fond of you. I love you."

Jacques wanted desperately to meet with my parents, but I felt no impulse to accommodate his insistence. Indeed, he was, from every angle, a well-to-do and erudite gentleman — a commendable catch, I guess! But his failure to meet my family never deterred him from pursuing new ways of getting my attention, nor discouraged him from communicating, over and over again, his desire to marry me!

CHAPTER 9

Jerry

Monday through Friday, Odile and I shared the same schedule at American Express. We were required to come to work every other Saturday. Accordingly, we alternated shifts.

I was invited by my cousin, Francois, and his family to spend the last weekend of August in their home near the Belgian border. Since I did not have to work on that Saturday, I could accept my cousin's invitation.

However, and unexpectedly, Odile approached me, asking for a favor: "Muriel, could you possibly switch Saturdays with me? My husband wants us to go away this weekend."

Without hesitation, I answered, "No problem, Odile. I will reschedule the visit with my cousins for next week."

Odile was very grateful and thanked me profusely.

****

I was sitting at my desk when the doors of American Express opened that early morning, Saturday, August 27th, 1960.

A young gentleman rushed in and came straight to me, with a pipe in his mouth.

"Can I help you, sir?"

"Not really. I saw you and I wanted to say hello."

"Bonjour! Welcome! I am pleased to meet you. How do you do?"

"I am fine. Last night, I went to see Fellini's, Dolce Vita. Have you seen it?"

"No, not yet. But I intend to go and see it soon. I really enjoy Italian films," I acknowledged, with a smile.

"Yes, you should!"

"Sir, are you visiting Paris? Do you need information or specifics regarding your stay in the French capital?"

"Non merci, je connais bien la ville et toute sa splendeur." (I know the city well and all its splendor.) "Amo Paris con todo mi corazón." (I love Paris with all my heart.)

"Monsieur, you are certainly multilingual!" I exclaimed.

"Yes, I am a polyglot with proficiency in several languages."

"Bravo, that is certainly noteworthy! Sir, can I help you with anything?"

"No, thank you. I am leaving Paris tomorrow, for New York. I was able to avail myself of American Express's 'poste restante' during my entire trip in Europe. I am here to check whether I have received some mail. I should go downstairs to the mailroom. By the way, my name is Gerald, but my nickname is Jerry. Call me Jerry."

"Jerry, I wish you 'un bon voyage' and a safe return. Now, I have to assist other tourists and translate some letters. Au revoir."

"Au revoir, so long, adios, ciao!" he uttered as he left.

When I lifted up my head some three hours later from the papers I was working on, Jerry was there at my desk, with his eyes focused on me.

Startled and very surprised, I inquired, "What are you doing here?"

"I was watching you from afar."

I thought that Jerry had left the premises. I just could not believe that for several hours, he had feasted his eyes on me. Why was he still here? What was he up to? I wondered.

He drew closer to me and said, emphatically, "Since American Express is closing today at one o'clock, I would like to take you to Versailles this afternoon."

"I guess that you were determined to spend the afternoon with me. I thank you for your cordial invitation, but I cannot go to Versailles with you. My friend Françoise is picking me up. We will have lunch together before making our way to the Galeries Lafayette department store."

For a moment, Jerry looked glum and somewhat dismayed by my response.

Riveting his eyes on me, he whispered, "Since you are not able to spend the afternoon with me, let's go out for dinner tonight."

"Well, since my plans with Françoise for the evening are not yet confirmed, I could possibly go out for dinner with you. However, you will have to pick me up from my parent's home, where I live."

"No problem. Just give me your address and I will be there at 7:30 p.m."

To this day, I do not know what made me accept Jerry's invitation for dinner.

Be that as it may, I found him to be a very engaging and pleasant, handsome young man. Consequently, I simply acquiesced to his wishes.

After all, since he was leaving the next day, for New York, I had no worries or feelings of disquietude! I would see him one evening and 'finito'! (finish! in Italian)

When Jerry arrived punctually at 7:30 p.m., my parents were not at home. However, he met my friend Françoise, who was still with me. She greeted him and then left right away.

Jerry wanted me to choose a restaurant. I suggested the Mexico Lindo, near the Boulevard St. Germain, a restaurant a la mode with an attractive decor, serving delicious traditional savory Mexican dishes. I always had a craving for exotic and colorful places. Little did I know that Jerry hated spicy foods! However, calm and undisturbed, he did not utter a word and went along with my preference!

All through dinner, in a long and leisurely narrative, Jerry talked so passionately about the amazing and challenging course of his life. Struck by curiosity, I was all ears to listen to his invaluable experiences. Furthermore, he carried an air of joviality by wiggling his ears for me.

Charming, he was. Amused, I was.

After dinner, we ambled to the picturesque banks of the Seine. What an amazing and romantic stroll that was! We hugged, we kissed, we smiled…

As Jerry was escorting me back to my home in a taxi, he repeated continuously, without interruption, that he definitely and unquestionably wanted to see me the next day, prior to his flight to New York. And casting his eyes on me, he persisted that he would not take 'no' for an answer.

He carried on and persevered until I finally gave in!

I never thought that I would capitulate to his request. But I did!

We agreed to meet in front of the Opera Garnier, Place de l'Opera, at 9:30 the next morning.

To my parent's great astonishment, I was leaving early on a Sunday morning! When I reached Place de l'Opera and stepped out of my taxi, Jerry was there, radiating a strong feeling of ecstasy and jubilation for my rendezvous with him. With a beaming smile, he welcomed me and embraced me.

So punctual were we that while we were enjoying our cafe and croissants, we actually had more time for a little terrace chitchat at the Cafe de la Paix. In an unrestrained and heartfelt way, Jerry voiced his opinion: "I believe that it is a good idea to share viewpoints. After all, they are to a great extent, consistent with our everyday experience of life."

"Yes, I fully agree with you. A person's perspective and interpretation of an experience can really be enlightening and open one's eyes," I said with a smile.

Enthusiastically, we spoke about our travel experiences, our hobbies and our leisure pursuits for an entertaining diversion. I discovered that our interests and our opinions on these subjects had a certain resonance. Last, but not least, we both loved talking.

After checking the time on his watch, Jerry suggested that before going to his hotel to pick up his luggage from the concierge, we take a little walk. A great idea, I thought.

As we were moving at a slow and relaxed pace, Jerry suddenly stopped. He looked at me and begged me to escort him to the airport. Without hesitation, I declined. "I do not take anyone to an airport," I said.

With a bewildered look, he was standing there, perplexed and confused. Acknowledging his dismay, I agreed wholeheartedly to accompany him to

Les Cars Air France at Les Invalides. Knowing that their shuttle service between Paris and the Orly Airport was excellent, I believed that it would be a good choice for him. He decided to go along with my suggestion. We walked back to his hotel, Rue Scribe. We picked up his luggage and proceeded by cab to Les Invalides.

As soon as we arrived at the bus terminal of Les Invalides, Jerry gave his airline ticket to one of the attendants. A couple of minutes later, the gentleman returned the ticket to Jerry and told him, with an apologetic smile across his face, that his flight had a delay of three hours!

Jerry could not contain his delight. His overwhelming feeling of great happiness was genuine.

"Now we have time to have lunch together at the Air France Restaurant!" he blurted out.

While we were enjoying the good food and drinks, Jerry talked about his career. Since his education, his experience and past achievements were all in the field of chemistry, he was happy and comfortable working for a French firm dealing with essential oils for perfume. He was, for sure, in his element.

As we were sharing our aspirations, dreams and ideals, our reciprocal exchanges were emphasizing the qualities and characteristics we had in common. But with that said, I did not expect or anticipate what was yet to come!

When the dessert came on the table, Jerry gave me a little more wine and stood up with his glass. "Here's to the girl I want to marry. I had to wait 31 years to find the dream girl of my life. I am passionate about you. You fill my heart. Sweetheart, I love you, I want you so badly — will you marry me?"

I was almost breathless. I needed a few minutes to understand what was happening.

Beyond a doubt, he was emphasizing the seriousness of his infatuation by proposing marriage the day after we met!

As we were savoring a magnificent strawberry tart with whipped cream, Jerry continued, with confidence, to proclaim that he was absolutely convinced that we belonged together: "Now that I've met you, I know that we are meant for each other. You are my inspiration. I could not even conceive a life without you. We are definitely perfectly suited and destined to be together. I love you, I love you. Please say 'yes,' that you will marry me. My life would be incomplete without you."

Smitten by his charm, I was attracted to Jerry and was falling in love with him. As insane as it was, I smiled broadly and finally came out with a "yes." We called it "le oui des Invalides."

Is love at first sight possible? Yes, I believe so. Two strangers meet and, in moments, they have an instant attraction for each other and simply know that they are meant to be together. Jerry and I felt it in our souls.

With our wonderful tête-à-tête, there was no time like the present. Extremely happy, our love was floating in the air.

Running out of time, Jerry needed to go and take the Air France shuttle service to the airport. Our goodbyes were not easy. Passionately, Jerry kissed me and then boarded the bus.

Overwhelmed with emotion, I was suddenly seized by the strange and astonishing sentiment that I knew Jerry from another life. This was not a dream or a trance — I sensed it. Swept away by this mystical persuasion, I left the bus terminal of Les Invalides.

I had no desire to go home right away. I did not want to be questioned by my parents. "Why did you leave so early on a Sunday morning?" "Where were you?" "What did you do?" I needed time on my own to understand what had occurred and not be exposed to cross-examination by Maman, Papa or my siblings.

As I was walking, I was thinking of Jerry's love for me, when he popped the question: "Will you marry me?" And then how he persisted resolutely, with no restraint or boundaries, that he would not take a "no" for an answer — that was undeniably phenomenal!

Reaching the Champs-Élysées, I needed to take a break. I ended up in a movie house to see a little comedy of which I have no recollection. My thoughts were somewhere else!

As soon as I came home, I was told by my parents that Jerry had called and that a priority mail express had been delivered for me.

I tried to avoid the inevitable questions from my parents by keeping quiet. Nevertheless, they conjectured that something was going on!

I could not believe what I was looking at. Jerry had written on an airport embarkation card: "Ne ten fais pas, tu n'as pas fait de gaffes. Tendresses, Jerry" (Do not worry, you did not make mistakes. Fondly, Jerry.)

The next day, I received two express letters from Jerry. He had just arrived in New York. He wanted to assure me that as unpremeditated and impulsive his desires were, they were not without merit. He also asserted, with deep confidence, that his strong feelings for me were acceptable justifications for his behavior.

To allay any doubts I had, Jerry was ready to prove the credibility of his aspirations of committing himself to "petit moi."

"So unexpected is this situation, I congratulate myself. I think I have won the jackpot!" Jerry emphasized in one of his missives.

I surmised that Jerry's proposal might very well be paving the way for new beginnings for both of us.

The sadness of being separated, when we had barely begun getting to know each other, was heart-wrenching. I could hardly concentrate on work.

Before I met Jerry, I had had in mind to visit the United States the following spring.

Be that as it may, on September 2nd, six days after I had, by chance, met Jerry, I was on fire. I decided to change my plans and go to New York in October and contacted my parents' friends, who had invited me to come and stay with them whenever I was ready.

My parents had left Paris with my two younger siblings, and had no idea of what was yet to come!

I wrote to Jerry to tell him that I needed to make sure that our feelings for each other were real and that the only way for us to know was to spend time together.

Overjoyed by my determination to cross the Atlantic Ocean, Jerry was absolutely elated by my decision.

****

CHAPTER 10

Check your List
Get Things Done
and Bon Voyage!

When a huge bouquet of red roses was delivered to my door on my 22nd birthday, September 3rd, my heart was filled with overwhelming emotions. The magnificent flowers were from Jerry.

Not only did he want to convey his birthday wishes to me, but he also recognized that it was our one-week anniversary of knowing each other!

Indeed, we had met a week ago! I was so touched by his thoughtfulness and his love for me.

My parents and my siblings Christian and Roxane were away on vacation in Belgium. My sister Ghislaine was staying with a family in Germany, to improve her German.

But I was invited out to dinner by my father's sister, Aunt Huguette, and my Uncle Roger to celebrate my birthday with them in a lovely restaurant in the Madeleine neighborhood.

After that, to add to my already enjoyable evening, my aunt and uncle had reserved seats at the famous Music Hall de l'Olympia to see Josephine Baker on the stage. Dressed in glamorous costumes, Baker's performance was an unforgettable experience and a wonderful surprise for me.

****

Notwithstanding that, thoughts regarding the nature of my significant project were preoccupying *petit moi*. I was still very busy with tourists pouring in the American Express office and I simply had to continue to do my best.

However, if I wanted my trip to the United States to succeed, I needed to make up my mind and start working on it, with a firm and unflinching resolution.

Yes, influenced by Jerry's infatuation with me and by my personal feelings for him, I had to definitely go ahead with my travel plans!

Decisions! Decisions! They are not always easy to make… Where do I start? Should I go by air or by sea?

What dates should I select for my departure and return?

Where should I stay, if my parents' friends cannot receive me in their home?

When should I go to the American Embassy for my visa? How long will it take to get it?

Will I be able to get a leave of absence from American Express?

Last but not least, when do I advise my parents that I am putting my plans into effect? Since they were still away on vacation, should I tell them right away? If so, should I write to them or call them on the phone?

"Make up your mind little girl! Go down the line and choose what makes the most sense to you. You have the final word!" I told myself.

For the question of crossing the Atlantic Ocean by plane or ship, the best alternative was, without question, to take a ship. After dealing with a heavy flow of tourists all summer long, I really needed to take a break and enjoy the fresh air of the ocean.

Consequently, the next day, September 5th, I chose to make a reservation on the French Line, SS Liberté, sailing from Le Havre on October 4, 1960. Later that day, one of the directors of the French Line called me back: "Mademoiselle, due to the pertinent fact that you are a full-time employee of American Express, working in the travel business, I am calling you to apprise you of what has happened."

"Monsieur, what's the problem?"

"Mademoiselle, there are no problems, I just wanted to bring to your attention that it is our pleasure to upgrade you. You will pay for a third-class cabin, and without a fee, you will have a first-class cabin. This, of course, applies to your round-trip as well."

I was surprised and delighted by the generous perk I was getting from the French Line.

Expressing feelings of joy, I wrote to Jerry that I would be disembarking on October 10th at the Port of New York, and that I would be returning to France at the end of December.

Jerry, who had been anxiously waiting for the good news, wrote back that he was overwhelmed with excitement. Elated by my terrific news, he told me that he could hardly wait until October 10th to see me again.

Now, I had to apply for a visa. I will never forget the interrogation I submitted to at the American Embassy. I was asked to swear under oath, to tell the truth, with my hand on the bible: "Are you a lawbreaker?" "Are you a criminal?" "Have you ever been arrested?" "Have you ever engaged in prostitution?" "Are you a communist?"

I found this hard to believe. In my twenty-two years, I had never been interrogated by anyone in this way. Well, lucky me, I was able to answer "no" to all the questions!

After making my travel reservation and getting my visa, I decided to see Mr. G, Director of American Express in Paris.

Very pleasantly, he welcomed me into his office and asked, "Mademoiselle, what can I do for you?"

"Well, Monsieur, all being well, I plan to leave in early October for the United States. I am here to request a three-month leave of absence, without pay, of course."

"No problem, Mademoiselle, but based on your good work, we definitely want to see you back in early January. We count on you," he asserted clearly.

I thanked him profusely for his understanding and benevolence.

I was relieved to receive from the friends of my parents in New York an acknowledgment that they would be waiting for me on October 10th with open arms.

As I was trying to sort out in my head how to approach my parents about the momentous decision I had just made, my mother called me from Belgium.

Without hesitation, I emphasized to my mother that in light of Jerry's strong feelings for me and my sentiments for him, I did not want to wait until springtime to go to New York. I told her that I had come to the inevitable conclusion that I was to cross the Atlantic Ocean on a ship sailing from Le Havre on October 4th.

Hearing no response to what I had imparted, I was concerned that I had lost the connection: "Maman, do you hear me? Are you still on the line?" I asked.

"Yes, I heard you, but I need some time to absorb the substance of what you are divulging to me. We will talk soon. Bye bye, my darling."

My mother was perplexed and somewhat troubled by my announcement of my firm intent to go to New York. Perceiving my mother's bewilderment, I became uneasy. But I had made up my mind. I could actually hear a little voice inside me saying, "Get up and go!"

As I returned home from work the next day, I was very surprised to be greeted by my parents and siblings. They were there, waiting for me. They had deemed it necessary to cut short their vacation and head home four days earlier than expected!

"Are you alright? I asked.

"Yes we are fine."

"So, why did you abbreviate your vacation in Belgium?" I asked, somewhat concerned.

"Your father and I need to talk to you," said Maman. "We want to understand fully why you desire to move so fast."

I sat down with them and went to great lengths to explain my reasons for going to the United States.

To my relief, both of my parents recognized and understood very well the intensity of my strong emotions.

With their sympathy and approval of my decision, I was in seventh heaven. Jumping for joy, I embraced them and thank them profusely for their support.

And to add to my jubilation, I received two letters from Jerry.

It may sound implausible, but up to the day of my departure for the United States, I received two or three letters a day from him.

At that time, mail was delivered three times a day, morning, noon and night, with the exception of Sunday.

Each and every Sunday at around 6 o'clock in the morning, the doorbell would ring. My father would get up and open the door and exclaim: "Good Lord, the American has again sent a telegram for Muriel!"

Jerry's intensity and devotion was characteristic of his heartfelt manner. He was firmly convinced that his profuse exuberance was not only due to the exhilaration of having met me, but to his thoughts of our sharing a future together.

Jerry's letters were absolutely enthralling. I delighted in reading them as much I had enjoyed listening to him in Paris. He wrote about his life in New York, his family, his friends, his work, stories of his youth during the war, his beliefs regarding religion, and his aspirations for the future. His long letters divulged so much of who he was.

With my departure approaching, I was extremely busy.

Even so, with the allegiance and loyalty I had for my job, I put forth a concerted effort to do my best up until my last working day, September 30th.

As might be expected, it was imperative for me to buy new fall and winter clothes. During my lunch hour, I would head to lovely boutiques on the Rue Royale or the Rue de la Paix, where I would find an array of high-quality and classy outfits.

Needless to say, the queen needed to look elegant for her prince!

Occasionally, my mother wanted to accompany me on my shopping sprees. I was so happy to have her with me. Her exquisite and refined taste enchanted me. We had a delightful time together as she helped me to pick and choose.

I remember the day when I left the office to buy a present for Jerry. What kind of gift should I purchase for him? I asked myself. Suddenly, an idea popped into my mind: "Jerry is a pipe smoker...Babies are soothed by sucking on pacifiers... a pipe has the same effect on Jerry!" I ran to a tobacco store and bought a gorgeous pipe for him.

Yearning to purchase something relevant to our meeting in Paris and to the "oui des Invalides," I bought a fabulous book of photographs, *The Paris I Love*, for Jerry. I still have that beautiful book on my book shelf!

No matter how busy I was, I did my utmost to see before my departure as many relatives and friends as I could. They all acknowledged that after my stunning and unexpected encounter with Jerry, my quick decision to leave as soon as possible for New York was totally understandable.

As I conveyed my farewells, goodbyes, *au revoirs, sayonaras* and *adieus* on September 30th to Odile and my colleagues at American Express, I felt the warmth radiating from their smiles and good wishes.

The momentous day of my voyage finally arrived. My father took me to the train station.

I have no recollection of my train ride to Le Havre. I was probably indulging in pleasant daydreams which would soon be a reality when I met up again with Jerry.

I was in awe by the magnificence of my first-class private room on the ship. Spacious, luxurious and comfortable, it was.

The first-class dining room was beautiful. The gourmet food would have enticed any passionate gastronome. The pleasures of the table were certainly there.

I enjoyed eating the caviar, the foie gras, the lobsters, and the *cordon bleu* cuisine was absolutely sublime.

However, due to an impressive windstorm, the dining room was often empty. The ship was bouncing around and people were seasick. Fortunately, I did not miss a meal!

I delighted also in the wonderful entertainment. As a first-class passenger, I had access to all three classes.

First class was definitely opulent, but the high spirits and the gaiety of youth were unfortunately missing!

So I would often go back to third class, where I shared activities with a group of young people.

When I would return to my room at the end of the day, I would find a radiogram hanging on the door. These were from Jerry. Receiving them warmed my heart immensely. I was very moved by his thoughtfulness.

Entering the gateway to the Port of New York at dawn on October 10, 1960, as the light of the sun appeared in the sky, was an experience for me.

The decks on the ship were jam-packed; everyone wanted to see the iconic Lady Liberty, representing freedom. Gorgeous it was.

I was utterly mesmerized by Manhattan's skyline, with the fabulous panoramic views of the city's skyscrapers. Filled with emotions, I was entering the port of New York.

Jerry was there to welcome me with a bouquet of red roses and a huge smile across his face. He was not alone; Mr. and Mrs. R, my parents' friends, were there as well.

But my impression of New York was underwhelming. I could never have imagined seeing so much filth in the streets. There was garbage all over the pavement! As Mr. R drove us to their home, I soon realized that the architecture had nothing in common with European buildings, that there were no cafés with outdoor seating, and that there were no trees on the streets. And then, to add to my dismay, Mrs. R apprised me that crime was rising rapidly in New York City and that I would have to be very careful walking around.

I attempted to conceal my perturbation. But, I asked myself, should I go back on the ship and return to France? My answer was no. Jerry was more important to me. I really needed to become better acquainted with him and understand the meaning of our infatuation.

We headed straight towards Mr. and Mrs. R's beautiful apartment, located in an elegant modern building on Fifth Avenue, near the Washington Square Arch.

As soon as we arrived, Jerry insisted on taking me out for lunch.

On our way to a very nice restaurant in the neighborhood, Jerry made me laugh when he divulged his father's concern earlier today: "Will you recognize Muriel? Do you remember what she looks like?"

Recognizing *petit moi* right away was not a problem for Jerry; he enthusiastically applauded my arrival. As for me, I could not forget his attractiveness and comportment — he had had such an impact on me!

Sitting *en tête-à-tête* in the lovely restaurant, we had a heart-to-heart conversation. I do not remember what we ate, but I can still hear Jerry, voicing softly and distinctly his thoughts: "Indeed, you are the girl I love and want to marry."

I had just arrived in New York, we had only spent two days together in Paris, but Jerry knew for sure that I was *"l'élue de son coeur"* (the chosen one in his heart).

Whenever Jerry could meet me for lunch, he would.

I will never forget the lunch I had with Mrs. R. a few days after my arrival in New York. She invited me out to a very nice little restaurant. I thought that it would be good manners to order the same thing as she did. Little did I know!

I could not believe what I had on my plate: a tiny scoop of cottage cheese, a little Jello and a few crackers. A colorful little appetizer, I thought. I was mistaken — this was the entire lunch!

As I do not like wiggly food, I left the Jello and ate the cottage cheese. The portion was just enough to fill a cavity!

When Mrs. R called the waiter, I though that she wanted to order the main course. Foolish, I was! She wanted the bill!

Jerry would meet me every day after work at around 6 p.m. at the super-classy Hotel Pierre for cocktails and dancing, before heading to all kinds of lovely restaurants for dinner.

We enjoyed thoroughly our evenings, and were so happy.

The weekend after my arrival, Jerry's parents came to Manhattan to participate in a trade show for hair products.

Jerry insisted that we should have lunch with them on Saturday at their hotel.

Apparently, Jerry's father told his mother, "I have been introduced to tons of girlfriends… This time, *you* be the judge. If she is pleasant and friendly, invite her to our home on Sunday."

Well, I met Jerry's mother and one of her friends. We had a very nice lunch together. I found her very pleasant. Lucky me, I passed the test and was invited to their home in Queens the following day.

Jerry's parents and grandmother were very friendly and cordial. I felt happy and accepted. In fact, Oma, the grandmother, took Jerry in another room to question him: "What are you waiting for? You should have married her yesterday!"

Jerry was naturally delighted that his family had expressed their approval. They wanted to find out more about what had brought me to America. As if they did not know!

But I wanted them to tell about me about their heroic determination to flee Europe and make it to the United States. Impressed by their extreme bravery, I will relate their story in my next chapter.

I definitely did not regret my decision to come to New York. Our strong feelings for each other were real.

No matter how much time passes, some memories never go away. There are noteworthy experiences and events that I could never assign to oblivion.

CHAPTER 11

Gerald and His Parents Escape the Nazis

Gerald was born Gunter on July 15, 1929 in Berlin, Germany.

William, Gerald's father, was raised on farmland owned by his parents, who were cattle dealers in Gondelsheim, near Baden-Württemberg in southern Germany.

As a young man, William moved to Berlin. By the time he met his wife, Lotte, he was a wealthy and successful professional who owned a bank.

Lotte, her parents and her five siblings were all from Berlin.

When Hitler came to power in 1933, Gerald's parents fled Germany for the Netherlands with the bare minimum, leaving their son Gerald, who was four years old, with his paternal grandparents, Amalia and Moses, in Gondelsheim.

Unable to establish themselves in Holland, Gerald's parents moved on to Brussels, where they found refuge.

Since the Nazis had blacklisted William, it was therefore out of the question for him to continue his career as an expatriate. Consequently, he created a new company, dealing with chemicals for hair products.

In 1934, under the escort of his Oma, Amalia, Gerald left Germany for Brussels to join his parents, who were by then well established.

When Gerald's grandfather, Moses, died in 1937, under Nazi watch, Amalia left Gondelsheim right away to move in with her son and his family in Brussels.

On May 10, 1940, at about half-past five in the morning, detonations were heard and were growing in intensity.

The shocking news was revealed on the radio — the Nazis had invaded Belgium.

William got dressed and hurried out to the bank to withdraw money and securities.

The situation was already chaotic. People were starting to leave Brussels to take refuge in France and England.

Later that morning, three Belgian soldiers came to arrest William and his family. Due to their German origin, they were now considered "enemy aliens"!

They were told to grab food for 24 hours and were taken by truck to a high school, which had been converted for internment.

By 6 p.m. all the women and children were released.

The following day, rumors started to fly that the Belgians had decided to ship their prisoners to somewhere in France. Lotte, who was bringing food to William, arrived just in time to see her husband rushed into a boxcar and taken away.

****

When the Nazis invaded Belgium in 1940, Gerald was almost 11 years old and had just about completed his primary education.

On May 12, in an attempt to leave Belgium, Amalia, Lotte and Gerald hired a cab to take them to the French border. But the road was totally blocked. They were ordered by the Belgians to return to Brussels.

Without news of William, on May 23, 1940, they made another attempt to flee with some of their friends.

They boarded a train going to Tournai, near the French border, some 85 kilometers southwest of Brussels. But Tournai's train station had just been completely destroyed by Nazi bombs, so the train had to stop at the outskirts of the city to let the passengers out. From there, they proceeded by taxi to a farm owned by friends of their traveling companions.

On the following day, they proceeded on foot to the French border. They were not alone. Thousands of refugees were fleeing, along with British, French, Belgian and Dutch soldiers. The state of panic was incredible.

Exhausted and in a pitiable condition, they finally reached Armentieres. The Allies' general headquarters was there. Afraid of falling into the hands of the Nazis, Lotte approached a British officer for advice. He brought the family to the cellar to meet with his commander.

During their meeting, there was an air raid and bombing over the city. With the situation worsening, they were given the name of a private chauffeur who would drive them to the coast. But that never happened — the chauffeur was killed by a bomb.

The next day, Armentieres had turned into a battlefield, killing scores and wounding hundreds. Armentieres had nearly been wiped off the map. Gerald's family decided to leave and walk back to Belgium by crossing the bridge joining the two countries.

Again, they were not alone. People were trampling each other. Exhausted they were! They finally made it to Ostende, where they took refuge in the dunes. But with the Nazis sweeping the resorts, they decided it was best to return to Brussels.

Gerald went back to school. But, with the daily fights and the prejudice against Jews, school evolved into an unbearable and appalling plight.

Through friends, news trickled out that William was being held in St. Cyprien or Gurs concentration camp, in the South of France. These were located in the Free Zone, where Jews who were expelled from Germany and Belgium were received.

Gerald was then able to correspond with his dad.

With the situation in Belgium rapidly worsening, Lotte decided to make an all-out effort for the family to leave for the Free Zone, where William was being held. From there they hoped that their American friends, Mr. L of Charles of the Ritz and his counsel, Mr. Hugo M, would be able to get them into the United States of America.

In order to acquire a permit from the Nazis to leave Belgium they needed visas. They could not get them for the USA, so Lotte tried to purchase visas for Thailand, but they were also denied. A new regulation made travel permits impossible to obtain.

Audacious and undeterred, Lotte decided to purchase "laissez-passers" (exit permits) from the Belgian Underground so they could to journey to France.

So as not to arouse suspicion, they brought along as little baggage as they possibly could. Money was carefully hidden in the handle of a knife, which had been bored out, and which Amalia was to carry in her hand-bag. Gold coins were hidden inside their clothing and in the handle of a trunk. Acute in perception and sound in judgment, Amalia and Lotte certainly were!

After much delay, Amalia, Lotte and Gerald were finally able to board a train to Paris. The train was packed; people were pressed together. They had to stand all the way!

At the Belgian border, they were checked thoroughly and their papers examined. Fortunately, they were able to make it through this precarious situation and arrived in the French capital on March 1, 1941.

Under the occupation, Paris was a very dangerous city. To add to Amalia and Lotte's consternation and anxiety, the Nazi authorities were forcing hotel owners to submit the names of their guests! Adding to their dismay, food was rationed and extremely expensive. It was actually a miracle that they were able to elude the Gestapo.

They were hoping to find a way to reach Marseilles, where William was living after having escaped from Camp des Milles, another concentration camp where he had been interned.

Lotte's main objective in Paris was to find an appropriate "passeur" (a person who helped people to escape to freedom during the war) to accompany them to the Free Zone.

In due course, Amalia, Lotte and Gerald were able, with a passeur, to board a train for Bordeaux, a city close to the Free Zone. Once on the train, the passeur recommended that they get off in Libourne, a small city in the outskirts of Bordeaux. Then, by cab, they reached Castillon, a small village bordering the Free Zone. But the passeur wanted to wait for the darkness of night to take them over the border.

In Castillon, they came upon a little restaurant where they were served a rabbit stew for dinner. But their senses gave rise to the suspicion that they were probably feasting on a wandering alley cat that had ended up in the cook's pot!

No need to tell you more on that subject!

The night was crystalline pure with a bright full moon, which guided Amalia, Lotte and Gerald, along with another family, as they approached the Free Zone. But a few feet away from the border, two uniformed soldiers with a large police dog started to chase them.

Their passeur took off into the bushes with the trunk, thus escaping capture and saving the hidden gold in the handle.

Amalia, Lotte, Gerald and the other family were ordered by the Nazis to march in single file to a dwelling a few miles away.

The weather was bitter, and the long trek was difficult and strenuous. To add to their precarious situation, they realized that if they were caught trying to get to the Free Zone with forged border-passes, the Nazis could severely punish them or put them to death.

When the Nazis discerned that they were both Jewish and German, insults and cursing erupted! They were in grave danger.

However, Amalia was able to convey to the soldiers that her grandson was terribly hungry and needed to be fed. Right away, they provided a loaf of bread.

Gerald could never forget the sight of his Oma using the knife, with the handle filled with money, to cut a piece of bread for him in front of the Nazi soldiers. (Actually, I still have the famous knife in one of my drawers!)

Meanwhile, Lotte was subjected to endless cross-examination. Then it was Gerald's turn to be interrogated by the Nazis. They seized his stamp collection and confiscated other belongings.

Subsequently, the Nazis escorted Amalia, Lotte and Gerald to another building, where they spent the rest of the night.

The next day, they were taken to the Kommandantur (the German commander's headquarters) in Libourne.

Upon their arrival, their forged border-passes were confiscated. Amalia and Lotte were extremely fearful that the Nazis would ascertain that their documents were phony. But to their great relief, it came to light that the Occupation authorities had for quite some time stopped issuing passes and laissez-passers were no longer required.

They were not alone in the German commander's headquarters; a couple was there as well, with their son Peter.

The two boys were separated from their parents and taken to a Catholic hospital for children. For the most part, orphans were housed there.

The youngsters slept in large dormitories, where an elderly matron, carrying a whip, patrolled constantly!

During this trying episode of separation from their families, a woman showed up unexpectedly. A bearer of good tidings, she gave Gerald and Peter candy and underwear, of which they were in dire need, since all their belongings had been taken by the Nazis.

This woman pretended to be the hostess of a hotel where their parents were staying. The boys didn't know that their parents were actually in prison. And the woman was the jailor's wife — and an underground agent, who was risking her life by visiting the boys!

After twelve days, a Gestapo officer took the boys to the Libourne prison, where they were only too happy to see their folks again. From there, they were all taken by truck to Fort du Ha, an infamous military prison in Bordeaux.

As soon as they arrived, the boys were once again separated from their families. They were taken a few kilometers away, to the reform school d'Eysines. They were lodged in wooden barracks, among young criminals, Spanish refugees and illegitimate children. The food in these ignominious quarters was repulsive; I will not go into the specifics. The whole experience was abominable.

After becoming sick with sore throats, Gerald and Peter were taken back two weeks later to Fort du Ha, where they were reunited once again with their parents.

Finally, after a long delay, the Nazis returned all their belongings to them, dismissed them and deported them back to the Free Zone.

They could now express their elation: "Yippee! Yippee!"

They took a train to Marseilles to join William, who was in a hotel room, semiconscious from a flea bite. Yet, as sick as he was, the family was thrilled to be back together after such a long time.

Soon after their arrival in Marseilles, they contacted their passeur, who, to their relief, returned the trunk with the precious gold right away. Fortunately, the trunk had escaped detection!

In their endeavor to get sponsored to the United States, they contacted Mr. L and Mr. S of Charles of the Ritz. Desiring to provide assistance, they appointed their lawyer, Mr. M, to aid them. William had a cousin who also expressed his determination to help. Consequently, various appeals to Washington were made.

However, considering the danger of William's re-arrest by the Vichy Police, his American friends chose to obtain a Cuban visa for him. From Cuba, he would proceed to the USA and hopefully be reunited with his mother, his wife and his son.

With a booking to board a vessel, William left his family behind, only to find out that the French ship had been confiscated by the British!

Consequently, since the French authorities collaborated with the North African countries, where colonialism and fascism coexisted, William was sent to an internment labor camp in the El Oued desert, not far from Casablanca, pending his finding another way to go to Cuba.

Meanwhile, Amalia, Lotte and Gerald were waiting for their American visas, to no purpose. But, since the Nazi's impact was increasing rapidly, a postponement would more than likely have been gravely dangerous for them. Hence their New York friends decided to obtain Cuban visas for them as well.

Amalia, Lotte and Gerald were about to leave Marseilles for Sevilla, Spain, where they hoped to meet William and sail to Havana, when they were notified that their motorboat crossing had been cancelled. Since they could not reach William, they decided to use their Spanish transit visas and left Marseilles by train for Spain on August 8, 1941.

After a few hours of travel, they reached Portbou, at the French/Spanish border, where they switched trains.

Gerald could never forget their irksome ride to Madrid in the primeval railroad cars, with windows that could not be closed and the creak of the insecure connections between the wagons. The train journeyed through lengthy tunnels from which it emerged thoroughly black from soot, which seeped through the open windows and corridors.

As I am sharing with you Gerald's story of his long journey to safety, I would like to quote his impressions of the Prado Museum in Madrid: "I was dazzled and shocked by the multitude of nude Madonnas! I was embarrassed by this immodest display. Without question, the Prado

Museum proved to be a liberal education for me!" Well, Gerald was 12 years old at the time, and too much was just too much, I suppose!

After their brief visit to Madrid, Amalia, Lotte and Gerald proceeded to Sevilla. And to their great surprise, William was waiting patiently for them at the train station. As a matter a fact, when William had arrived earlier that day from Tangiers, he had been made aware of the boat cancellation. Luckily, his instinct to go to the railroad terminal augured well. It was, without a doubt, the best place for them to meet up!

Great and extraordinary was their reunion.

Staying in a small hotel in the center of the city, the torrid heat of the August sun did not dissuade them from visiting a few great sights, such as the Giralda with its the famous Moorish bell tower and the Cathedral de Sevilla, with its massive monument to Christopher Columbus.

Unfortunately, the extreme poverty and the critical need for food was everywhere. Homeless children of all ages were begging. Heartbreaking, it certainly was!

Since the motorboat had been cancelled, they got a booking on the SS Nyassa, a cargo ship departing from the Port of Lisbon and bound for Cuba.

By train, on August 30, 1941, they arrived in Lisbon, Portugal. Since they had several days prior to their departure, they hoped to recover from the austerity, deprivation and hardship they had endured in the past months and find their bearings by opting to stay in one of the best hotels in Lisbon.

Finally, after waiting many, many hours under a burning sun for the Portuguese authorities, they were able to embark on the SS Nyassa on September 9, 1941.

As they were leaving Europe, in which they had experienced so many difficult and hostile encounters, a wave of sentiment and emotion filled their hearts. With the fear of an unknown and uncertain future lying ahead of him, Gerald was kind of despondent.

The ship was jam-packed with Jewish refugees from all over Europe. No war refugees were allowed into the United States! Consequently, they were all on the way to Cuba.

A frightening and severe storm, with the sea rising in huge waves, terrified the deck passengers, who were tumbling all over as they struggled against the tempest. What a scary and distressing event it was for them!

Fortunately, the grueling and exhausting crossing would conclude. As they finally reached the Cuban shores on September 22, 1941, the ship sailed slowly along the gleaming lights of El Malecón, Havana's beautiful sea-side avenue. A very touching Yom Kippur service, with all the spiritual richness of the Jewish tradition, was held for the passengers before they disembarked.

Just after the ship docked, the passengers were taken to Tiscornia, the Ellis Island of Cuba, where they were greeted by the local Hebrew organization, which invited them to a feast to commemorate their arrival in a Free World.

However, due to complicated administrative procedures and rigid regulations, Gerald and his family were put under quarantine for several days, after which they were finally released.

As Gerald recollected, the family's four-year sojourn in Cuba was comfortable and quite good for them.

That said, the tropical, steamy climate was a strain. They were just not accustomed to dealing with such sweltering and oppressive conditions. Hence, they spent most of their free time at La Concha Beach resort, where Gerald overcame his fear of water and enjoyed swimming.

Amazingly, Gerald was able to conquer a manifold of difficulties. Not only did he have to go back to school, but he also had to master two new foreign languages — English and Spanish. Nonetheless, with his acuity, his wide-ranging knowledge and his good ear for languages, he was able to overcome the challenge and keep up at the British school he attended. In fact, Gerald completed middle school and high school in four years instead of six!

Notwithstanding his shyness, Gerald was able to strike up new friendships with classmates who originated mostly from England, Germany and Belgium.

Gerald had his Bar Mitzvah. Though celebrated during the heat of the war, on July 19, 1942, the simple service in the temple was conducted in German and was apparently lovely. Neighbors and friends joined the

1942

family to honor Gerald and give him presents such as books, wallets and fountain pens.

Finally, on April 4, 1946, Gerald and his family were able to obtain their visas for the United States of America.

They boarded a plane for Miami on April 10, 1946 and then continued their journey to New York, never forgetting their appreciation and gratefulness for their years in Cuba.

CHAPTER 12

It Takes Two to Tie a Knot

While Jerry was busy at work, I wanted to experience the authentic New York — a very different city from Paris. Exploring New York was definitely a great adventure for me. The sheer variety of the city's cool and unusual sights was dazzling! I was mesmerized by the soaring skyscrapers around Rockefeller Center, by the stunning views from the top of the Empire State Building, by Wall Street — the famous financial district in lower Manhattan — by the historic landmarks, by my visit to the fabulous Metropolitan Museum and more.

The department stores on Fifth Avenue were outstanding. My very first purchase in New York was an elegant black velvet beret from the luxurious Bonwit Teller. I still have that little chapeau in my closet! Whenever Jerry saw me wearing it, he would call me "Princess"!

I would meet Jerry every day. Our superb get-togethers were, to say the least, always delightful. We were deeply in love.

****

My stay with Mr. and Mrs. R seemed to work out well.

I had brought light to why I had decided to cross the Atlantic Ocean so precipitously by explaining to them that I was in New York to get better acquainted with Jerry and that I needed to determine whether our feelings were genuine or not!

I was very grateful for their kindness towards me and I certainly did not want to abuse their generosity. I spent time with Mrs. R. We would have some very nice conversations and we would occasionally go out together.

Not quite two weeks after my arrival, Mr. and Mrs. R left New York to spend a few days in their country home. Unexpectedly, early the next morning, their daughter showed up. I had never met her before.

She walked into the apartment and approached me with a troubled expression on her face.

"Bonjour! How are you? Is there something wrong with your parents?" I asked.

"No, my parents are well."

She paused for a minute, and then in a loud voice she exclaimed, "Muriel, you are using my parents' home like a hotel!"

Shocked by her presumption and her arrogance, I kept quiet for a moment.

Somewhat bewildered, I looked at her and retorted, "Do not worry. I will pack my belongings and I will go to a hotel today."

Pleased with my answer, she reminded me, as she walked out, to not forget to leave the key behind.

As soon as she closed the door, I telephoned Jerry to let him know that I was leaving the R's apartment and that I was going to move to a hotel.

"No way! The girl I am going to marry is not moving to a hotel." He paused for a minute and went on to say, "I am going to call you back in a few minutes — start packing!"

Busy gathering my belongings, I was trying to stay calm. Then, as I was pulling the sheets off the bed, the phone rang. It was Jerry.

"My parents are on their way. They will pick up your luggage."

It was Friday. Jerry's parents were working in their office, some twenty-five blocks away. I did not have to wait long before they showed up. As they were putting the luggage into the car, they told me that I was more than welcome to live with them, as long as I needed to.

I highly appreciated their courtesy and gentility.

Before leaving Mr. and Mrs. R's apartment, I wanted to write a note expressing my gratitude for letting me stay with them for almost two weeks. I could not underestimate their kindness. But considering their daughter's assertion that I was using their home as a hotel, I had decided to leave their home.

I tried in vain to call them, but they never answered. They had Jerry's phone number, but they never called. I never heard from them again!

After I left the R's apartment, I met Ethel, an employee of Mr. R's, for lunch.

As a buyer for Mr. R's firm, Ethel would go overseas quite frequently. Not only did she visit my father in his office to buy goods for export, but she enjoyed socializing with my parents. Whenever I saw her in Paris, I enjoyed her friendliness.

When I apprised her of what had happened to me earlier in the day, I perceived Ethel's strong feeling of aversion towards the R's daughter. Disconcerted, she looked at me and said, "This is objectionable and totally inappropriate! Would you like to stay with me, in Brooklyn?"

I thanked her profusely for her offer and told her that Jerry's parents were going to put me up.

I remained in contact with Ethel. Occasionally we saw each other, but the R's name was never brought up!

****

Later that day, I met Jerry in his parents' office. We all headed to their home in Queens. Jerry's grandmother, his "Oma," was there, filled with delight at seeing me again. She welcomed me with open arms.

It was decided that I would have Jerry's bedroom and that he would sleep on the sofa bed in the basement. The large room was used as a home office. He had no computer — a typewriter was on the desk!

What is a typewriter? the young generations will ask. Well, it is a machine with keys that you use for typing letters and symbols directly onto a sheet of paper wrapped around a roller. Indeed, things change!

I received a warm welcome in Jerry's home. Amused, I was when I found out that Jerry's Oma would go up and down the corridor during the night to ensure and verify that her grandson kept away from his bedroom, and that he would go straight down to the basement after using the bathroom! She was, most certainly, a superb night-watch!

A few days later, Jerry found me an exquisite room in the house of one of his mother's friends in nearby Forest Hills.

Jerry's father drove us to Mrs. B's home. After introducing me to the affable host and bringing my valise and travel bag upstairs, they left. Jerry told me that he had to do an errand and that he would come back to pick me up in a couple of hours.

Engaged in an enjoyable exchange with Mrs. B, I felt very much at ease. Before leaving her to unpack my bags upstairs, I told her that I would like to pay for my accommodations, and asked her to establish a set price per week.

She immediately acknowledged that Jerry would take care of it and that in no way did he want me to pay.

****

Now, three weeks had elapsed since the French Line, SS Liberté had dropped its anchor in the Port of New York and I walked off the ship to reunite with Jerry.

He had definitely not changed his mind. I was still *"l'élue de son coeur"* (the chosen one in his heart).

While we were walking from Mrs. B's house to the subway station, Jerry wanted to share again his sentiments and express his feelings for me. He stopped and looked at me; he suggested that we get officially engaged.

I smiled.

We continued ambling down the street until Jerry stopped again. Facing me with a grin from ear to ear, he said: "Cherie, I want you to know that committing the rest of our lives to each other would be the first major step in the planning of our wedding date! Think about it — it would put the icing on the cake!"

I was, to say the least, amused by his ideas.

Without a doubt, we were head over heels in love with each other.

As soon as we reached the platform, the train arrived. We stepped in and sat down.

I was sitting quietly on the train, totally absorbed by Jerry's suggestion of getting officially engaged, when all of a sudden, he got up from his seat. Smiling, he went down on his knees, urging me to give him my left hand.

He took hold of my hand and as he was slipping a diamond ring on my fourth finger. He affirmed with a tenderness that with this ring, he wanted to solidify our commitment to each other.

There we were, on our way to town, riding on the subway with people all around us. Not on your life could I have anticipated what had just happened!

Actually, I had never met anyone like Jerry! When I think of his marriage proposal the day after we met in Paris, and his slipping a diamond engagement ring on my finger on the subway, he was definitely one of a kind. He was not idiosyncratic or temperamental; he had just a strong fancy for petit moi and he knew what he wanted! Unique, he certainly was!

After that phenomenal subway ride, we had a very lovely dinner on the west side of Manhattan at Les Pyrenees, a French restaurant on 51st Street. Then we headed to Broadway to see a show. I was far too absorbed in thoughts and emotions to be able to concentrate on the musical. I do not remember what we saw!

****

Now, we were in November. I would see Jerry every day after work. We would often meet at our favorite, the super-classy Hotel Pierre, for cocktails and dancing before heading to a restaurant for dinner.

We both agreed to commit ourselves to a permanent relationship and get married soon.

Having made up his mind to accompany me to Paris,

I switched my return booking on the SS Liberte to an Air France flight, on December 23.

Owing to the strength and authenticity of his feelings for me, Jerry asserted that we should get married before we leave for France.

Undoubtedly, Jerry was anxious about my parents' reactions to the unexpected rapidity of our commitment. He was afraid that they would ask us to postpone our marriage or try to dissuade me from leaving their home.

Jerry did not want to expose himself to the danger of losing me. His heart was set on tying the knot! With these thoughts in mind, he preferred that I return to France with the wedding band on my finger!

I failed to resist. I simply yielded to his overpowering appeal.

Now the process of drawing up plans for successfully achieving our goal was in the making.

As we sat together in a quiet restaurant, Jerry declared that he was eager to live in a nice house with a garden in Westchester County, an area known for its beautiful villages.

Firm and resolute, I told him that being a big-city person, I needed to be in a metropolitan apartment and that a house would be completely out of question. Furthermore, while on vacation, I would not want a house either; after all, hotels, clubs and cruises do exist! Who wants to know where the kitchen is on vacation? Not *petit moi*, for sure!

Jerry appeared somewhat disconcerted by my answer.

"If you do not agree to live in an apartment in the city, I am not the wife for you," I blurted out.

With a burst of strong feeling and without waiting for a second, he acknowledged: "You are certainly more important to me than a house. We will look for an apartment in Manhattan."

I was so very happy to hear that I was of greater importance to him than a house!

Then, adding to my crucial prerequisite, I told him that it would be mandatory for me to visit my family at least once or twice a year.

"Absolutely, my *cherie*, you will cross the Atlantic Ocean at least once a year, I promise."

After Jerry agreed to my essential necessities, we talked about a possible date for our marriage.

Since Jerry's father was going to be hospitalized for hernia surgery on December 5th, we finally opted to get married at City Hall in lower Manhattan on December 3, 1960.

Now, it was vital for us to find an apartment in the city.

I had no idea where to look for one, but my savvy future husband selected the superb neighborhood of the Upper East Side of Manhattan. I kept very busy hunting for an apartment until I came across a delightful one on Madison Avenue, close to the fabulous Central Park. Both Jerry and I agreed that we had found a very pleasing place of residence for ourselves.

When it came to selecting furniture, carpets and curtains for our future home, Jerry insisted on buying the "in" Danish modern designs of the '60s. It was certainly a big change for me from the 17th and 18th-century furnishings of my parents and grandparents! But I went along with it.

The target date for our defining moment and point of no return was fast approaching. We needed to gather documents and fill out applications for our marriage license and present them to a city clerk downtown.

****

Since my parents and family were not going to be present for the exchange of our vows, Jerry did not want his Oma or his parents to come. However, to make our union legal, we needed two witnesses. A lovely couple, Fred and Mary H — friends of Jerry's — were there to watch the two of us sign our marriage license.

Jerry wanted a simple and short ceremony providing the essentials and nothing fancy — no breathtaking long white gown, no white bridal veil, no bridal bouquet for me. Jerry said that as long as the young lady he had set his heart on was at his side, that was all that mattered.

I was not impressed by the little ceremony, but the meaning of our vows was far more important; we belonged to each other and that prevailed over everything else.

After being joined in marriage, we left City Hall with our witnesses and met up with Jerry's Oma and his parents for a lovely lunch in a good French restaurant.

In the afternoon, we moved into our new home, to start our lives as husband and wife.

****

I made certain that an express letter would reach my parents on December 3rd to let them know that Jerry and I were getting married on that day.

My mother responded right away with a telegram: "Congratulations! No need for you to come to Paris for your engagement!" Fortunately, a few hours later we received another telegram from my mother saying, "Please come to Paris, introduce Jerry to your family and friends, and exchange your vows again, in a synagogue." I was so relieved by the second telegram; we could keep our plans and fly over to France on December 23rd.

Since Jerry had to work until our departure for Paris, our post-nuptial vacation had to be put aside.

Never mind — I spent my honeymoon in the hospital with my father-in-law, who was slowly recovering from his hernia surgery.

With heavy snow falling all over New York, my mother-in-law was unable to leave her house for several days. So, I volunteered to go every day and spend hours with my father-in-law, who seemed enchanted to have me at his side.

As I was writing to my family and friends that I had tied the knot in New York with Jerry, and that I was going to take again my marriage vows in Paris, I thought that I should send a note to Jacques, who was waiting impatiently for my return and give him the news that he would probably totally dislike.

Well, Jacques wrote back right away: "I wish you everything you deserve."

What did he mean by the word "deserve"? His words could be interpreted as signs of pure abhorrence for *petit moi* or as good wishes. Who knows? In any case, this was the last exchange we had with each other! I never heard from him again.

It was also important for me to communicate to Mr. G of American Express that I had gotten married in New York and that I would not be returning to work in early January.

With his congratulations, he said that he was very sorry that I would not be back, but that he could write a letter of recommendation for me to the American Express travel office downtown, on Wall Street.

When I mentioned to Jerry the golden opportunity of getting a job in New York at the American Express travel office, he freaked out and was dead set against it.

I am sure that he was not in favor of me taking the job because it would be far too dangerous. I could meet another nutcase who would have his eyes on *petit moi*!

****

The day had come for Jerry and me to leave New York and start our journey to "*mon Paris.*"

As we were flying over the Atlantic Ocean, I was thinking of the pain I had unconsciously caused my parents by letting my sentiments talk and carrying on with my strong feelings. I just hoped that Maman and Papa would not perceive our action as an indignity, notably an offense against them and that they would understand our decision.

Papa was waiting for us at the Orly Airport. I hugged him and in a soft voice I uttered, "Papa, I want you to meet Jerry, my husband."

Papa greeted Jerry with a polite word of welcome and invited us to follow him to his car in the parking lot.

Within a short time, we arrived at my parents' home, where my mother received us with open arms. Since she was known for her hospitality and courtesy, her friendliness did not surprise me.

I was obviously relieved by my parent's wonderful welcome.

The holidays of Christmas and New Year were, like always, warm and delightful. We shared them with my father's sister's family.

On January 3, 1961, Jerry and I got married religiously at the rue Copernic synagogue, the oldest Reform synagogue in France. Complying with the traditions, we stood under the *chuppah*, (a canopy that symbolizes the home that the couple will build together). Christian, my brother, was Jerry's witness and Papa was my witness. A few family members and friends were present as well.

After a short ceremony performed by the rabbi, we exchanged our vows, signed our marriage license, and Jerry smashed the glass — a beloved tradition that symbolizes 'the absolute finality of the marital covenant."

Later that day, my parents opened their home to about fifty to sixty people for a beautifully catered affair. The buffet was absolutely lovely. Seeing family and friends was a huge joy for me.

With Jerry's rendezvous for work at his French company and with the time I had to spend in the American Embassy filling out the immigration papers required to get the Green Card that would allow me to reside in New York, we only had three days left for a honeymoon.

Jerry asked me to select a place of my choosing for our short post-nuptial vacation. To this day, I do not know what made me choose Amsterdam. I loved the picturesque Dutch capital city with its bountiful canals and its lovely surroundings, but going there during the freezing days of winter was pretty unpleasant. Furthermore, Jerry wanted to see customers, visit his aunt and uncle and spend time at Anne Frank's house, where she lived with her family during World War II. It had recently been turned into a museum, exhibiting lots of memorabilia of the persecution of the Jews.

Our newlywed escapade was certainly totally unlike a traditional honeymoon. But I must acknowledge that we stayed in a fabulous hotel and that, with the exception of the popular raw herring that I loathe, I enjoyed the food.

After returning to Paris, we only had a couple of days left. Then it was time for our goodbyes. I knew that I would be back in the summer, but an *au revoir* is never easy — especially when you feel the heavy heart of your parents.

When the plane took off from Orly Airport, I had tears in my eyes. Jerry put his arms around me and reassured me, with compassion, that his profound love for me was real and as each day passed, his love for me was growing.

****

CHAPTER 13

Leslie

A few days after our return to New York, Jerry's parents wanted to celebrate us — the newlyweds — by inviting family and friends to a lovely catered party in their home.

With the exchange of our vows in New York and the exchange of our vows in Paris, with the reception in my parents' home and with the reception in Jerry's parents' home, our marriage was certainly celebrated by many events!

Now it was time for us to begin our life together in our enchanting new home.

Jerry was totally against me working. He was still from the old school, when the role of a wife was to stand by her husband, give him unconditional love, support him in his endeavors, nurture the children to come and, last but not least, take on the duties of the home.

"Cherie, I earn a good living. You do not need to work," he stated with a smile from ear to ear.

He just did not want me to take on the jobs that I was offered by American Express and Air France.

After a moment of respite, I responded without resistance: "Okey-doke, I will not go into the business world and I will commit myself to you, but I do want to complement my role as a wife with the important role of being a mother as soon as possible."

"You are right. We should start having a family soon."

In February I went along with Jerry to Montreal, where he had a couple of appointments, during which I enjoyed visiting the picturesque colonial district with its old buildings.

Notwithstanding the cold, snowy winter weather, we continued our journey to Niagara Falls and spent the night at the fabulous Marriott Fallsview Hotel. Scenically beautiful, the breathtaking vistas of Niagara Falls were just a pure delight for us.

Shortly after our return from Canada, I found out that I was expecting a baby. Filled with joy and overpowering emotions at the idea of having our first newborn in November, Jerry and I were absolutely ecstatic.

In our building, we met a young couple, Michael and Barbara. We socialized with them right away.

Too unlikely to be believed, but Barbara was expecting, as I was, her first child in November.

Being that Barbara was like me, a stay-at-home wife tending to household affairs, we enjoyed seeing each other and going out together. A sense of camaraderie was kindled between us, which helped me to endure the slow pace of my new lifestyle, compared to the tempo of my Parisian life.

****

As promised by Jerry, towards the end of July we were on our way to Paris. I was delighted to spend time with my family and my friends. And then, to add to my happiness, my mother decided to join us with Roxane, my six-year-old little sister, for a two-week vacation in Switzerland — Jerry's favorite country.

Jerry had selected to go to the peaceful small village of Mürren, perched on the edge of a high cliff rising from the Lauterbrunnen Valley, located in the Jungfrau region. The impressive and amazing panoramic views of the Swiss Alps, with the mountain peaks soaring up in the sky, were breathtaking.

We were staying in the one and only hotel in the village. Built on the edge of the cliff, it was somewhat scary for me to look down!

Other than the scenic views and the mountain climbing, there was basically nothing much to do!

Being seven months pregnant, I could not possibly hike on the steep hills with Jerry, who was a definite pro at it. Fortunately, I was not alone. I had my mother and my sweet little sister Roxane with me. Together, we enjoyed talking and playing games.

All in all, Jerry and I had a good six weeks in Europe.

We went back to our New York way of life. The next few weeks passed swiftly.

****

On November 8, our little baby boy was born. We named him Leslie.

I will never forget Jerry's call to his boss the next morning, when he told him, "I am exhausted. I gave birth to a baby boy during the night."

When he was off the phone, I looked at him and said, "Jerry, you are hilarious! How long did your labor last? Tell me."

In the hospital, I shared a room with a lovely young Belgian lady who had just given birth to a stillborn baby. As I was breastfeeding my little Leslie, I could hear her weeping and lamenting. She was heartbroken. I tried to do my best to ease her grief and console her by showing her solicitude and compassion.

Jerry and I were so happy to go home with our little bundle of joy.

A couple of days after my accouchement, Barbara gave birth to a little baby girl. We shared a lot of time together. During the winter months, we would go to each other's apartment. I can still see our two babies eying each other on my bed. They were adorable.

Two weeks after Leslie's birth, my parents came to New York. I will never forget the Thanksgiving with them when they invited Oma, my in-laws and us to dinner in the beautiful restaurant at the Carlyle, on Madison and 76th Street.

The elegant dining experience in the Regency room was, to say the least, memorable. I still have the menu! When I look at it today, I cannot believe the array of lovely choices for each course. The options were phenomenal, just to mention a few hors d'oeuvres: Supreme of Fresh Fruit au Kirsch, Ecuadorian Shrimp Cocktail, Cape Cod Oysters... Among the variety of choices for the main course: Roast Vermont Turkey with chestnut stuffing, Pilaf of Fresh Maine Lobster Newberg, Roast Rack of Spring Lamb with mint sauce, Long Island Duckling and more. The choices were absolutely incredible! The fine and scrumptious six-course dinner ended with a demitasse and after-dinner mints — all for eight dollars per person!

And that was expensive in 1961. Today you would not get a sandwich for eight dollars!

****

When Leslie was six months old, I had an appointment for him to have a regular check-up and a vaccination. It was Good Friday, April 20, 1962.

We were taken right away to an examination room. The pediatrician came in and asked the nurse to send in another doctor. I found it somewhat bizarre, but in an instant, there was a knock at the door and the second doctor came in.

Leslie was lying on the table quietly. Nodding their heads, the two doctors were not uttering a sound.

As soon as the second doctor left, the pediatrician turned to me and said: "Leslie is a Down syndrome baby."

I stood there speechless. I had to sit down.

"Down syndrome is a genetic disorder caused when a baby has an extra chromosome 21."

Totally tongue-tied and dumbfounded, I remained speechless. However, I had to get up and shake the emotions clouding my head.

"Doctor, why did it take you six months to give me the horrifying news?"

"Well, it was not clear to us. We thought that it would be smarter to say nothing until we were certain that this was the case."

I was so shocked by the doctor's inability to detect and recognize Leslie's condition before!

The pediatrician glanced at me and uttered: "In order to detect if the abnormality is in your genes, you and your husband must go to Mount Sinai Hospital on Monday and take a chromosome test.

Flabbergasted by the horrendous revelation, I barely had time to take a breath, but I had to telephone Jerry.

As I did not want to divulge that our baby boy was abnormal on the phone, I simply told him that our Leslie had medical problems and that he should come right away to the pediatrician's office.

As I was sitting, waiting for Jerry, my thoughts turned to the time of Leslie's birth when I was sharing the room with the young Belgium lady who had given birth to a stillborn baby. How tragic that was! Little had I known what was coming! Not for a moment could I have imagined that six months later, I would find out that my Leslie was a Down syndrome baby.

As soon as Jerry stepped into the examination room, the pediatrician appraised him of Leslie's unpleasantly difficult situation. And then, as if to add to our stupor he said that our baby's flow of blood through the lungs was limited.

After hearing the pediatrician's unsettling prognosis, Jerry and I were, to say the least, dumbfounded. Staggering to our seats, we tried to catch our breath.

We went home without uttering a word.

I do not remember how we spent Easter weekend, troubled we certainly were. But I did my best to keep our routine going.

After the doctor's recommendation, the following Monday, Jerry and I were on our way for a chromosome test.

Jerry asserted that if they detected an abnormality in the chromosome analysis, we did not need to know in whose genes they were. I wholeheartedly agreed with him.

We did not have to wait very long for the results of our tests. We were told that we had no genetic chromosomal abnormalities and that we should have children.

Jerry stated clearly and strongly to me that we should take a break and a pause from the sudden upheaval in our lives. Owing to the recent gripping tragedy, I came to the same point of view. Jerry and I agreed. We needed to spend a few days away.

We opted to take a one-week cruise out of the Port of New York to Nassau and back. Leslie was in the good hands of the baby nurse we had employed during his first week at home.

On our cruise, Jerry said that he did not want to get involved or make any decisions concerning Leslie. He told me that it was up to me to research and determine what we should do.

He just could not face the actuality of our baby boy's condition.

The weight of it all seemed tremendous to me, but I needed to stay strong. I was only 24 years old, but I knew that there are instances in one's life that one cannot obliterate. They are an actuality and one has to face it head-on and do the best one can.

Soon after our return to New York, I had a rendezvous for Leslie with the pediatrician. He greeted us. Then, turning to me, he uttered: "Leslie is a Down syndrome child who suffers from a chronic bronchial condition which requires special care in a mountainous climate. You should look into the possibilities."

I started my exploratory investigating right away. I got in touch with several organizations and I spoke to many physicians. My probing went on for a good couple of months. Difficult it was, but I was not going to leave my Leslie just anywhere. It was absolutely vital to find the right place for him and it was also crucial that I would be able to look at myself in a mirror and know that I was living by my moral principles, by doing my utmost for my baby boy.

A few weeks after our cruise, I found out that I was pregnant. When I think that on Easter Monday, we were told that our genes were normal, Jerry and I had certainly not wasted time!

Coming back to my research and decision-making for Leslie: I definitely did not care for the facilities that I visited on the East Coast. So, I thought of crossing the Atlantic Ocean and carrying out my research by contacting doctors and organizations in the Western Alps. With this systematic search, I found several possibilities.

It was decided that Jerry and I would take Leslie to Europe in August and that we would select one of the homes for him.

Well, without going into the details of our visits to three homes, with my parents who joined us, it was not difficult to opt for the beautiful home near Mont-Salève run by Mademoiselle P.

Right away we knew that we had found the place. I liked the fact that Mademoiselle P had a dozen employees to assist her in the care of the ten children she was responsible for, and to add to my relief, the little ones were all under six years old. To my surprise, the youngsters came from different parts of the world!

Mademoiselle P asserted that our nine-month-old Leslie would be sleeping in her bedroom and that she would watch him attentively.

As much as I had a heavy heart leaving the little pearl of my heart, I knew for sure that I had discovered the perfect environment for him.

Jerry had made reservations for us to head to Florence, Italy. I could well imagine how this lovely city, in the beautiful Tuscany region, could have inspired the Renaissance painters, but my thoughts were with my Leslie.

Coming home empty-handed was not easy. Fortunately, Mademoiselle P was constantly in contact with us. She kept us abreast of Leslie's latest developments, she sent us pictures, and she kept us up-to-date on the events and celebrations taking place in the home. Notwithstanding the thousands of miles that separated us, I could always feel her warmth and devotion. My parents visited him, and we made visits as well.

On August 15th at 4 A.M. we got a phone call from Mademoiselle P attesting tearfully that, suddenly breathless with a sharp chest pain, Leslie had expired in her arms.

Leslie was 21 months old.

Mademoiselle P had our little angel for one year. And now, he had left the world.

The little pearl of my heart was no longer in existence; a part of me no longer existed.

CHAPTER 14

Anecdotes and Encounters

Heartbroken as I was with the death of my Leslie, I was thankful that I had Marc in January. And grateful to have Richard, two and a half years later.

As I am reminiscing and pondering my memories. I cannot believe how the palm reader could have foretold so clearly my future in July 1960!

"I see you going way over the seas."

Well, after meeting Jerry at the end of August, I crossed the Atlantic Ocean in October!

"You will be married before the end of the year"

Well, I married Jerry on December 3, 1960!

"You will have three children; however, you will have a lamentable tragedy."

Well, I had three children, and I certainly had an unmeasurable tragedy with my Leslie.

"You will have a long life."

Well, I am still here, writing about it in my eighties!

There I was, a total stranger to this lady, yet in a few minutes, she was able to divulge to me what was going to happen, exactly, in my future. It was just too extraordinary to believe! Her insight into the reality of what was yet to come was, to say the least, fascinating to me.

I am really in awe of palm readers and fortune-tellers. Their spiritual practices enable them to discover, untangle and interpret an individual's life path. Incredible for sure!

****

Jerry and I were certainly blessed to have our two boys. We felt so fortunate to have them.

Every stage of their development, from their infancy to their adulthood, was animated with their imagination, their youthful mischievousness and their unpredictable prankishness.

I'll never forget that afternoon in the playground on Fifth Avenue and 84th Street. Rick was quietly playing in the sandbox, while Marc was going in circles on his tricycle, a little boy speeding along at his side. The youngsters stopped and confronted each other. I went over and queried, "Boys, are you okay?"

A lady appeared before me asserting, with a snobbish and arrogant tone: "I am Mrs. Kennedy."

Looking at her, I imitated her stuck-up demeanor and replied, "I am Mrs. Bessinger."

She lived across the street, but I never saw her again.

****

Marc, you pushed it!

Ricky, you wanted it!

Dad, you fancied it!

But Mom allowed it!

What am I referring to? Well, it was a quiet autumn day. Jerry needed to rest and recover from pneumonia, so I decided to take the boys to the playground.

On Fifth Avenue, between 86th and 87th streets, a man standing by a huge container filled with tiny kittens was bellowing repeatedly, "I am looking for a good home for my kittens."

The boys ran to see the tiny kittens. They were thrilled and did not want to leave. After quite a long while, I was able to get them to the playground.

Once there, they refused to let go of me. They pleaded for my understanding and begged me to take a kitten home.

"Mom, this is the only thing I'll ever want from you," Marc shouted out.

On our way home, the boys ran ahead of me. Seeing Marc with the tiny bundle of fur in his arms, I finally gave in and brought the kitten home.

Jerry took hold of the kitten and inspected the feline. He declared, emphatically, "No, I will not accept a female cat in the house. You must take it back and ask the man for a male cat."

Somewhat disconcerted, Marc implored that I go with him and ask the man for a male kitten.

Well, we were lucky. Marc succeeded in carrying his new playmate home, tucked into his coat.

Jumping up and down with happiness, the boys' spirited outburst electrified the already sparkling atmosphere with even more enthusiasm.

Then, whispering into my ear, Marc uttered, "Mom, this is the best day of my life. I love you. Thank you for letting me bring Kitty home."

Kitty's bicolored silky fur coat gave him a definite air of elegance. The contrast of his cameo-white chest and white paws with his striped grey body endowed our pussy cat with a certain touch of class! Furthermore, his almond green eyes sparkled with intelligence.

Kitty followed Marc and Ricky everywhere, and he took part in all of their activities. He snuggled against them, crouched on top of the glass doors, watched them taking their baths, and slept with Marc.

At meal times, he was a well-mannered pussy cat, but at other times, he could be an incorrigible thief!

We loved having him for about thirteen years. Kitty was certainly a joy for all of us.

****

Our two boys had both parents in common, but like most siblings, they had different inclinations.

Early on, Marc had great fun with his G.I. Joe toys and their multiple accessories. He enjoyed playing with his cars, trucks and trains as well. And last but not least, he loved watching TV shows and listening to the rock and pop music of the 60's, 70's and 80's.

His favorite costume for Halloween was definitely the jumpsuit with the big S on the chest, the large cape and all the little odds and ends that completed his accoutrement as the invincible alien hero *Superman*.

Richard's first choice was to play with his puppets. Young as he was, his imagination and creativity were unbelievable. Jerry and I gave him a puppet theater. We loved watching him manipulating his marionettes and listening to his wonderful made-up stories.

As I am enjoying reminiscing about the young years of my boys, I could never forget when my ten-year-old Richard was chosen, out of his entire school, to pose as a model for The New York Times. As I am glancing at his picture, I laugh. Unsmiling but adorable, he was!

Browsing through my photo albums, I fall upon Marc's picture, at the age of fourteen, standing with his arms in the air at the top of a human pyramid — his classmates. With his skill and his balance, he could have worked for a circus!

They both were engaged in playing soccer and baseball.

****

As Jerry promised, we would go at least once a year to Europe.

In spite of the considerable distance between New York and Paris, my family was always of utmost importance to me. Consequently, I had the earnest wish that my boys have a bond with my parents and my siblings and get to know them.

They certainly did and it warmed my heart to see their strong connection.

Every summer, we would spend six weeks in Europe. My parents invited us on a couple of scenically beautiful trips to Southwest France. The

Atlantic coast region was always my father's favorite destination. The boys enjoyed the beaches and so did we!

At times, my mother and Roxane would join us at a Swiss resort like Grindelwald in the Bernese Alps or Verbier in the canton of Valais, but I will never forget our enjoyable vacation in 1967 when we stayed along the charming Riviera di Levante in Santa Margherita Ligure in Italy. Marc and Richard were enthralled to have their teenage aunt and their loving grandmother on the beach to play with them, and I can still see my boys jumping up and down on the ferry boat heading to the picturesque fishing village of Portofino. Our few hours there were absolutely enchanting.

Nevertheless, the mountains of Switzerland were of paramount importance for Jerry. It was his world. But to go every summer to a small resort on top of a mountain and stay in a little chalet hotel without any ambiance for three weeks was not for *petit moi*!

After a stay in the gorgeous Swiss resort of Zermatt, famous for its fabulous Matterhorn, we returned to Paris. I met up with my Aunt Huguette and told her that as much as I appreciate the beautiful scenery of the mountain resorts, I found that by eight o'clock in the evening, there was no *joie de vivre*. The elderly would retire to their rooms and the mountain climbers would go to bed early to leave at five o'clock in the morning for their hikes.

My aunt looked at me and said, "You should try a Club Med vacation. They have seaside villages and mountain villages in different countries and they offer all kinds of sports and activities. They also provide amusement and enjoyment for every age."

Jerry understood my strong desire to try something different.

The following summer, after spending a couple of weeks in the Swiss mountains, we proceeded to Donoratico, a Club Med village on the Mediterranean in the heart of Tuscany, where we sojourned for another two weeks.

Without a doubt, it was a thoroughly enjoyable and unforgettable experience. A magnificent forest along the sea adorned the glorious landscape. The beach did not only offer sand and water; you could play volleyball, sail and go swimming in the sea or in the swimming pools, play tennis, go for archery, aerobics and more. Games and activities were endless. The entertainment on the stage of the outdoor theater was a pleasure. The discotheque, the bar and the restaurant were always filled with a marvelous *joie de vivre*.

The gourmet cuisine and the table delicacies were sublime, but they had nothing in common with our accommodations in the straw hut village.

We had to use flashlights to find our way in the dark of the forest, and we needed them in our hut as well. We shared the shower rooms with a number of people at the same time!

Believe it or not, it reminded me of my camping days as a Girl Scout.

The boys were enthralled by the wide range of sports, games and activities offered by the Mini Club.

With the feasting and the sociability between the hosts and the guests, the village was a wonderful bubble of conviviality.

Jerry agreed with me that Club Med vacations would be ideal for our family and that he would concede to it, but that he needed a village with the comfort of a room with a bathroom!

The following year, we went to the Club Med in St. Moritz, Switzerland, but our favorite Club Med in Switzerland was definitely Villars-sur-Ollon

— we vacationed there at least thirty times! There we could enjoy our favorite activities. Jerry could always find people to hike with. He also

delighted in riding a cow on the grasslands. He asserted that mounting a cow was less snobbish than mounting a horse! Ha Ha! Funny Jerry.

I liked going on a few hikes as well, but I preferred the aerobics, the tennis, the swimming in the pool and last but not least, the Scrabble tournaments which were always a pure joy for me. I won a gold medal for Scrabble.

The boys had a great time sharing all kinds of fun with their newly made friends. They also loved participating in stage shows.

My Club Med experiences in Switzerland, France, Corsica, Italy, Greece, Martinique, Florida, the Dominican Republic and Mexico were always a pleasure. Faithful for at least forty years, I was definitely a fan of Club Med.

When Marc and Richard turned thirteen, we celebrated their Bar Mitzvah — an important milestone — and to add to their joyous occasion, Jerry and I decided to take them for new discoveries to Israel. The trips were fascinating and magnificent.

I certainly believe that traveling and exploring different countries is not only awe-inspiring and amazing, but it also enriches one's life. Visiting sights and hearing about the history are important, but learning about the culture and the everyday life of people around the world is even more significant.

* * * * * * * * * * * * * * * * * *

Jerry and I established a secure routine of school, homework, sports, entertainment and birthday parties for our boys.

We would spend every weekend in Queens with Oma and my in-laws. Jerry had a set belief about treating his Oma — la doyenne — and his parents with the reverence and the respect due to elders. With my humble submission and deference to Jerry's wishes, I agreed.

The boys enjoyed the garden with its inflated pool; they loved helping their grandfather with his gardening and more.

I remember telling Opi, my father-in-law, that I loved his roses, his lawns, his bushes, his raspberries, his tomatoes and his green peppers, but that his garden was missing a fruit tree!

On these good words, Opi invited me to go with him to the tree nursery. There, he ordered a cherry tree, which was delivered and planted a few hours later!

What a treat it was! The cherries were succulent. I can still see my boys climbing up and eating them off the tree!

When Jerry would go for a nap in the afternoon, I would play Scrabble with my father in-law. He loved the game, but he was a poor loser!

****

Richard was four years old and he was going to begin preschool.

With the two boys in school, I was thinking of starting a business of my own, importing ornaments for home decor from countries around the world.

As soon as Jerry understood that I had a strong desire to work outside of the home, he immediately put forward for consideration that I teach French. He emphasized that, even though I could make more money in a business, a career in the teaching field would work out well for me since I would have the same schedule and vacations as our boys.

Taking into account the pros and cons, I took heed of Jerry's suggestion and decided to contemplate a possible future for myself in the teaching field.

As I was checking several potential schools, I heard that my boys' private school had just lost one of their two schoolmistresses teaching French.

After a few significant interviews with the headmistress and some board members of the school, I was told that I would certainly be a good candidate for the assignment, but that I needed to take a few psychology classes — a program which would help me to communicate with the students and better understand their behavior!

I understood that this was mandatory, so I went along with it and got the position.

For ten years, I put my heart and soul into my teaching. I had classes from kindergarten to the eighth grade.

I can still see myself with the kindergarteners. There I was, on the floor with them. We would build a village or a town with houses, people, animals, trees, cars, etc. Then, I would pick up one item at a time and ask them to repeat after me: *la fille* (the girl), *le garçon* (the boy), *la maison* (the house), and so on. They loved it and retained everything. They were my best students!

I always made sure to come well prepared for each of the levels that I taught. I invested a great deal of time in my work. Anxious to impart the language to my students with frequently used vocabulary, I also wanted to bring a sparkle of the excitement and humor of my French background with artifacts, pictures of France, games, puzzles and records with songs in French.

I wanted them to have more than the language. I wanted them to have some knowledge of the social and traditional culture of France.

I was not only a member of the school staff; I was also a member of the school parent group. I served on the Parents' Committee. Very involved, I chaired for many years an event, a carnival and bazaar to raise money for children whose parents could not afford the tuition and needed assistance.

I am happy to say that my long-range planning to strive for a high goal was very successful.

For decades, I volunteered to help and participated in many, many events: book fairs and carnivals in my boys' high school, events at the synagogue to help raise money for poor people.

My efforts and endeavors were always rewarded by an overwhelming feeling of having been able to give a hand to underprivileged human beings.

I was also there to help family members, neighbors and friends, as well.

****

On December 4, 1982, my father-in-law passed away. My mother-in-law's weakness from a stroke and her despondency had turned into depression. On that day, I told Jerry that his mother needed to come home with us and that I wished to take care of her.

Marc had left our home for the university and Richard was in his last year of high school.

For the next four months, I nursed Omi morning, noon and night until I was able to put her back on her feet. Then, I emptied her house, found an apartment for her near us and hired a live-in aid. During the day, I would take her to a museum and wheel her around, take her to see a movie, organize tea parties for her and more. We invited her to go with us to Paris and to the mountain resort of Villars-sur-Ollon as well.

****

I had been so absorbed with my mother-in-law that it was only after her death that I realized the huge void left by my best friends' departures from New York: Tatiana had gone back to Rio de Janeiro, Paule and other pals had returned to France…

Now, I needed to make new friends.

As I was pondering how to go about it, the idea of launching a Scrabble club in French jumped into my head.

In the early fall of 1985, on a Tuesday, I approached the French Institute/ Alliance Française and told them that I would like to gather a group of people at their location for tournaments of *Scrabble en duplicate*.

"Very nice, but Scrabble is not for us. You should go on Thursday to the French Consulate and ask about "Accueil New York." Their mission is to welcome, inform and entertain French expatriates. Put forward your suggestion to them."

I was ready to take a chance and hopefully achieve my desired aim. So, without hesitation, on Thursday I made my way to the Consulate and met some charming hostesses, members of Accueil New York. The organization had an impressive range of activities, but a Scrabble club was missing!

I decided to become a member of Accueil New York right away.

The ladies were extremely happy and absolutely excited about my idea.

No need to say more. The following Monday, I had in my living room sixteen Scrabble fans of all ages, and for about thirty years I opened my door every Monday afternoon. Every player had to bring their own game. I picked out the letters randomly, gave everyone three minutes and took the scores. We continued with the best-chosen word. They had a choice of tea, coffee or cold beverages and cookies.

Shortly after, I launched a Mahjong club on Thursday afternoons in my home.

Along the way, I made some wonderful friends. But unfortunately now, they all have left New York.

But to this day, every Monday, via Skype, eight of us from the original group, play Duplicate Scrabble.

For the two players in the United States, it is 8 am. For the four players in France and the player in Belgium, it is 2 pm, and for the player in Japan it is 9 pm. Notwithstanding the time difference, we are faithful players who share the same interest.

****

When I think of these years, my life was, to say the least, filled with diverse experiences. Besides being a wife and a mother who was totally engaged in doing the best for her family, I was still able to pay close attention to my teaching and participate in many events to help the underprivileged or simply be compassionate to others.

CHAPTER 15

Life is a Double-Edged Sword

As the years passed, the boys were going on with their lives studying, dating, traveling, working…

After my precious mother's passing away at the end of August 1986, Papa was never abandoned. My siblings were always there for him, and I continued crossing the Atlantic Ocean twice a year to visit him. Papa came several times to New York. I remember our walks in Central Park, when he admired the green glow of the trees with the sunlight through the leafy branches. He also enjoyed going to the Metropolitan Museum to visit the galleries of the 17th and 18th century European paintings, his favorite époque. Papa would stand in front of a canvas, without moving, checking every detail for at least ten minutes!

I must admit that, at times, I found it a little tedious!

Papa seemed to find joy in all the happenings and activities during his visits with us.

Flashing back to our good times together, the summer of 1988 comes to my mind when we invited him to spend a week with us at the Club Med of Villars sur Ollon. Papa loved the scenery, the garden, the walks, the food and more than anything, playing bridge — his passion!

In January 1996, Papa passed away. I was in Paris, at his side, the last three weeks of his life.

Sad I was; both my parents had left this world, but they will always be in my heart.

****

Life is a double-edged sword — a mixed bowl of blessings and troublesome challenges.

Now, I would like to share with you some of the beautiful and wonderful experiences I had traveling with my Jerry. Our wide-ranging trips have certainly enriched my life.

How could I ever forget our 1991 summer vacation in Turkey! We started by spending a week in the fabulous European-Asian city of Istanbul. On the evening of our arrival at the delightful President Hotel, Jerry was going down to ask the concierge for the name of a good restaurant on the waterfront. Strangely enough, a lady walked into the elevator with him and was heading to the concierge with the same inquiry!

Without hesitation, the concierge gave them the address of a renowned fish restaurant. Jerry introduced himself to Dominique, who had just arrived from Paris with her husband Hichemi and their daughter Sarah. After consideration, they decided that we should all meet in the lobby and go out for dinner together.

In an instant, we became friends and spent our entire week together. I would see them in Paris, in New York; we traveled to Montreal and Quebec together and more. To this day, I am in contact with Sarah. Sadly, Dominique has passed away.

Now, coming back to our stay in Istanbul, we certainly enjoyed ambling around the beautiful mosques, palaces and museums. We loved cruising down the Bosphorus with views of the Orient and the Occident. We had fun looking around the Grand Bazaar, the largest underground market. I had never encountered so much haggling!

As we were ambling through the fashion district, we came across stores filled with designer dresses. Dominique and I were totally enamored by the style and the elegance of Turkish clothing. She bought a dress and I bought an exquisite evening gown. I still have it hanging in my closet!

Jerry and I did not want to miss the flavor and customs of Turkish culture. Our dinner at the Orient House Restaurant was amazing. While we were savoring our excellent meal, the sensual belly dance performance went on, and then, to our astonishment, Jerry and I were asked to join them on the stage! I must admit that wiggling my belly is not up my alley! But high-spirited, we were animated by the lovely music and we danced. It was, indeed, a night to remember!

After our goodbyes to our new friends, we sailed across the Marmara Sea to Izmir. Cruising the Turkish coast was phenomenal. The ship passed Gallipoli and then funneled into the Dardanelles straits.

Our sojourn in Izmir was filled with the discovery of an abundance of sites. The lovely promenade along the Aegean Sea was delightful. We enjoyed our stroll around the bazaar district; smells and flavors of spices came from all sides; food vendors were everywhere.

Our day in Ephesus, which was originally part of Ancient Greece, was a wonderful experience. We saw the ruins and the archeological museum, which was prodigious.

Jerry and I were absolutely enthralled by our unbelievable venture into the Turkish world.

****

Exploring the sights on our unforgettable Greek Island cruise the following year was a fabulous experience for Jerry and me. We were completely enamored by all the Greek Islands. I was totally enraptured by the white architecture of Santorini and the famous island of Mykonos. For Jerry, who had dreamt of being an archaeologist, the vestiges of the archaeological sites of Rhodes were enthralling.

****

Our cruise, a year later in 1993, from Oslo to Bergen, was certainly very different. The Norwegian fjords, surrounded by the mountain scenery, were impressive.

I will never forget the colorful facades of the houses in Bergen and our stop at the picturesque fish market. The variety of fish was unbelievable. In the evening, we were invited to attend a beautiful Scandinavian folkloric show. Watching the old Norwegian traditional dancing was a pleasure.

After our superb cruise, we stayed for a couple of nights in Oslo. I can still remember our emotions when we caught sight of the granite, bronze and wrought iron sculptures of the naked figures in the Vigeland Park. The sexual positions were certainly more than what Jerry and I ever expected!

From Oslo, we cruised to Copenhagen. Visiting the Danish capital reminded me of my trip with the Girl Scouts, years back! But for Jerry it was all new — he had never been to Denmark before.

We enjoyed our boat ride along the canal. The red, turquoise, yellow, pink, green and orange 17th and 18th century houses on the waterfront of the Nyhavn district reminded us of Bergen. On our stroll along the Langelinie promenade, we stop to admire the iconic bronze sculpture of the Little Mermaid sitting on a rock by the waterside. We dined in a lovely restaurant at the Tivoli Gardens. The famous amusement park, with its manicured garden and twinkling lights, was magical and enchanting.

The next day, we crossed the sound by ferry to the scenic coastal city of Helsingborg, in Sweden. Walking around the old city and the medieval fortress for a few hours was a pleasure.

Before leaving Denmark, we visited the magnificent Kronborg Castle in Helsinger, the splendidly decorated Rosenberg Castle in the heart of Copenhagen, and last but not least, the 17th-century Rundetaam Round Tower.

After this superb Scandinavian trip, we stopped for a few days in Paris before returning to our New York life.

* * * * * * * * * * * * * * * * * *

Motivated by our curiosity, desire and eagerness to see the unique and beautiful treasures of different countries, Jerry and I had a thirst for travel.

Indeed, we continued…

After our usual great vacation in Villars sur Ollon in 1994, we proceeded to Genoa, Italy, to board the SS Monterey.

Jerry and I loved cruises. For one thing, one does not have to worry about packing and unpacking; the luggage followed us, and one can hop off the ship and venture anywhere unencumbered.

Our first stop was Valencia, Spain. We walked around the lovely city. When we returned to the ship that evening, Jerry and I were invited to the captain's table for dinner. The warmth of our Italian host, the soft music and the excellent candlelight dinner added up to an ambiance like no other. What an awesome evening that was!

Sailing down the Mediterranean Sea was delightful. When we got to Gibraltar, Jerry and I had such great fun playing with a bunch of little macaques.

Then we visited St. Michael's cave; we were in awe of the rock formations in the massive cavern.

Our exhilarating cruise continued in the Atlantic Ocean, with wonderful stops on the island of Madeira and in the Canary Islands, Tenerife and Lanzarote. Sauntering around the pretty islands was pure joy, but the volcanic landscape with craters and lava was definitely a new experience for us.

A couple of days later, the ship dropped anchor in Casablanca. Passing through the typical villages on our way to Marrakech was delightful. Historic Medina, with its colorful souks and the mosques, was fascinating to Jerry and me. But the most striking of all was our buffet lunch in a "caidale" tent, with an amazing folkloric show with Moroccan singing, music and horseback riding. It surpassed our expectations.

In hindsight, as much as I was captivated by the beauty of the town, I am still carrying terrifying memories of the snake charmers, with their snakes draped around their neck and wiggling out of baskets all over the Central Square. Entertaining for some people, but definitely not for *petit moi*!

As we were passing through the Strait of Gibraltar, where the Atlantic meets the Mediterranean, Jerry and I were relaxing on the deck when, to our surprise, a dazzling display of whales and dolphins was flipping around in their natural habitat. It all happened right in front of our eyes. What an unforgettable show that was!

Our ship stopped in Malaga, from which we visited Granada. Then, before reaching Genoa, our final destination, we were able to enjoy a wonderful day in the beautiful metropolis of Barcelona. All in all, our cruise was delightful.

As I am writing about my wonderful trips with Jerry, I must not forget to mention our 1994 Thanksgiving weekend in the attractive capital of the United States — Washington D.C. In addition to the White House, the Albert Einstein Planetarium and the many historical monuments, Jerry insisted on going to the Holocaust Museum. When I saw the railway car used for deportation on display, I was too upset to continue the visit. My thoughts were with family members who had been deported. Jerry followed me out. Unhappily, we both left with a heavy heart.

With our positive approach to embracing new horizons and different cultures, Jerry and I had a strong desire to continue to take trips.

After our faithful stay in Paris to see my family and our vacation in Villars-sur-Ollon, we left the Swiss Alps to go once again to Genoa, to board one of our favorite ships, the SS Monterey.

As soon as we reached Naples, we hopped off the ship and headed for Pompeii. Seeing the vestiges, the artifacts and the skeletons of this ancient buried city was, to say the least, harrowing to us. As much as Jerry was always fascinated by archaeological sites, I could see a feeling of apprehension on his face. He was actually concerned that the active volcano of Mount Vesuvius would erupt again! Fortunately, we made it back to the ship safely and we were able to enjoy the swimming pool, the good food, the shows, the dancing and the romantic pleasures of being in each other's arms as we were sailing on the Mediterranean.

After arriving in the Port of Alexandria in Egypt, we headed to Cairo on a tour bus to see the pyramids of Giza and the Sphinx, built on the sands of the Sahara Desert. I could not believe that a huge modern hotel was erected so close to these monumental sculptures. The architectural contrast was, for sure, ridiculous.

We went with our guide and our group to a typical Egyptian restaurant for lunch. The Eastern Mediterranean cuisine was certainly a pleasure to eat, but the succulent dessert with dates, almonds and honey was a treat beyond words!

In due course, we arrived at the Museum of Egyptian Antiquities. We tried to appreciate the valuable, extensive collection from days of yore, but with the unbearable heat and no air in the galleries, Jerry and I could hardly breathe. To put it mildly, our visit was utterly exhausting!

At the end of our trying day, we were returning to our buses when we discovered, to our horror, that they were surrounded by policemen on motorcycles. Apparently, gunmen were opening fire on tourists. The air was thick with apprehension and dismay. We did not feel safe.

Fortunately, we made it back to the ship.

When we arrived in the Port of Ashdod in Israel, we met Jerry's cousin Michael and his wife Sima. Michael drove us up to the Old City of Jerusalem where we were able to see, once again, the wall of the Jewish temple, the Muslim Dome of the Rock, and the Christian Church of the Sepulchre. We had an enchanting day together.

Rhodes was our next stop. Jerry and I were enthralled by the magnificent Gothic architecture of the palace of the Grand Master of the Knights of Rhodes, which overlooks the medieval city. Then, to Jerry's delight, we visited, once again, the archeological site in Lindos.

Fortunately for us, it was never a problem to return to interesting places. Hooray! It was a good thing since our next port was Istanbul!

What a treat it was for us to go back to this magnificent, historic Byzantine city on the Bosphorus!

Our last stop, before returning to Naples, was Messina, on the east coast of Sicily. Before getting off the ship, Jerry and I went down to have breakfast. The waiter approached our table and asked us if we had heard tumultuous and loud noise during the night.

"Yes," I answered. "Something was going on at the pool deck above us during the night. Furthermore, we saw several police guards on our deck."

"Do not worry. Buscetta, the head of the Sicilian Mafia, was removed from the ship by helicopter in the middle of the night. While he was sunbathing and dancing in the ship's ballroom, he was identified and photographed by a journalist."

I could not believe that such a man was on our August 1995 cruise. Not only were we neighbors on the ship with him, his wife Cristina and their son Stephano, but I was at his side in the hot tub the day before!

After our waiter's disclosure, I was not too sure that I wanted to get off the ship in Messina, a city well known for members of the Sicilian mafia. But Jerry insisted that we should go on our tour to Taormina.

The views of the sea and Mt. Etna from Taormina's rocky terrace high above the Ionian Sea were superb. Strolling the streets and the gardens and climbing up to the castle held my attention. I could put to rest my Mafiosi phobia!

To this day, I still have the copies of articles in the Italian newspapers *Corriere della Sera* and *La Republica* and the magazine *Oggi* about Buscetta's removal from the ship, with pictures!

When we reached the vibrant city of Naples, we ambled around the winding cobblestones streets.

Our cruise was coming to an end. Jerry and I were, of course, thrilled to experience some of the magic of these different port cities.

****

A few months later, Jerry and I opted to spend Thanksgiving weekend in Philadelphia, so that we could see more of America. We stayed in the downtown Ritz-Carlton. We were enthralled by the elegance and luxury of our hotel.

Our guided sightseeing tours encompassed the Philadelphia Museum of Art, the Rodin Museum and more.

Philadelphia's historic district was definitely interesting. But our Thanksgiving repast at the City Tavern surpassed our expectations. We were told that Washington ate there and that Jefferson, Adams, Franklin, and Paul Revere held meetings there. Unfortunately, we came too late to see them! We could not have picked a better place for our holiday celebration. The ambiance and the food were superb.

The following year, in May 1996, Jerry and I wished to visit the Pennsylvania Amish countryside.

A farmer and his lovely wife gave us a buggy ride tour along the winding country roads, through the tranquil farmlands. Since the horse-and-buggy was the only mode of transportation for the Amish, we were not alone on the route — the clippity-clop of horses was everywhere.

Passing by the simple log cabins in the Amish villages, I noticed that the men and the young boys were all wearing black attire and black felt hats and that the women and the young girls were all wearing plain long dresses with white or black bonnets. It gave me the impression of crawling into the yesteryear of the 18th century. Without a doubt, the country landscape and the atmosphere had nothing in common with our urban environment!

Jerry and I wanted to know more about the Amish way of life. The friendly couple responded right away by explaining that the Amish lifestyle was based on Christianity, on simple living, plain dressing, inflexible rules, discipline and hard work. The children do not attend regular schools; they are not allowed to leave the Amish community.

Jerry and I were rather disheartened by their austere way of life. Their culture and customs were not for *petit moi*! But it is so important to open our eyes to different lifestyles and surroundings. Without a doubt, these experiences enrich our lives.

****

For our August 1996 cruise, after Villars sur Ollon, Jerry and I made our way to Genoa to board the Rhapsody. Some of our ports were *du déjà vu*, such as Naples, our first stop.

As soon as we reached Volos, in Greece, Jerry and I elected to take a tour bus to visit the unique Orthodox monastery built on natural pillars on the very top of the Meteora. Monks were living there. The views and the landscape were phenomenal. But when we started our descent on the very narrow, winding road, I was so scared by the steep slope that I ended up sitting on the floor of our bus. I did not want to see the precipitous wall of rock.

I have never been so frightened!

To our great joy, Istanbul was part of our itinerary. Jerry and I were enchanted with our visit to Topkapi, the beautiful imperial harem where the Ottoman sultan lived with his concubines. Seemingly, it was in a sultan's power to own women!

Our visit to Istanbul would never have been complete without seeing again the artistic Byzantine Grand Mosque of Sophia.

My favorite island, Mykonos, with the iconic windmills, was our next port. Jerry and I spent the day on a paradisiacal sandy beach with lovely surroundings. Heavenly, it was.

Then, back on the Turkish coastline, the ship stopped in another brilliant destination, the city of Bodrum. From there, we could not miss visiting the remains of the Mausoleum of Halicarnassus, one of the Seven Wonders of the World, which was destroyed by many earthquakes. Walking around the ruins was impressive.

Then, Jerry and I proceeded to the Bodrum Amphitheater, dating back to the 4th century BC. Not a soul was there, and we went up the steps to the top to admire the magnificent views of the mountains and the sea.

As soon as our ship docked in the Port of Rhodes in front of Catherine's Gate and the remnants of the old ramparts, Jerry and I were on our way to the old Kahal Synagogue before visiting, once again, the Palace of the Grand Masters.

Since our ship remained tied to the dock for the evening, we had time to have a glass of ouzo, the widely consumed anise-flavored aperitif, and some little appetizers in a delightful bar-restaurant along the Aegean Sea. The ambiance there was simply alluring.

Our next venture was to Heraklion, the capital of the island of Crete. As we meandered around the vibrant and attractive old city, we walked into the magnificent Agios Minas cathedral. Jerry and I had never expected to see such richness in the interior; the frescos and stained-glass windows were stunning.

Then, after enjoying a delicious Greek salad, some goat cheese and some sweet red-skinned grapes, we joined a tour to visit the archeological site of Knossos, to see what is left of the Palace of the Minoans. To set foot once again in a place of mythology, history and legends was somewhat bewitching for Jerry and *petit moi*!

After our ship docked in Syracuse, Jerry and I had a thirst to discover the city's rich Greek and Roman heritage. We started our day by going to the city's grandiose and ancient Greek Theater. For sure, it was not to be missed.

Then, we headed to the lovely Baroque city of Noto. What a delight that was to walk around this truly unique little 18th century town at the foot of the mountains!

On our last evening on the ship, we were invited by the captain to a cocktail party. It was such an engaging and congenial soiree, but it was time for us to say our *arrivederci, adieu*, bye-bye, *sayonara* get-together.

Our zig-zagging cruise between Italy, Greece, Turkey and Sicily was unfortunately ending. But without a doubt, discovering the historical beauty along the way was fascinating for Jerry and *petit moi*.

After disembarking in Genoa, we traveled by train to Milano for an overnight stay. In the afternoon, after our guided tour of La Scala, the prominent opera house, we had a leisurely stroll under the arcade of the famous Galleria.

On the next day, we boarded a train for Brussels. There, we met up with our adorable niece Emmanuelle. Jerry was eager to show us the nice neighborhood where he had lived during all of his primary school years. Overcome with emotion, he pointed out the house.

We moved slowly to the magnificent Grande Place. We strolled along the Rue des Bouchers, a street with lots of chocolate boutiques. *Miam! Miam!* Since I know that I am a chocolate connoisseur, I believe that the best tasting chocolate in the world is, for sure, Belgian!

The following day, Emmanuelle invited us to go to Bruges. With its unique architecture along the river, canals and old bridges, it did not surprise me that people called it the "Venice of the North." We continued our journey to the seaside resort in Zeebrugge. Walking on the beautiful sandy beach, surrounded by dunes, was delightful!

Our last pause before our return to New York was obviously *mon* Paris. Notwithstanding that we wanted to spend as much time as possible with family and friends, we decided to take a day trip to Giverny. Visiting Claude Monet's charming house and colorful gardens was a real treat for us. It so happens that Impressionism is my favorite period in art. I love the clarity with which the artists express their ideas and feelings.

Our entire dazzling summer vacation had a marvelous golden glow for Jerry and me.

When I expressed to Jerry my desire to go to New Orleans, he liked the idea and told me to make plans right away for Christmas/New Year's week.

After our arrival on Christmas eve at the lovely InterContinental Hotel, Jerry and I wanted to have dinner in a restaurant near the Cathedral Basilica of Saint Louis, before heading to the midnight mass. We had no reservation; all the restaurants were booked solid or they were closed! Finally, we were able to get a table at Patout's, a restaurant in a historic building. While we were consuming our oysters and Cajun seafood, we heard some enchanting live Cajun music. Then, promptly, we made it to the cathedral to listen to the lovely prelude and the beautiful midnight mass.

As soon as we left the church, I started to feel very nauseous. I made it just in time to our hotel room. I had a dreadful night with no sleep, feeling queasy. People were dying from an outbreak of oyster-related gastroenteritis in New Orleans. After a day in bed, I was fortunate to recover.

Jerry and I were able to discover the beauty and grandeur of the Oak Alley and Laura Creole plantations. We loved taking the exquisite trolley ride through the Garden District. Visiting the old south swamp was certainly an adventure. Walking around the French Quarter and listening to a concert at the Jazz Bistro was a real joy. It was a celebration of New Orleans' culture.

While there were some zig-zags on the path, my wonderful voyages with my Jerry will always stay with me.

CHAPTER 16

Wonder, Amazement or Disquietude

In March 1997, I crossed the Atlantic Ocean with Jerry, Marc and Richard to attend my nephew Philippe's amazing wedding to Sophie.

After their ceremony and ring exchange in the elegant 16th Arrondissement Town Hall, we were all invited to join them at the Place du Trocadero for some photo-taking.

I'll never forget our rides on the merry-go-round. Sitting on vintage carousel horses with a view of the Eiffel Tower was, beyond doubt, an unusual thrill for Jerry and me!

In the evening, we were invited for a high-end dinner and dance reception at the sumptuous Pavillon Dauphine, situated at the edge of the Bois de Boulogne.

Needless to say, my handsome nephew Philippe and his beautiful bride were absolutely enchanting.

While enjoying the very happy, animated party, I was elated to be surrounded by all my siblings, their families and my cousins.

* * * * * * * * * * * * * * * * * *

A short time after our return from Europe, Jerry set forth that he wanted to take *petit moi* to Bali, Indonesia, in August. I was surprised. This was, for sure, completely unexpected.

We left New York in late July and journeyed to Oahu via Los Angeles. Jerry wanted us to take a few days in Hawaii on our way to Asia and on our way back from Asia.

I'll never forget the mesmerizing sunset over the sweeping Pacific Ocean and the attractive harbor from the terrace of our Prince Waikiki Hotel. The view was breathtaking.

We appreciated the scenery and the beach, but we could not leave Hawaii without visiting Pearl Harbor, the site where so many sailors and crewmen lost their lives on the sunken battleship USS Arizona in 1941. As our guide explained the horror of it all to us, I could not fight back my tears!

On August 3rd, we boarded our plane at the Honolulu Airport for our flight to Denpasar, the main airport in Bali.

I could not believe that we had arrived in Indonesia!

Close to the beach, our pretty hotel was in the midst of grounds made more attractive by the addition of fabulous hand-carved stone Buddha statues, a swimming pool surrounded by beautiful Balinese tropical plants and a charming outdoor restaurant.

Notwithstanding the attractiveness of our resort, Jerry and I wanted to spend our time experiencing the high spots of Bali.

We had a keen interest in getting around and seeing how different the cultures and customs were.

Jerry hired a private tour guide for several days. With our guide, we headed to the Tirta Empul temple, located in the village of Manukaya, near the town of Tampaksiring. Built below the Presidential Palace, the temple provided fascinating views. But seeing the holy water gushing out from taps into the sacred pool of purification — where an incredible number of Balinese people were washing themselves in the blessed water — was a sight not to be forgotten!

The next day, our guide escorted us to the Gunung Kawi temple, located at the bottom of a beautiful river valley. Jerry and I were amazed to discover such a phenomenal collection of ancient shrines carved into a rock cliff. It was a unique archeological site.

Another day, our guide drove us along the coastline to see the ancient Hindu temple Tanah Lot. Jerry and I were so impressed by the icon sitting on a rock in the middle of the sea, carved by the tides. The view of it all transported us into another world!

That being said, I will never forget our visit to the Sangeh Monkey Forest.

Monkeys were everywhere. I remember seeing several cunning long-tailed macaques snatching things from the tourists. Believe it or not, I witnessed a monkey climbing on the shoulders of a lady and ripping off her glasses in a split second, while another monkey was grabbing the camera from the hands of the gentleman standing next to me!

Well, as much as Jerry and I cherished the magnificence of the tall nutmeg trees, the waterfalls and the beautiful birds of the forest, our willingness to tolerate more of the unacceptable behavior of the macaques exceeded our patience. We just wanted to leave!

In our hotel, we met a friendly Australian couple. They joined us, with our guide, to visit the volcanic region of Mount Batur.

On one of the hills surrounding the lake, we came upon a cremation! But the people attending the ceremony did not appear troubled by the vicissitudes of life — they were ebullient, dancing, singing and laughing. They were full of *joie de vivre*!

Seeing our consternation, our guide told us that the soul was going to be reunited with the gods and that in order to be reincarnated into a new body, it has to be released through the cleansing fire of cremation.

Then, he added that in the Balinese culture, a cremation is the most significant ceremony in a life. Together, family and friends celebrate that the spirit of their loved one is heading into the next life, hopefully to a better life.

In the evening, we were invited by our guide to see a Kecak show, also known as the Ramayana monkey chant, with tons of performers, mostly men, lying down on the ground in a circle, throwing up their hands and arms. For Jerry and me, this was definitely another out-of-the-ordinary Indonesian experience!

We dined in a lovely restaurant the next day. I will never forget the grace and the elegance of the dancers in their impressive, colorful, traditional Legong costumes. Wrapped in mostly red cloth embellished with golden-printed patterns and embroidery, and wearing crown head-pieces which added richness to their already colorful and gorgeous outfits, their live performance on the stage was absolutely enchanting.

After our magnificent stay in Bali, we boarded a flight to Yogyakarta, bordering the Indian Ocean, on the island of Java. Renowned for its art and culture, the city was interesting to visit.

Jerry hired a tour guide for an excursion to the beautiful ancient Mendut Buddhist temple in Borobudur. Like most tourists, Jerry and I did not want to miss the fun diversion of an elephant ride on the high grounds around. We enjoyed our tour so much; the views of the temple from the hills were such a pleasure for the eyes.

Afterwards, we visited the grand Prambanan temple compound with its superb archaeological park. This was also an unforgettable and sensational experience for us.

On our way back, our guide drove us by the heavenly, hilly rice fields surrounding Yogyakarta. We caught sight of the hard-working men and women wearing their traditional conical hats, farming the rice paddies. Another fascinating vista not to be missed!

On August 10th, we left Yogyakarta for Singapore, where we boarded the cruise ship Sun Viking for two weeks. For day one and day two, the ship was our hotel. We were allowed to go out to the clean streets of the modern city in Singapore, with its tall buildings, as often as we wished.

We came upon the Sri Srinivasa Perumal Temple, with rows of statues of gods and goddesses, sculptures and paintings. Jerry and I were amazed by the unique Hindu design of the temple.

Our walk around the lush botanic gardens and the lovely lake with its statue of swans was stunning, but the heat and the humidity of the day made it almost unbearable! Furthermore, we were told that Singapore has lots of snakes and that many of them could be potentially dangerous. Venomous or not, they disgust and scare me!

Now, to change the subject to a more pleasing topic, our exquisite afternoon tea at the famous, elegant Raffles Hotel was, for us, an unforgettable experience.

After our two days in Singapore, our ship headed to Bali, Surabaya, and Semarang in Indonesia; Kuala Lumpur in Malaysia; and Songkhla, Koh Samui, and Bangkok in Thailand.

On the 12th of August, we were on board for the crossing of the equator that separates the North and South Pacific. Everyone on the deck was excited and wanted to celebrate crossing the line! What an experience that was!

Jerry and I were happy to return to Bali and visit more temples with their superb panoramic views, and enjoy a wonderful lunch in a tropical paradise close to a magnificent waterfall, with our new acquaintances from the ship. Without a doubt, it was a pleasure to go back to the delightful Indonesian province of Bali.

To add to the joy of the day, we were invited in the evening to a fabulous Balinese Gamelan performance on the ship. Watching the lovely dancers in their colorful attire was certainly an appealing and fascinating treat.

Immediately after docking in the port of Surabaya, the second-largest city in Indonesia after Jakarta, Jerry and I sallied forth and went to the Kebun Binatang, the Surabaya Zoo. I am still wondering what was our reason for heading straight to such a dreadful place. Seeing this virtual hell for the animals, cramped in their squalid and filthy, small cages, was very painful for us. We were not hallucinating, this was an absolute nightmare!

Before getting back on board, Jerry and I went for a walk along the waterfront, at a slow and relaxed pace, to try to recoup from our frightful experience.

As soon as we arrived on August 17th in Semarang, the capital of Central Java in Indonesia, we left the bustling city with a private tour guide and headed for the countryside. We were enthralled by the exotic and lush landscapes, terraced rice fields, coffee plantations and more, with active and extinct volcanos in the background, on top of the mountains. The vistas were superb.

Then we stopped with our guide at the Railway Museum in Ambarawa. Jerry and I were amused by their collection of steam locomotives and railway memorabilia. I have a picture of Jerry standing up in one of their steam locomotives. Actually, it reminded me of the train I traveled on with my parents and my sister Ghislaine when we returned to Paris after World War II.

Before returning to the ship, our guide suggested that we stop at Kreo Cave to see the monkeys. When he saw our expression of despair, he wanted to reassure us by saying, "The monkeys here are not as dangerous as those in Bali."

Daring and adventurous as we were, we agreed to go and observe the little primates. Watching them jump from one branch to another on the trees was awesome. They were sweet and entertaining.

After leaving Semarang, we had two very relaxing days at sea before reaching the port of Kelang in Kuala Lumpur, Malaysia.

Jerry and I enjoyed touring the capital of Malaysia with two couples from the ship. Visiting the huge Sultan Salahuddin Abdul Aziz Mosque with its large dome and tall minarets was very interesting and fascinating to see.

At the Thean Hou Temple, I stood in awe of the grand Buddhist pagoda with dragon-inspired columns. This was, without a doubt, a jewel not to be missed.

And seeing the splendid view of the city from the observation deck of the Menara Kuala Lumpur Tower was phenomenal.

The city, with the National Monument's bronze memorial statue, the court and the palace, was spectacular. Jerry and I were certainly not disappointed with our day in Malaysia.

On the ship at sea the following day, we were able to relax on long reclining chairs and enjoy the sea breeze. After our beautiful, easygoing day at sea, we were invited to a fabulous black-tie party in the evening. The elegance and refinement of men in their tuxedos and women wearing fashionable evening gowns was a pleasure for the eyes.

On the thirteenth day of our cruise, we entered the port of Songkhla, in southern Thailand.

With our private guide, we visited the revered and historic Buddhist Wat Machimawat temple, and the little museum in an old wooden structure next to it. Seeing the lovely collection of ancient artifacts was a joy for us.

When we approached the beach in Songkhla, Jerry and I were surprised at the sight of the magnificent Golden Mermaid statue. I can still visualize Jerry sitting on the rock at her side. It reminded me of the smaller mermaid statue in Copenhagen!

Then, before returning to the ship, we stopped in the fishing village of Kao Seng. The view of the sea, with the colorful fishing boats anchored on the beach, was truly an unforgettable picture before our eyes. All in all, it was a day to remember.

We spent our fourteenth cruise day on the exotic tropical island of Koh Samui, off the east coast of Thailand. The beaches, with the crystal blue sea, were beautiful. But with our enthusiasm, eagerness and curiosity to visit more famous landmarks, Jerry and I were not about to give up our keen desire to continue...

As our guide was driving us along the Northern coast, to our surprise, we discerned at a distance the big gold Buddha statue of Koh Samui. We could not believe the sweeping scene before our eyes. It was astonishing and awe-inspiring. Then, Jerry and I ambled around the surrounding temples with smaller ornate Buddhas everywhere. Fascinating, it was!

From there, our guide drove us around. We enjoyed the awesome scenery, the interesting sights and the beaches, with stunning vistas.

After leaving this phenomenal island for our ship, we had an unexpectedly heavy storm during the night. Aboard, we could feel the rage of the China Sea, as the waves rocked the ship almost to the tipping point. With the turbulence, the captain and the crew ordered all the passengers to gather at the center of the ship.

Fortunately, the next day we made it to Bangkok, where we disembarked with our belongings. Our cruising adventure had ended.

From the port, we headed to The Royal Orchid Sheraton, situated on the Chao Phraya River. The view from our hotel was spectacular.

As soon as we found our bearings, we went on a full-day tour around Bangkok. The temples and palaces were absolutely enchanting.

Our first stop was the Wat Pho, known as the Temple of the Reclining Buddha. Not only were we impressed by the giant reclining Buddha covered in gold leaf, but Jerry and I were also in awe of the great architectural treasures around it.

Afterwards, we reached Wat Traimit, in the Chinatown area of Bangkok. The huge solid gold Buddha and the sculptures in the temple there were striking.

Our tour came to an end with a visit to the marble temple Wat Benchamabophit. Filled with ancient objects of art, it turned up to be another fascinating stop for Jerry and me. Our day had certainly been packed with high-quality sightseeing.

Before leaving Bangkok the next day, we cruised along the banks of the Chao Phraya River. This was a lovely escape from the heavy traffic of the city. As the boat meandered gently, we were able to enjoy the fascinating vistas of temples and quaint markets.

We had concluded our wonderful voyage through Indonesia, Kuala Lumpur, Malaysia and Thailand.

Now, we were on our way toward Hawaii …

****

Our thirteen-and-a-half-hour flight from Bangkok to Honolulu was very pleasant.

We had a few idyllic days by the beach of Oahu. And to add to our joy, we were entertained every evening by some wonderful Hawaiian music and traditional dances.

All in all, Jerry and I were enchanted with our adventurous trip.

Nothing can enhance one's life more than discovering new places in the world. One should always open the door to new opportunities and fulfill one's dreams, which provide meaningful inspiration.

"If you want to fly, give up everything that weighs you down."

— The Buddha

The Buddha was right!

On our way back to New York, we stopped in Los Angeles in a hotel near the airport for one night. As we were eating in the hotel's restaurant, the waiter came to our table and said, "I have some bad news. Princess Diana was killed in a car accident in Paris." Shocked to hear the tragic news, Jerry and I sat there, speechless. This was on August 31, 1997.

The next day we flew back to New York.

Very soon after our return, Jerry was having back trouble. He had complained a few times during our vacation that his back was killing him, but the pain did not stop him from carrying on.

But now, his pain was becoming impossible to bear. Was it lumbago, sciatica or a slipped disk? He definitely needed to be checked by a doctor. He tried it all, but the chiropractic and physical therapy did not help; the epidural injections did not help; the acupuncture did not help. Nothing relieved the severity of his painful condition.

He was finally told that he had a cervical disk rupture and that he needed surgery. Besides the fact that the surgery did not help his pain, he was left with a staph infection in his spine!

He endured one operation after the other.

After many, many interventions, he was still unable to walk, sit or stand.

My sixtieth birthday was rolling up. Jerry was in no shape to plan some festivity for me. Furthermore, all of my friends were going out of town for Labor Day weekend.

To this day, I do not know why my big 6-0 was so important to me. But the thought of not celebrating it was definitely troubling to me!

Then unexpectedly, the idea of inviting Jerry, Marc, Richard, their girl-friends and my sister Ghislaine to join me on a cruise from New York to Bermuda for my birthday, came to mind.

I could not have had a better objective. Jerry, who could not walk, sit or stand, could make it with a taxi to the port and a wheelchair to the ship.

For Jerry, relaxing on a chaise long in the fresh air on the deck was a huge advantage for him, considering what he had gone through with the innumerable failed surgeries.

Our crossing to Bermuda was delightful. Visiting the well-preserved historic town of St. George's and the nearby fortress was interesting, but we preferred ambling around the picturesque city of Hamilton, graced with great shops.

Yet nothing could surpass the beauty of the pink houses sitting along the pinkish-white sandy beaches with turquoise water, under the blue sky. The beautiful sight was, most certainly, a feast for the eyes. Furthermore, the lively ambiance of joviality created by my entourage for my big 6-0 was absolutely unforgettable.

The sailing on our way back was horrendous. The high waves and the strong wind were pushing the ship in every direction. Our captain ordered everyone to stay away from the decks, leave our cabins and go to the center of the ship. It reminded me of our dreadful experience caused by the rage of the China Sea. Thank goodness we were able to get back to New York safely.

Notwithstanding Jerry's inability to move around, the voyage at sea perked him up. The change of air was definitely beneficial for him.

In the fall, Jerry had to go to the hospital for another failed intervention for his back. From there, he called me early in the morning to tell me, in total dismay, that he needed to have a dialysis shunt implanted in his arm the next day.

I responded by telling him that I was going to call his nephrologist right away.

Fortunately, I was able to reach the doctor instantaneously and communicate my consternation and disquietude concerning my Jerry.

I needed to pause for a moment, to take a breath, before questioning him. Then, in a decisive way, I asked him, "Does my husband need dialysis tomorrow? Next week? In a month? Or later?"

The doctor replied promptly: "No, not yet. I am not sure when he will have to start the treatment, but one day, due to his renal condition, it will be imperative for him to have dialysis."

Without waiting a minute, I answered, "but since it is not tomorrow, next week, or in a month, I will not allow the implantation of a shunt in his arm tomorrow. He is going through enough with his unsuccessful surgeries."

Luckily, the nephrologist understood my veto, and did not push me further!

Nevertheless, I wanted Jerry to get back on his feet, and I was not going to give up my search to find the right surgeon for him!

When I mentioned this to my family and my friends, they all told me that, after all the failed attempts, I was insane to even think about it.

But I listened to my little voice saying: "Jerry has nothing to lose. He is still unable to walk, sit or stand. Get on with your research!" And I did!

I was able to connect with a surgeon specializing in orthopedic surgery at the Hospital for Special Surgery and I asked for his opinion. He answered: "Yes, it is a difficult and perplexing situation, but he has nothing to lose and should take a chance with another operation."

The decision was made. Jerry had his last spinal surgery in early 1999. As a result, he could now walk, sit and stand again. I made the right choice and found the right surgeon. Hooray! Hooray!

CHAPTER 17

As Long as You are Alive, You Need to Put One Foot in Front of the Other

The following April, Jerry was able to travel to Paris with me to attend the marriage of my niece Emmanuelle to Peter. Our boys succeeded in getting there as well.

The wedding cocktails and dinner party took place on a Bateau Mouche on the River Seine. Cruising along the Seine and seeing the magnificent monuments of my favorite capital all lit up was an unforgettable event. Furthermore, having all the family together was such a delight for me.

Our sojourn in Paris was very social. Jerry and I had such a wonderful time spending time with family and friends.

After our return from Paris to New York, we went back pretty much to all our activities.

But there are always exceptions to the rule!

On Father's Day, Jerry took part in the Road Runners' four-mile walk in Central Park. It was a real delight for our sons Marc and Richard and *petit moi* to watch him ambulate with such a charismatic demeanor, when only a few months before, he could hardly put one foot in front of the other! It made me think of my Girl Guide motto: "Never give up!" I know that is easier said than done. But it is still of utmost importance to always go forward!

* * * * * * * * * * * * * * * * * * * *

Just as I had my heart on celebrating my big 6-0, I wanted to do something special for Jerry's big 7-0 in July. And what could be better than going on a cruise for his birthday? I invited Marc, Richard, their girlfriends and my sister, Ghislaine, to join us on a cruise, leaving from Miami.

Our cruise on the Majesty of the Seas, owned by Royal Caribbean, was very satisfying and entertaining.

Our first stop was Labadee, on the north-central coast of Haiti. Our beach day there was heavenly. The fine white sand, the turquoise waters of the Caribbean and the palm trees were so delightful to the eye and mind. Whether we were relaxing in a hammock, reclining on a long chaise or unwinding on a floating mattress, we were in an idyllic paradise.

I also cherished the beauty of the exotic landscape and the magnificent waterfalls of Jamaica. That was an extraordinary day, filled with adventure and fun. I can still see the boys and the girls bouncing around the cascades and tumbling over the limestone steps! It was an electrifying place.

On the 15th of July, after spending a few hours on the beach in the Cayman Islands, we returned to the ship to celebrate Jerry's big 7-0.

It was a soirée of elegance. Jerry and I were treated as VIPs, with a bottle of Moet & Chandon from the captain. Jerry conveyed his jubilation with a constant beaming smile. And we all had a good time.

I must admit that I was very pleased with the choice I made for the birthday boy — the cruise was definitely a winner!

The effusively ecstatic summer of 1999 was far from over.

In August, our son Marc married the love of his life, Christina, in a delightful club overlooking a pretty lake in the foothills of the Berkshires in Connecticut. It was a whole-day affair. The guests were able to undertake all kinds of water sports — water skiing, boating, swimming — or simply embrace the *dolce vita* and sunbathe on chaise lounges, before the formal ceremony, the feast and the party. What a gorgeous day that was!

A few members of my family and friends came from France for the magnificent occasion. Hechemi, Dominique and Sarah, whom we met in Istanbul, were among them. With our mutual strong desire to visit Quebec, we had decided to take a trip together to Canada. After the wedding, the five of us spent the night at the Rosewood Meadow Bed and Breakfast in Connecticut before hitting the road the next day. Hechemi and Dominique shared the driving. Great chauffeurs, they were.

On our way, we stopped for lunch at a Hooters restaurant. *Oh là là! Il faut de tout pour faire un monde!* The Hooters girls serving in these restaurants were known for their revealing outfits and sex appeal! Well, it takes everything to make a world and one should see it all!

As we continued our journey, we appreciated the magnificent countryside along the Saint Lawrence River. We stopped here and there and loved discovering the region.

I will never forget, on August 10th, the Festival de Montgolfières in Saint-Jean-sur-Richelieu. The sight of the hot-air balloons hovering above us was amazing and spectacular. That was a novelty for all of us!

When we reached Quebec with no hotel reservation, we soon realized that everything was booked solid! We were told by a travel agent to go to the Auberge de Jeunesse, a youth hostel, situated in the heart of the city and within walking distance of the Château Frontenac.

Hooray! Hooray! A few bunk beds in the dormitories, with a common bathroom, were available. Without hesitation, we opted to spend a night there.

Since the dorms were separated by gender, I never expected Jerry to show up in my four-bed room and say, "I want to be with you."

I can still hear one of the two women respond: "It is a female-only dorm, but let him stay!"

With their consent, Jerry climbed up to the bunk bed above mine and slept there! Oh là là!

Fortunately, the next day we were able to find a wonderful bed and breakfast along the Saint Lawrence River.

A couple with two teenage children, friends of Hechemi and Dominique, joined us in Quebec. We loved the unique character of the old francophone city. Walking around the charming narrow cobblestone streets with quaint shops was delightful. Historical scenes, frescoed on the walls of some of the old buildings, were eye-catching. The splendid and imposing perspectives of the Château Frontenac, at the top of Cap Diamant, enchanted us. The wonderful panoramas of the city and the Saint Lawrence River from the Observatoire de la Capitale were remarkable. Our visit to the Musée d'art Inuit, with their exceptional collection of Inuit sculptures, was extraordinary.

After sightseeing, we enjoyed a lovely, easygoing day in the field and pastures of the Île d'Orléans, located in the Saint Lawrence River.

The following day, Hechemi drove us to the spectacular Montmorency Falls Park, fifteen minutes away from Quebec. The beauty of the landscape surrounding the cascading river swept us off our feet.

Our adventures in the Quebec region were far from over. Our scenic drive to Charlevoix was alluring. Visiting the very old and famous windmill in Isle-aux-Coudres was also very pleasurable. But the most exhilarating experience of all was our whale-and seal-watching boat ride from the little town of Tadoussac, situated at the confluence of the Saguenay and Saint Lawrence rivers. Feasting our eyes on these giants of the sea, jumping with high energy above the water was, despite the splashing that drenched us, an exceptional and unforgettable escapade.

We continued our journey along the Saguenay River. When we reached le Parc National du Fjord-du Saguenay, we hiked around the gorgeous waterfront and forest.

The next day, we had a ravishing time exploring le Parc National des Grands-Jardins in Charlevoix. The lush boreal forest and the tundra, carpeted in lichen, and the surroundings with the lovely flora, were all eye-catching. Bright-eyed and bushy-tailed, we ambled around with enthusiasm and intense enjoyment.

Naturally, we did not want to miss seeing the spectacular Canyon Sainte-Anne with its waterfall. I cannot even begin to describe the many scenic vistas from the three suspension footbridges crossing the canyon, but I can assert that I had a strong feeling of reverence for nature. The panoramas filled me with wonder.

Le Parc de la Gorge de Coaticook was captivating as well. The beauties and diversity of nature were a definite treat to our eyes.

We ended our trip in Montreal. Before our au revoir, we visited an exhibition at the Canadian Centre for Architecture, an important stop for Hechemi, an architect.

Goodbyes are never easy, but our friends were heading for the airport while Jerry and I were proceeding towards Montreal Central Station to take our train back to New York.

****

After returning to our regular daily routine, Jerry and I decided to finish 1999 with a one-week cruise on the Holland American Line, leaving from Fort Lauderdale, Florida on December 23rd.

Our first stop was a private resort owned by the Holland American Line on San Salvador, an island in the Bahamas southeast of Nassau.

What could be more relaxing than spending a day on that spectacular white-sand crescent beach and swimming in the Caribbean Sea?

The next two days onboard were heavenly. *La dolce vita* continued on the sunny deck during the day and under the celestial sky at night. Sublime, it was! We enjoyed the sensational meals and the great entertainment aboard as well.

On our arrival in Guatemala, at the Port of Santo Tomás de Castilla, Jerry and I left the ship and boarded a tour bus for a very interesting excursion.

The picturesque hills around the port and the rainforest were a pleasure to see, but the amazing Mayan ruins at the archeological site in Quiriguá National Park, with its standing stones, carved stelae and sculpted calendars, were astonishing and very impressive.

Then, to our surprise, at the end of the beaten path we were sauntering on, there was an outdoor market selling clothes. Of course, I could not resist. I had to take a look and came back with a colorful Mayan dress. Bravo! Bravo!

Our next cruise stop was in Cozumel, a Caribbean island off Mexico's Yucatan Peninsula. Since Jerry and I had been there before, we just relaxed on a pristine beach by the crystal-clear sea.

On December 29th we were back in the U.S.A. Our ship docked in Key West, Florida. Since Jerry and I had never set foot in that resort, we decided to take the Hop On-Hop Off trolley historic tour. We were very happy with our decision. It highlighted the fascinating treasures not to be missed. We stopped by the Audubon House and Tropical Gardens. We appreciated the unique art collection and furnishings, which certainly reflected a certain elegance.

Then, we went on to visit the famous aquarium. The marine life was quite fascinating, although I must admit that I would definitely not like to swim with sea turtles and sharks!

Finally, before returning to the ship, we walked around the tropical gardens and caught sight of Ernest Hemingway's house, known today as a National Historic Landmark.

After a lovely evening onboard and a night at sea, our cruise was over. We headed for the airport in Miami and flew back to New York.

****

Jerry and I were home to greet at the beginning of the year 2000. We were back to our routine until our flight to Paris in April. Getting together with our family and friends was, as always, a delight.

After our return to New York, Jerry was told that — even though it was not for tomorrow — he needed to have a dialysis shunt implanted in his arm. Now he had no choice. He went along with it.

In June, I chaperoned Jerry for his regular check-up. The doctor said that Jerry would definitely need to start dialysis in about a month and that we should take our vacation right away.

As soon as we returned home, I gave serious thought to the doctor's deliberate communication and felt that, due to the circumstances of Jerry's condition, I needed to think about the type of vacation we should have. If Jerry required dialysis earlier, we needed to be in a city with medical assistance, rather than in a resort in the middle of nowhere!

Where should we go? That was my question. Well, all of a sudden, I had a brainstorm!

"Eureka! London would be a perfect destination for us," I exclaimed, triumphantly.

Jerry looked at me with a smile from ear to ear and acknowledged that embarking on a journey to England would be appropriate and enchanting. He paused for a second and then uttered, "*Petite cherie*, get on the phone right away — make our flight reservations and book a hotel for us."

Recognizing that we should not waste any time, I arranged our trip for early July.

Jerry and I were very happy with our beautifully located hotel, in the heart of Kensington. We were in walking distance of one of my favorite stores, Harrods — *oh là là!* — and very close to the Victoria and Albert Museum of Art and Design, which we visited with pleasure.

Our recreational pursuits were filled with such a variety of wonderful activities. Name it, we did it! Like all the tourists, we hopped on a double-decker sightseeing tour bus. Sitting on the upper level, we enjoyed the perspectives of the stunning landmarks of the city.

We visited the fabulous Westminster Abbey, famous for coronations and royal ceremonies. We hopped off to take pictures at Buckingham Palace. I guess that the monarchs of the United Kingdom were too busy to invite us for tea! Ha! Ha!

We had fun visiting Madame Tussauds' Wax Museum. Gazing at the lifelike wax figures of all kinds of celebrities was, for us, an unforgettable experience. We had a lovely evening at the Prince of Wales Theatre, where we saw the delightful musical *Fosse*.

But the best was yet to come. Our dinner in a restaurant with my niece, Joanna, and my nephew, Jocelyn, was such a great pleasure. We were also happy to meet up with Peter, Jan and Roger, who were like family to us.

But the pinnacle was when my sister, Ghislaine, crossed the English Channel to spend a day with us.

Together, we ambled along the colorful Portobello Road on a market day. Though famous for antiques, one could find everything. Bargain lovers were certainly in their element; that was the place to acquire loads of vintage and unique treasures. We had so much fun wandering around the charmingly painted houses, the stores, the cafes and the collectibles. The atmosphere of the bustling street, with music and food of all kinds, was so jovial and entertaining.

I still have photos of Ghislaine and me wearing top hats with the Union Jack on them. Original that was, but we did not buy them!

Desiring an easy escape from the city, Jerry and I decided to spend a day in Brighton, a resort on the southern coast. We started our day by spending a couple of hours lounging on the boardwalk. The beach was simply miles of pebbles! Never mind — we were there to take in a breath of fresh air. The gentle breeze from the sea was delightful.

Then, along the seafront, we stumbled upon the Melrose Restaurant for lunch. Since we both had a yen for seafood, this was the place for good fish and chips with wine. *Que c'était bon!* It was so good!

After lunch, we walked over to the magnificent Royal Pavillon. When Jerry and I saw the impressive palace, we were transported in another world. The colorful and elegant building belonged in India or China, we thought. It was definitely different from British architecture!

Not only were we in awe of the Royal Pavillon — the surrounding gardens, with their array of beautiful flowers, plants and trees were enchanting as well.

All in all, our vacation in England was exhilarating and thoroughly enjoyable.

****

Soon after our return to New York, Jerry had to start dialysis. With his problems caused by kidney failure, he could no longer wait. He had to go three times a week to the Rogosin Institute, for his four-hour hemodialysis treatment.

Determined to keep Jerry going, I was adamant that we should not stop traveling. I was ready to schedule appointments for his dialysis treatment, in whatever place, anywhere in the world.

My perspective has always been to focus on the manner in which an issue is handled. Circumstances are a problem to tackle. As long as you are alive, you need to put one foot in front of the other and knock over that stumbling block.

That said, I wanted to do something special for our 40th wedding anniversary in December. Weighing the reasons for or against a cruise, I decided to find out which cruise ships provided dialysis services onboard.

Hallelujah! Hallelujah! The ten-day cruise on the MS Zaandam, operated by Holland America Line, leaving from Fort Lauderdale on December 3rd, had dialysis services onboard.

Right away, I made reservations for Jerry, Marc and Christina, and Richard and Tamar — who was soon to be his wife. I did not only want to celebrate our 40th wedding anniversary. I had invited my boys for my big 6-0 in 1998 and Jerry's big 7-0 in 1999. Why not have memories of a cruise together in 2000?

We all had such a good time together. Jerry did not miss a port. He had his hemodialysis treatment at night and was ready to join us on our adventures in Antigua, Barbados, Guadeloupe and St. Thomas.

We had such a great time. We enjoyed them all.

CHAPTER 18

2001: A Year to Remember

On our Caribbean cruise, the dialysis treatment had never deterred Jerry from joining us in all the activities of the day. His courage and determination were definitely there.

Now that Jerry was no longer working, traveling would keep him going and help him and *petit moi* continue a worthwhile life.

Right away, I decided we should set forth on a meaningful and inspiring venture: a three-week cruise around South America.

On January 21st, 2001 we boarded a plane for Santiago, Chile. On the 22nd, after a good flight, we arrived at Hotel Kennedy, only minutes from Parque Arauco. I had scheduled a rendezvous for Jerry at a dialysis center close to our hotel. The treatment was on schedule and went well.

During our two days in the Chilean capital, we did not waste our time. Along with a sightseeing tour of the beautiful city, Jerry wanted to meet up with the director of a grapeseed oil refinery, with whom he had communicated regarding essential oils. When he showed us his factory, I was surprised to see the professional attire of his employees — just like doctors and nurses, they were all wearing white coats and hats!

After this nice visit to the lab, the friendly gentleman suggested that we accompany him for a guided tour of Viña Veramonte. We toured the vineyards, we visited the production warehouse, we proceeded to the wine cellars and last but not least, we were invited to taste a selection of their wines. *Ooh là là!* I still wonder how we made it back to our hotel!

The following day, our newfound friend picked us up from the hotel to take us to the major seaport of Valparaiso. On our way there, we stopped in Viña del Mar to take a walk along the beach on the Pacific Ocean. It was idyllic.

But it was time for us to board the Holland America MS Ryndam, sailing away at 5 P.M. The energy and *joie de vivre* at the pool party that evening was fabulous.

We were at sea the next day. It felt good to just relax after our long flight to Santiago and our two hectic days visiting different areas in the vicinity.

Puerto Montt was our first stop. With a small group of people from the ship, we headed to the Parque Nacional Vicente Pérez Rosales, located in the Los Lagos region. We enjoyed the flora and the fauna. But when we reached the shores of Lake Llanquihue, the views of the snowcapped Osorno Volcano and the Petrohué Waterfalls were definitely a sight not to be missed. It was just spectacular, but the best and the most unexpected adventure was yet to come.

When we were invited to go ziplining, we were somewhat flabbergasted. But it exceeded our expectations in every way. We would never have imagined that a seventy-year-old man and a sixty-one-year-old lady would ever be invited to travel from the top of the hills down to the green fields, attached to a moving pulley suspended to a cable!

I never imagined ziplining, but we went for it! I must say that, notwithstanding our apprehension, we had an awesome experience with our feet dangling in the air!

Well, rest assured we had no traumatic brain injury. Jerry's poor renal function did not impact his soundness of mind and alluding to the wisdom of age, I still had a good head on my shoulders!

But we never knew what was waiting for us around the corner. It could have been everything or it could have been nothing. We just needed to keep putting one foot in front of the other and then…Surprise! Surprise!

A moment after we had reached our destination, I saw Jerry, with a snobbish demeanor, facing a highbrowed and pretentious llama! Their supercilious haughtiness made me laugh!

I could never forget the out-of-the-ordinary events of our day in the region of Puerto Montt.

Then, after our marvelous and fascinating discoveries at the southern end of Chile, we had two days at sea. The *joie de vivre* on board was phenomenal and, hurrah, Jerry's dialysis treatments were excellent!

We enjoyed so much the scenic cruising through the Chilean fjords and Patagonia (the Tierra del Fuego provinces of Chile and Argentina). At the head of the picturesque Eyre Fjord we admired the Pio XI Glacier.

Jerry and I were absolutely exhilarated by the wonderful panorama of the region surrounding us.

We were told by our shore excursion advisor that as soon as we reached Punta Arenas, we should take a penguin tour by boat to the Isla Magdalena in the Strait of Magellan, in southern Patagonia. He added emphatically, "The island has the most important Magellanic penguin colony and is totally uninhabited by humans. You should not miss it!"

Jerry and I were always curious and decided to go for it. Little did we know what to expect. Well, we had arrived in Penguin Heaven! Seeing these appealing and playful tuxedoed, flightless seabirds in their natural habitat, nesting and waddling around, was a wonderful and unforgettable experience for us.

Back on our ship, we cruised to Ushuaia, Argentina's southernmost city — a lovely town with beautiful surroundings. From there, we journeyed to Tierra del Fuego National Park, home of the "Post Office at the End of the World." Our guide told us that, indeed, we had reached the last outpost of civilization, "*El fin del mundo.*"

We may have reached the end of the world — ha ha! But with the scenic beauty of the lakes, waterfalls, mountains and glaciers, I would simply call this a striking and significant Patagonian adventure!

As I am writing about my memorable experiences, the navigation around Cape Horn, where the Atlantic and Pacific oceans meet, enters my mind.

Despite the massive waves, the strong wind and the frigid temperatures, brave Jerry and brave *petit moi* were solo on the deck! After all, our primary aim was to always satisfy our curiosity! And that was, for sure, a not-to-be-missed experience!

After a couple of delightful days at sea, our ship dropped anchor in the port of Buenos Aires.

With a group and our escort, we headed to the Tigre and Paraná River Delta. Jerry and I admired the attractive region and the jungle-like islands. They were such a pleasure for the eyes.

We were invited to a dinner show in the evening. As we were enjoying the excellent cuisine in a beautiful relaxed atmosphere, we immersed ourselves in Argentina's most famous cultural tradition in music and dance — the tango. Watching the sensuality and the elegance of the dancers was, most definitely, a sensational treat for us.

Another unique experience was awaiting us the next day. With our tour guide and a nice group of people from our ship, we wandered around Buenos Aires' old neighborhoods. Looking at the architecture, the boulevards and the parks, the European heritage was evident. I literally felt at home! When we stopped to visit the spectacular Teatro Colón, it was like *déjà vu* for me! The magnificent opera house reminded me of la Scala di Milano and l'Opéra de Paris.

The beautiful city of Buenos Aires enchanted us, but there are always things that exceed all expectations! Well, without a doubt, the uniqueness of the neighborhood of La Boca, with all the buildings painted in bright colors, the cobblestone streets, the cafes and the tango and gaucho dancers on every corner, was, to say the least, fascinating to us! The charismatic charm of these men and women added such an immeasurable atmospheric ambiance to the neighborhood that it was not surprising to us that the area was swarming with tourists!

Our delightful day ended at the famous Café Tortoni, the city's oldest cafe-restaurant, with another authentic Argentinian soirée — and a fabulous tango show. *¡Que espléndido y magnifico!*

After a night at sea, we arrived in Montevideo, Uruguay's capital. We strolled around the old town and admired the grand Plaza

Independencia. Then we decided to continue our leisurely walk on the lovely Rambla along the coastline.

After two relaxing and pleasurable days at sea, our ship approached, early the next morning, the harbor of Rio de Janeiro, Brazil. Watching the vistas of the surrounding mountains from our deck was absolutely spectacular.

This was the last port on our cruise. We were still able to come and go from the ship as we pleased for the next two days.

As soon as the ship anchored, we were on our way for a day trip with our guide. I will never forget the ride on the cable car up and down Sugarloaf Mountain (in Portuguese "Pão de Açúca"). The eye-catching and breathtaking panorama of Rio de Janeiro and the view of Corcovado's famous sculpture of Christ the Redeemer from Sugarloaf Mountain was just incredible!

The following day, after taking a tour of the city, Jerry and I ambled along the scenic promenades of the beautiful coast and stopped on the famous Copacabana beach to bask in the sun.

The awe-inspiring Brazilian city of Rio de Janeiro was the grand finale of our fabulous trip around South America. Our exciting voyage was coming to an end — certainly the experience of a lifetime.

On February 10th, the time had come for us to say our *au revoir* and head to the airport for our flight to New York.

****

After making appointments for Jerry's dialysis in Geneva and Paris, we flew over to Europe to visit family and friends in the spring of 2001. It was a delight as always to spend time with all of them and then, to add to our joy, we attended the beautiful wedding of Noemie, my cousin François' youngest daughter, to David.

****

As soon as we returned to New York, I was determined to do some research for our next two trips. Since Jerry and I chose cruises as being the most suitable for us, I had to research which ones had dialysis on board.

Yippee! I was able to make reservations for a seven-night cruise on Celebrity Cruises' Horizon, leaving New York on June 16th for Bermuda.

And yippee! After some pondering, Jerry and I decided to opt for an Alaskan cruise leaving Vancouver on July 16th. We invited Marc and Christina to join us. Richard and Tamar were deeply immersed with the plans for their wedding the following month.

Our cruise to Bermuda was very comfortable and entertaining. Given that we had been to Bermuda several times, we simply enjoyed the beauty of the island and the lovely beaches.

On July 12th we flew with Marc and Christina, who was expecting their first baby, to Seattle. Marc rented a car and drove us up to Mount Rainier National Park, in Washington State. The massive and prominent mountains, the Cascades, the spectacular meadows and the towering forests were amazing sights to discover.

We were fortunate to find accommodations for one night at the Paradise Inn in Mount Rainier. The next morning, we hiked around the grounds. Along the way, we saw some friendly marmots. I must admit that I am not a fan of rodents, *mais que faire?* (But what could we do?) We were the trespassers in their paradise!

Then, Marc drove us to the area surrounding the famous volcano of Mount St. Helens. We could not believe the scars from the volcanic eruption of May 1980. The ashes had devastated the forest — the shattered stumps were all that was left! Sad it was, to see such ravages.

From there, we went back to Seattle. Seeing the enchanting city from the top of the Space Needle observation deck was awe-inspiring.

After spending a night in a hotel, we were en route for Vancouver, Canada. The scenery along the way was very pleasurable. Then, before boarding Royal Caribbean's Vision of the Seas, Marc drove us around the pretty city of Vancouver. A few hours later, we were on our way to Alaska.

July 15th was our first evening on the ship. Jerry was celebrating his 72nd birthday. It was a soirée filled with joy.

After two alluring days of cruising, passing through the gorgeous fjords with beyond-expected vistas of massive white glaciers, we arrived in Skagway, the gateway to the trails of the Gold Rush! Our ship dropped anchor there for two days.

On our first day, we took a streetcar tour of the charming little city of Skagway and all its surroundings. With our spirit of adventure, the next day we boarded a scenic railroad journey. From the vintage coaches, we enjoyed the breathtaking panorama of the mountains, the glaciers, Bridal Veil Falls and the historic sites. We stopped to visit the Gold Rush Cemetery and walked through a short forest trail to Lower Reid Falls. All in all, our couple of days turned out to be noteworthy and significant.

As soon as we arrived early the next morning in Juneau, we headed to the Mount Roberts Tramway for a lift to the summit — 1,800 feet above. The views of the city, mountains and waterways were superb. After our beautiful scenic jaunt, we still had time to take a city trolley tour.

I will never forget the contrast between the old-fashioned trolley we were sitting in and the strikingly modern sites we were riding through! *Il faut de tout pour faire un monde!* It takes all sorts to make a world!

Our last port in Alaska was Ketchikan. We only had a few hours to spend there. As we ambled along the waterfront, we arrived at the Totem Heritage Center. The artifacts and the colorful Totems poles from the Tlingit and Haida villages were different and interesting for us to see.

Then, taking a stroll along Creek Street, we were told that the street used to be lined with bordellos — salons that, after their exhausting chores of the day, the hardworking miners, loggers and fishermen headed to for female companionship! The houses had been converted into restaurants and shops for the tourists. But there is always an exception: 24 Creek Street, the house where the most famous "madam" entertained, had been converted into Dolly's House Museum. Curious, we did not want to miss it. We waited on line and bought tickets to visit it. I must confess that, when I saw Dolly's bedroom, I could imagine her rambunctious past! *Ooh la la!*

Back on our ship, we enjoyed the spectacular, misty fjords and the rock walls jutting out of the ocean.

This picturesque area has abundant wildlife, but we never saw the bears or the whales!

Up to the end of our cruise, the picturesque vistas from our decks captivated us. Our vacation turned out to be an exciting and delightful experience.

In addition, Jerry's dialysis on board was successful. He had hit the jackpot and was able to strike gold! Ha ha! Furthermore, he was able to hit the trails of the gold rush!

As soon as we had reached Vancouver, we were on our way to Seattle to catch our flight back to New York on July 22nd.

****

We actually had very little time to get ourselves ready for our next major event — Richard and Tamar's wedding in Baltimore on August 11th.

Having a strong desire to have as many family members and friends as possible, Richard had sent a "save-the-date" card a year ahead to give them plenty of time to get organized and come over for the marriage ceremony.

Jerry and I, parents of the groom, invited Tamar's parents, Avi and Jaffa, and their family to join our family and friends who were coming from overseas to a rehearsal dinner in a very pleasant French restaurant the night before the wedding.

Our soirée turned out to be marvelous. After an aperitif, an exquisite dinner and a few words on my part — surprise, surprise — Marc took part in a hilarious game with his seven European cousins and his cousin Philippe, who had flown in from Tahiti. The youngsters had prepared four horizontal, rectangular signs on sticks. On two were written "Yes" and on the others were written "No." Richard and Tamar were to respond instantly, by holding up a "Yes" or a "No," to the questions they were asked.

The purpose of the game was to find out how well they knew each other and how well they were matched. Ha ha! The questions were amusing; the laughter, the energy and the fun were beyond words. That was not all. The vitality and the ebullience of these young people were on display in their comical acting and their dancing as well.

The high-spirited atmosphere, along with the togetherness of family and the warmth of friendship, united us all. I simply loved it.

The following day, we celebrated Richard and Tamar's nuptial vows. The reception at the majestic Belvedere in Baltimore was enchanting.

Being escorted down the aisle to the chuppah by Richard, who had me on one arm and his dad on the other, was unforgettable. I could not believe that my baby boy was tying the knot. Where had the years gone? It seemed like it was only yesterday that I was holding him in my arms! *Mais c'est la vie!* That is life!

After the bridesmaids and the groomsmen reached the altar, Tamar and her parents walked down the aisle. With her beautiful demeanor, Tamar looked regal in her lovely gown.

The exchange of the vows, the wedding feast, the musicians playing music for us to dance to were all delightful. And having my siblings, nephews, nieces, cousins and some of my best friends there was positively wonderful.

The following day Avi and Jaffa invited us to a brunch at the Inn at the Colonnade to continue to celebrate Tamar and Richard with them, before the goodbyes.

Just one month after Richard and Tamar's wedding, on September 11th, almost 3,000 people were killed by two planes that crashed into the Twin Towers of the World Trade Center in New York. These dreadful and hideous attacks were carried out by Islamic extremists.

I believe that everyone in the world remembers where they were and what they were doing at the time when the Twin Towers collapsed in a massive cloud of dust and smoke. Millions saw it happen on their television. I will not dwell on the horror of it all. I want to extend to the victims and their families that I share their tears, but death cannot be the only focus of your life — we have to move on. I know that it is easier said than done, but do as much as you can.

Well, the year was not over. I do not recall the exact date, but I do remember inviting Christina's family and friends to a baby shower, a perfect American invention for the expectant mummy to collect layettes, outfits and toys for the baby.

On November 11th, Christina was celebrating her 25th birthday with family and friends in a restaurant when she had to be rushed to the hospital.

I was so moved when Christina requested my presence in the room where she was giving birth. Marc, the papa, was obviously there to take part in this most blessed event — the birth of their first daughter, Emily.

I am unable to express the extent of my jubilation, marked by this triumphant, monumental and unforgettable happening before my eyes — the coming into existence of my first grandchild on November 12th.

Viva 2001! What an enriching year that was, with the incredible experiences traveling with my Jerry. Notwithstanding his dialysis, we kept on going and discovered so much. Then, the beautiful wedding of my Richard with his lovely bride, Tamar, and last but not least, the birth of our magnificent Emily.

CHAPTER 19

The Unimaginable Becomes the Unforgettable

In 2002, we still had the drive and the energy for yet more journeys.

Hence, in spite of Jerry's dialyses, with my spirit of get-up-and-go, I continued researching possible options for more adventure travel or resorts, for a simple *dolce vita* for Jerry and *petit moi*.

In April, our seven-night Eastern Caribbean cruise aboard the Explorer of the Seas was very entertaining. And to add to our pleasure, all the ports of call were delightful.

Exploring the streets of Old San Juan, Puerto Rico on foot was absolutely enchanting for Jerry and *petit moi*. The historic fort and the old Spanish colonial architecture fascinated us.

We saw lots of people stepping into the Basilica de San Juan Bautista, a historic landmark in the heart of the old city. Without hesitation, we followed them and entered the magnificent church.

Filled with astonishment, we stood there gazing at a beautiful bride and groom with the maids of honor at their side, tying the knot. Witnessing their exchange of vows was awe-inspiring!

As soon as the ceremony ended, the elegant guests went along with the newlyweds through a decorated door for a joyous celebration. Jerry and I were kind of despondent that we were not summoned to the banquet and the fiesta! I am sure that with the *"joie de vivre"* — or *"la alegria de vivir"* of the Puerto Rican people, the party was very lively and cheerful. Well, we cannot win them all!

In June, we invited Marc, Christina, their darling Emily, Richard and Tamar to share with us an enchanting cruise to Bermuda. Together, we were able to enjoy, once again, some of the prettiest beaches in the world.

On my voyages, I have come across many, many unexpected and unique sights and events; the unimaginable becoming the unforgettable. Things end, but memories last forever.

Well, on this particular cruise, I will never forget the sight of Emily lying naked on her parents' bed, holding with her two little hands the Celebrity Cruises Horizon Daily.

She was a seven-month-old infant and she was already a passionate reader! I am not sure whether she was selecting her preferences for the following day, but she was definitely absorbed by her reading, and was not ready to put it down when I came into the cabin! Hilarious, it was!

Jerry and I needed to get away in July. From a range of possibilities, we chose to spend two weeks at the lovely Sandpiper Club Med in Florida. This was a very good destination for Jerry, who had less than a ten-minute taxi ride to the dialysis center.

We always enjoyed the relaxation, the atmosphere and the table delicacies of Club Med. But of greatest importance, we appreciated the kindness and the enthusiasm of the G.O.s, *"gentils organisateurs"* or "nice organizers," they are always the soul of the villages.

At the end of August, Marc invited his dad and *petit moi* to join his little family on a trip to Virginia Beach.

I will never forget the ferry ride on the mid-Atlantic coast from Cape May, New Jersey to Lewes, Delaware. Seeing the almost seven-kilometer Chesapeake Bay Bridge connecting the eastern shore to the west was quite a vista!

The vibrant coastal city of Virginia Beach was very pleasurable. Jerry and I were delighted with our few agreeable days on the beach.

Before the end of the year, Jerry and I had a strong desire to return to the island paradise of Puerto Rico, an ideal tropical escape for us with *"la alegria de vivir."* Once again, we were enamored by the island's appealing beauty.

****

In January 2003, despite Jerry's dialysis, we were still eager to get up and go back to the picturesque Sandpiper Club Med for a lovely week with Marc, Christina and Emily. Together, we celebrated Marc's 40th birthday. I could not believe that we were drinking a toast to my boy's four decades! Our cute Emily was taking her first steps, but she was not ready yet to play golf with her parents!

In June, after spending two delightfully charming weeks in our paradise of well-being, the Sandpiper Club Med, we extended our holiday with a leisurely, short visit to The Breakers in Palm Beach. This was, for us, another escape to paradise.

We were back in New York in good time for the birth of Ariel, Richard and Tamar's firstborn. Jerry and I were ecstatic to have another beautiful granddaughter.

Jerry and I were eager to celebrate, but we were not alone — all of America had flags out. They were eating, drinking and being merry, just like us, celebrating the 4th of July! Ha Ha!

I can still see Jerry holding Emily in one arm and Ariel in the other. I was sitting at his side, sharing with him the joy of our enrichment.

Whenever we could spend time with our two little darlings — at home, in the park or wherever — we could not take our eyes off them. We were mesmerized.

There's a saying that "Your children are your rainbows, your grandchildren are your pot of gold." Indeed, I agree.

Emily and Ariel gave us such enjoyment, and seeing Jerry's radiant smile when he looked at them was heartwarming and beautiful. Actually, they were not the only ones to bring a smile to his face. Richard's lovely dog Duchess, who spent every weekday, from morning till night with us, was such an affectionate delight. Our furry friend had been such a faithful companion to Jerry when he was bedridden with back problems.

Our Duchess was such a pleasure. We loved her.

****

In October, Jerry and I crossed the Atlantic Ocean to spend a couple of weeks in Paris.

Notwithstanding his appointments for dialysis, Jerry was able to enjoy our get-togethers with family and friends. And to add to our pleasure, Scott and Gillian, two first cousins on my mother's side, came from England to meet us for the first time. They were absolutely charming. It was truly enchanting getting acquainted with them.

Scott had tried to contact me when I was away on a trip with Jerry. He left his phone number with a message: "Are you Muriel Kiefe? If that is the case, I need to talk to you. I am telephoning you from Spain, where I work. Please call me as soon as possible."

How was he able to find me? I had never heard of him. I did not know that he even existed!

Well, daring as I was, I phoned him.

Scott explained that we were first cousins, that his mother had set her heart on talking to me, and that I needed to call her without delay.

He paused for a moment and went on to say, "My mother, Leah, is failing rapidly. She is near death in a hospital in London. She is anxious to know more about her sister Sybil — your mother — from whom she was separated when their parents divorced after World War I. My mother was only three years old!

"It seems that on one occasion before World War II, the two sisters had gotten together. They were both young adults."

I was, to say the least, completely surprised by Scott's request to call the auntie that I had never encountered or even heard from in my life!

I remained silent for a moment. I needed to catch my breath. Then, I ended my conversation with Scott by expressing my good wishes to him and my desire to get together in the near future.

Shortly afterwards, I called my Aunt Leah.

As soon as she answered the phone I uttered, "Scott, your son, was able to reach me in New York. He told me that you have questions about my mother and that I should call you as soon as possible."

"Yes, Muriel, I wanted to talk with you. As you surely know, Sybil, your mother, was raised by our father from age five. She never saw our mother again. I remained with our mother and had a very unfortunate childhood with no love."

I was disheartened by the hopeless situation she had had to deal with during her youth.

After a short pause, Leah went on to say, "Sybil was very fortunate to be with our dad."

"I guess so," I replied. "My mother adored her father, yet she had to accept the demands of a stern stepmother. It goes without saying that it must have been difficult for her."

"Yes, I understand. I had a stepfather and two half-brothers that I had to tend to," Leah expressed with deep emotion.

I heard her sigh, and then she went on to say, "In all likelihood, Sybil was determined to build an easier life for herself when she married a Frenchman, your father."

I burst out laughing and acknowledged that my parents definitely loved each other, but as we all know, life is never a straight line and that I was sure that they had, like everyone else, challenging moments.

"I couldn't agree more. That's true," Leah said.

She paused for a second. "Is your mother still alive?"

"No, she passed away in August 1996. She was 73 years old."

"What does her life say about her?" Leah asked.

"My mother was one of the kindest people I have ever known. She was a wonderful wife and a warm and loving mother to her four children. To put it simply, she was a remarkable human being."

"Did she express any grievance over her mother's absence?" asked Leah.

"My mother refrained from talking about her, and simply kept her feelings to herself. How could a mother ignore her five-year-old daughter and never see her again," I said.

"It eludes me as well. But I as I told you, Muriel, our mother was a person of bad character. Fortunately, your mother and I had nothing in common with her!"

Noticing my auntie's fatigue, I realized that our heart-to-heart exchange had to end.

She sounded very sweet, but it was time to say our *adieu*.

I never saw my aunt. She died shortly after our goodbye.

****

Our October visit to family and friends in Paris was our last trip in 2003. A few days before the year ended, during the night of December 26th, Jerry fainted and was transported by ambulance to the hospital, where he stayed until the 31st.

****

By January, Jerry had improved and was given the green light by his doctor to leave the frigid temperatures of New York for the warm climate of Florida. Our week at the Sandpiper Club Med, our home away from home, was always a wonderful energizer for us.

The beginning of the year was not only crowned by our escape to Florida — on February 20th, Abby, another amazing granddaughter, was born. The happy couple, Marc and Christina, were now the parents of two beautiful little girls and Emily had a sister.

There was no denying that Jerry and I cherished the gift of having a third granddaughter to fill our lives with love, laughter and endless joy. We were simply delighted!

CHAPTER 20

A Painful Decision

In 2004, after much cogitation, Jerry and I decided to go to Puerto Rico for a relaxing, paradisal week in May.

Keeping in mind Jerry's dialyses, I researched and decided to make our reservations in San Juan, at the Caribe Hilton.

On May 16th, we arrived at the enchanting hotel, situated on a lush, tropical landscape overlooking the Atlantic Ocean.

As soon as we had unpacked our valises, we made our way to the lovely gardens with their stunning views.

Then, before heading to the delicious buffet in the dining room, we relaxed in this tropical haven, sipping our Piña Coladas and listening to the birds chirping. What a delight that was!

The waiters in the restaurant were wonderfully friendly, accommodating Jerry's wishes. They were amazingly helpful.

After dinner, we went on a stroll and enjoyed the clear night sky displaying the bright stars and the moon.

Jerry stopped for a moment and, with a massive smile on his face, expressed that he was intensely happy to have me in his life. I was too deeply moved even to speak. I embraced him and we proceeded slowly to our room.

At one o'clock in the morning, I heard Jerry howling with chest pains. Without delay, I called the concierge for help. By the time the ambulance arrived, Jerry had fainted. I went with him to the emergency room. He had had a heart attack and needed to be transferred right away to a major hospital for his dialysis treatment, which, as a matter of fact, did not go well. He had to be moved immediately to intensive care.

I was told that Jerry had a limited chance of survival. I called my boys. Marc flew right away from New York and Richard came without delay as well. But they could not stay long. They had to go back to work.

When the staff in the hotel heard that Jerry had been hospitalized, they tried to ease my distress by sending a huge basket of goodies to my room. And they were all ears and paid attention to me in the restaurants. Their kindness warmed my heart.

The concierge arranged a car service to chauffeur me every day to the hospital.

During the mornings, I would laze in the hammocks of the glorious gardens, have lunch and head out in the afternoon to see Jerry.

In intensive care, visitors were not allowed to stay more than a few minutes.

Following my short visit with Jerry, I would see his doctors and nurses to get up-to-date developments concerning his health issues. I must say that my Spanish was really helpful!

Afterwards, I would spend a long period of time on the phone with our international insurance company arranging Jerry's repatriation, which could only occur with the doctors' consent. This was, to say the least, a daunting job, but I was not ready to give up!

Believe it or not, it took me three weeks to get the doctors' approval and make arrangements to fly Jerry back! Fortunately, I had taken the insurance for repatriation!

I could never forget our private medical flight from San Juan, with life support and equipment for Jerry, in the company of the pilot, the co-pilot, Jerry on a stretcher and two medical escorts at his side. I was sitting, crammed in the narrow back of the plane with our luggage. I could hardly breathe and, to add to my ordeal, we were going through an electrical storm and the plane was bouncing around!

When the pilot announced that the plane would have to land in Miami for refueling, I toyed with the idea of getting off and continuing my journey on another flight. But a little voice in me said, "You cannot abandon Jerry. You must disregard your discomfort and buckle down!"

I always listen to *petit moi*, and with a concerted effort, I remained in my tiny seat.

Oh, I was so thankful that the second part of our flight to New Jersey was easier and smoother. The storm had calmed down.

When we landed on the tarmac of Teterboro, a private jet airport, an ambulance was waiting for Jerry.

They transported Jerry on his stretcher from the plane to the back of the ambulance, the two medical escorts staying at his side. I was invited to sit in the front, next to the driver.

I had never anticipated such a terrifying experience. Apparently, in a traffic jam, emergency vehicles have the latitude to zigzag in the opposite lane, with cars moving towards them. When we were practically head-to-head with a car, I thought that I would suffer a heart attack and would need a hospital bed next to Jerry's!

Fortunately, we finally made it to New York-Presbyterian Hospital, where Jerry had to stay for a while. I went home to recover from the horrendous, harrowing drive.

For the next few months, Jerry was in and out of hospitals and rehabs.

Jerry was off the respirator in a nearby rehab when Ariel took her first steps, which brought smiles to him. Whenever Jerry could feast his eyes on his little granddaughters, he gazed upon them with joy, pleasure and love, which warmed my heart.

Mid-October, Jerry's doctor came to our home to see him. He told him that due to the cirrhosis of his liver, he would depart from this world in less than three months.

Then, he paused for a moment and added, "If you wish to stop your dialysis treatment, you will have six days to live. It is your choice!" The doctor voiced emphatically.

I was totally devastated.

As soon as the doctor left, Jerry turned to me in distress and asked me to contact the rabbi of our synagogue to find out if stopping dialysis was committing suicide.

Without delay, the rabbi came over and apprised Jerry that stopping dialysis was not committing suicide and that he was not born attached to a machine, but that he could in no way tell him what to do and that it was totally up to him.

In the evening, Jerry asked me to make the decision for him.

I was conflicted, but I was able to respond instantly that I would not make the decision for him and that it was up to him. I told him that I would support him all the way with the love I had for him.

Jerry opted to stop his dialysis.

Up to the last day, with the help that I had hired, I made sure that he had the best of everything. I bought all the food he had been craving and was not allowed to have because of his kidney problems — herring, potatoes, pickled olives, bananas and more. I tried to alleviate his fear of dying by telling him that he would join his parents, his beloved grandmother and the little pearl of our hearts, our Leslie.

The doctor wanted to move Jerry to a hospice, but I did not allow it. I wanted him to be in his own home until his last breath.

On his last day, I wheeled him with Maria, my helper, to the park to see the changing color of the leaves, the birds and more. He loved it.

A couple of hours before he departed, during the night of October 20th, his last words were: *"Je n'ai jamais regretté le oui des Invalides"* — "I have never regretted your 'yes' at Invalides."

CHAPTER 21

Little Girl, You Have to Move Forward

After facing a rough and challenging period, my Jerry had crossed over to the other side.

Was our sad parting a final goodbye?

Hopefully not.

Since I believe in an afterlife, I expect that we will run into each other someday and be reunited.

Meanwhile, after sharing 44 years with the love of my life, I was left alone.

I can still hear Marc on our way back from the cemetery: "Mom, we are here for only a fleeting moment."

It is so true; the time will come, but it is vital for us to get on with life and do our best to overcome the bumps along the way.

In spite of the grief I felt, I could hear a voice saying: "Little girl, you have to move forward."

As I was recalling the marvelous trips I shared with my Jerry, I realized that I should continue to embrace my passion for travel.

I started by inviting my two families to a Club Med in Punta Cana in the Dominican Republic in January 2005. On the pristine beach with powdery sand along the perfect turquoise water, the resort was an ideal Zen oasis for my children, grandchildren and *petit moi*.

In New York, I continued my usual activities: babysitting my grand-children, charitable work, keeping up with finances, playing Scrabble, mahjong and more…

But I was not going to give up crossing the Atlantic Ocean twice a year to visit my family and friends in Paris.

Nor was I going to cease inviting my two families to a Club Med or a resort or on a cruise or a sightseeing trip every year. My aspiration was to expose my children and grandchildren to lots of fascinating experiences in diverse countries.

When I hear today that my granddaughters' favorite destinations are Greece and Portugal, I am amused, but not surprised.

Besides my habitual voyages, I set my heart on embarking on journeys to discover other wonders of the world.

When I think back to my three weeks in China with a group of travelers in 2006, many memories come to my mind.

I could never forget the prodigious sight of the Forbidden City in Beijing, the immense Imperial Palace in Tiananmen Square, and the amazing Great Wall of China, snaking its way across the mountain.

We were not alone in exploring these fabulous landmarks; in fact, I had never seen as many people per square meter!

In contrast to these jam-packed sights, our ambling along the quiet Way of the Spirit, an alley lined with stone sculptures of animals and weeping willows on the way to the Ming Tombs, with soft music playing, was peaceful.

Our soirée at the Peking Opera was delightful. The singing, dancing and colorful costumes had, naturally, little in common with the opera I knew. But to be introduced to a new perspective has always brought enrichment to my life.

The lunch at the home of a Chinese family the following day was awesome. Our hosts were gracious and the food was delicious. Needless to say, the people-to-people experience was, without a doubt, most important for *petit moi* — the inquisitive traveler that I was and still am!

Our next venture was to Xi'an. Seeing the unearthed life-size sculptures of the famous and ancient terracotta warriors and horses was simply incredible.

However, I could never forget the notorious air pollution and dreadful smog in Xi'an. When I raised my hand in front of me, I could not see it! Breathing was hard, yet to my surprise, people were doing Tai Chi in the street!

I enjoyed our excursion to the famous Buddhist Big Wild Goose and Small Wild Goose pagodas. They reminded me so much of my trip to Asia with my Jerry. Then, to add to our awesome day, we were invited to go for a great dinner and theater show at the Tang Dynasty. The exotic Chinese music, dance and acrobatics were a pleasure to behold.

As soon as we pulled into our hotel in Hangzhou, our guide asked us if we wanted to have a massage. I did not hesitate and went for it right away. Little did I know what was in store for *petit moi*!

There I was, in a room with twenty people on huge recliners, at the hands of a masseur who treated my body as if it were pastry dough!

After trying to put my legs behind my head, he stopped.

"What about the feet?" I asked.

"Feet do not belong to the body," he replied.

I could not believe that I had exposed myself to such a dreadful experience.

Fortunately, I was able to leave behind the horrifying manipulations of the masseur and enjoy cruising the beautiful West Lake. The Buddhist treasures along the way were magnificent and the eye-catching, immense statue of the laughing Buddha at the Lingyin Temple made me smile!

The next day we had a delicious lunch at a farmer's home, where the two daughters-in-law had prepared a banquet for us. Inquisitive, I wanted to know if these lovely women lived on the farm.

The answer was, "Yes. The cultural way in China is for sons to bring their wives into their family."

How tough it must be for a young woman to be forced to live with her in-laws! I thought.

We continued at a hectic pace to Shanghai.

Our walk on the Bund promenade offered a unique atmosphere, with the river on one side and buildings in the Baroque, Gothic, Romanesque and Renaissance styles on the other.

On our night tour, the panoramic view from the observation deck of one of the tallest buildings in the world, with all the colorful lights of the city, was spectacular. The Bund and the skyscrapers appeared like a set of golden jewels!

After our sensational sightseeing in and out of Shanghai, we went to Yichang to embark on the Victoria Katarina, for a four-night cruise on the Yangtze River.

Relaxing on my private balcony, I enjoyed watching the changing landscape of gorges, majestic cliffs, and mountains dotted with pagodas and villages.

I had fun playing mahjong with a couple of Chinese women. They played differently, but I adopted their version — after all, the game is Chinese!

The evening shows, with the Chinese girls dancing in their traditional dresses, were a pleasure to see.

There were also some interesting lectures on Chinese customs. Just to mention a few that come into my mind: the father of the groom always pays for the wedding; the entire family, including aunts, uncles and cousins, picks up the bride to take her to the wedding; one child per family is mostly the case, but there are exceptions...

To hear about other people's *modi vivendi* and traditions has always captivated me. I believe that another important venue for learning about a people's lifestyle is their food markets; the variety and colorful displays say a lot about a country.

Moving on, we flew to Guilin, where we spent a couple of surreal days.

Our four-hour cruise on the Li River was probably the highlight of our trip. The unusual limestone formations and the hazy mist conveyed such a sense of mystery that I was not surprised that they had inspired painters and poets. And catching sight of the water buffalo plunging in the languid waters was certainly amusing.

Our cruise ended in the charming little town of Yangshuo, where we had a lovely dinner with a show. I was, once again, smitten by the graciousness and the talent of the Chinese dancers.

Our visit the next day to the multicolored Reed Flute Cave was a pleasure. The extraordinary stalagmites and stalactites reminded me of a set from a science fiction movie! What an impressive grotto that was!

Hong Kong was our last destination. The modern, bustling, cosmopolitan city reminded me of New York.

I was definitely more enthralled by mainland China, where the diversity of the landscapes, historic sites, markets, food and shows, and more importantly the people, made my trip so worthwhile and special.

****

I had always dreamt about going to India, but Jerry had no desire to go and see the grim malady of poverty.

When I got there in February 2007, I thought of my Jerry every inch of the way. He would have felt a repugnance for the indescribable indigence.

Our guide assured us that the poor accept their fate and believe vehemently that their suffering will make good in their next life!

Rich or poor, I found the men of Rajasthan very handsome, and the women, dressed in their saris, radiant and warm.

But the lack of empathy for the animals horrified me. Skeletal cows, considered sacred by Hindus, were roaming around. Famished camels and donkeys were meandering in the traffic, carrying enormous loads. Emaciated dogs and farm animals were attached by very short cords to poles. It broke my heart to see such dismal scenes.

Bewildered, I was. Elephants and sauntering monkeys were everywhere as well. The chaos in the streets and thoroughfares of Rajasthan was simply horrific!

Thinking of the fascinating city of Mumbai, also known as Bombay, our visit to Elephanta Island comes into my mind.

At the bottom of the 129 steps leading to the cave temples, we were told to sit in armchairs in which we would be carried all the way up. I declined. I did not want to abuse mankind. I had seen enough with the ill-treating of animals.

But, our guide protested, "This is their livelihood — they need the money!"

So, I conceded. Like a queen, I was transported up the steep steps by four elderly men! I must emphasize that I was filled with admiration for the stone sculptures, which were spectacular.

That evening, after dinner, we were all invited to travel back to Queen Victoria's reign by taking a ride on an ornate silver horse-drawn carriage. But going through the slums in such a flamboyant rig was not acceptable to me, nor my traveling companions. And to add to our dismay, the poor horses were constantly whipped! We all detested that tour.

Moving on, we stopped in several captivating and engaging cities:

Udaipur, set amid lakes and dotted with palaces, was a pleasure to visit.

In Ranakpur, I was smitten by the eye-catching sculptures of the Jain Temple.

Jodhpur was definitely not a disappointment; I loved seeing the houses, all painted in blue!

The walled Jaipur, known as "The Pink City" was fascinating. The domes, floral patterns and fluted pillars of the palace of Hawa Mahal were truly alluring. But we could not be in Jaipur and not go on an elephant ride! I was the first one to climb up the thin iron ladder. I had just sat down when the wacky beast stood up on his hind legs, ready to go on a rampage!

With my heart pounding hard, I cried, "Get me off! Get me off!"

No need to say that after that, I had no desire to take a ride!

The next day, we convened at 6 a.m. to go on a safari at the Ranthambore National Park to see tigers. Failing to fulfill our expectations, the tigers were not detectable! But we did catch sight of monkeys, gazelles and birds!

On our way to Delhi, we stopped at the ancient imperial city of Fatehpur Sikri and continued our journey to Agra to feast our eyes on the Taj Mahal. The ivory-white marble mausoleum was, for sure, grand.

Then, unexpectedly, we visited the SOS Village for abandoned children. I had plenty of admiration for the caregivers addressing the youngsters' emotional needs and giving them, hopefully, a better future. After making our donations, we left for New Delhi, for the grand finale of our trip to India.

I could never forget touring the ancient streets of Old Delhi. Filled with traffic, noise and congestion, the chaos and utter confusion on my rickshaw ride were, to say the least, unbearable.

India was a country of contrasts. In close proximity, you had the rich and the poor, the luxurious and the squalid.

Different and unusual, India was at times shattering, yet at other times fascinating for *petit moi*!

****

On the subject of exotic and cultural journeys, my trip to Vietnam and Cambodia in January 2008 comes to mind.

After hours and hours of travel, with several delays, I finally made it, in the middle of the night, to Ho Chi Minh City (formerly Saigon), only to find out that my suitcase was missing! As I was filling out a form for lost luggage, our escort appeared at my side to tell me that a man from our group had grabbed it by mistake!

Early the next morning, we hopped on our bus for a full-day tour. While I was watching the pulsating city from my seat, our guide never stopped talking about politics. With candor, she told us that she hated the Americans.

She paused for a moment, and added, "We do not call the war the Vietnam War, we call it the American War."

I was astounded that she had the guts to make such comments on a bus filled with American tourists. I looked at her and asked, "Do you like the French?"

"I hate the French as much as I hate the Americans," she blurted out.

For sure, with my two nationalities — French and American — I felt doubly blessed!

Thank goodness we were able to get off the bus for a visit to the Saigon Central Post Office. Built when Vietnam was part of French Indochina, the colonial architecture was certainly noteworthy.

However, when it came to crossing a street in the midst of thousands of speeding motorcycles carrying three or four people, zigzagging in all directions, with no traffic lights, Ho Chi Minh City was definitely a nightmare!

Another distressing jaunt for me was Cu Chi. Walking through the dismal maze of tunnels in which explosives were rigged during the war was unsettling.

In contrast, our day trip to the ancient city of Hôi An was very interesting. The lovely 18th century Japanese Covered Bridge, the Phuc Kien Pagoda, the Tan Ky House and the narrow streets with their exquisite frontage were all fascinating. I just loved the blend of foreign influences.

Among our large group of 34, there was Jack. I can still hear him saying, "I am married. After decades spent with the wrong shrew and our two sons, we separated, but we never divorced. I met the love of my life who has, after a few great years together, sadly passed away. Now I am solo, but I have met my French bonbon!"

Jack had taken a fancy to me and would clamor repeatedly, "I want to sit next to my Frenchy."

He would sing love songs into my ear and tell me sweet things. He made me laugh. A character, he was! But poor Jack was not my type of guy!

To return to my voyage… After a scenic drive along the China seacoast and through mountain passes, we arrived in Hue, famous for its imperial citadel.

Unfortunately, the skies were grey and the rain was drizzling during our dragon boat cruise on the Perfume River and our stop at the iconic Thien Mu Pagoda. Nonetheless, I liked the scenery.

Later that evening, our group was invited for a dinner at the home of Dr. Phan An and his wife — a princess. Their impressive house had been in her family for several generations. After an interesting lecture given by our host and a superb dinner cooked by his wife, we were introduced to their family. I was enthralled by their warm hospitality.

Although drenched to the bone, our visit to the Imperial Citadel of Th ng Long was nevertheless delightful. And — surprise, surprise — we were invited to a show. Strongly influenced by the royal courts, the Vietnamese music and dancing were very engaging. I had a great time.

On our way back to our hotel, we stopped at a conical hat workshop. I tried on a few hats, but I did not find them comfortable to wear. Yet nearly all Vietnamese people crown their heads with them. The conical hat is an exotic feature of Vietnam!

Cruising through the wonderland of the limestone dolomite karst dotting the pristine Ha Long Bay was probably the pearl of our voyage in Vietnam.

I felt so enriched and enlightened by Vietnamese culture and art.

But our trip was far from over. From Hanoi, we flew to Siem Reap, Cambodia.

The gateway to the famous Angkor temples was spectacular. During our dinner in the Angkor village, we were entertained by Apsara dancers performing traditional dances. Their refined and delicate gestures reminded me so much of the dancers I saw in Thailand with Jerry.

Our venture, the next day, on the Tonlé Sap Lake, was an unusual and somewhat daring experience. Getting on our boat was tedious; we had to step from one boat to another and another. A man in our group fell in the water; some in our group had to be carried. Amazingly, I was able to keep my balance!

The goings-on on the lake were startling — men fishing from their floating homes, vendors of all kinds trying to get our attention, women on tiny rowboats with very young children holding huge snakes and begging for money. We even saw a small baby floating in a tub, alone, crying, in the middle of the lake! How odd and disturbing that was!

I do not know how I was able to endure sitting for hours in an old beaten-up motor coach, with no air conditioning, rolling slowly on a dilapidated road, with the driver honking throughout the entire journey from Siem Reap to Phnom Penh, as he tried to avoid people running across the road, cows standing in the middle of the road and more. The coach was zigzagging so much that a bag fell on my head! Lucky me, I have a hard head! This was a grueling and challenging trip!

As we passed through villages, our guide apprised us that the wooden houses were built on stilts to avoid trespassing animals!

The houses were surrounded by rice paddies, where stooping men, women and young children have to toil hard for long hours in the sun. No wonder they designed the conical hat for them!

Cambodia was slowly recovering from the horror and genocide of the Khmer Rouge and the long period of civil and political instability. Despite it all, Phnom Penh retained its colonial charm. I was smitten by the beauty of the sublime and impressive temples, palaces, pagodas and the serene park. They reminded me so much of my visit to Thailand with my Jerry.

However, to see poor children and disabled beggars everywhere in Cambodia was so disheartening.

Unfortunately, the world is far from perfect.

****

Exploring the languages, religions, cuisines and ideologies of the different countries around the world that I have visited, I have accumulated a wealth of fascinating and meaningful experiences. Without a doubt, some memories will never fade!

CHAPTER 22

The Unexpected

Indeed, some memories never fade!

Good or bad, they remind me of my past.

Life is certainly not simple and can be, sometimes, hard to understand.

Has this ambiguity affected or changed the outcome of my life?

Well, I always tried to recognize the ambivalence that I feel about matters when it behooves me. Although it's challenging at times, I am sure that the intricate complexities of my life paint an authentic picture of who I am today!

I have had many insights in the dénouement of my traveled path, but I never expected the Coronavirus, a pandemic that has, since March 2020, impacted people's lives worldwide.

The long confinement and great mortality of the plague were beyond what anyone would have expected.

The isolation and loneliness caused such annoyance for me.

But once again, I heard a little voice telling me not to be exasperated, and that I should relive my life by writing my memoirs.

As always, I listen to *petit moi*. I must say that reminiscing about my well-traveled path through my writing helped me tremendously.

My other penchant, even with a mask, was to go on my walks in beautiful Central Park.

Fortunately, the long confinement that prevented everyone from traveling ended. I was able to go in July to a resort in Mexico and to go to Paris in September and be reunited with my family and my friends.

I'm glad to say that life is picking up slowly… but we never know what is around the corner!

A couple of weeks ago, I was ambling in the park, ready to sit down, when I heard the voice of a gentleman: "You are pretty. I would love to invite you to a restaurant for dinner."

I was stunned, and responded, "I am in my eighties!"

"Well, I am one hundred years old," he answered with a grin. "You know, when I was 96 years old, I ran the New York City Marathon."

With his high spirit, the gentleman was for sure an example of what I have always known: we must put one foot in front of the other and get on with life.

Behind each face there is a story.

This is my epilogue.